CREDO.

BOSTON:
LEE AND SHEPARD, PUBLISHERS.
NEW YORK:
LEE, SHEPARD AND DILLINGHAM.
1872.

Stereotyped at the Boston Stereotype Foundry,
19 Spring Lane.

TO

MY WIFE,

WHOSE PATIENT ASSISTANCE AND CONSTANT ENCOURAGEMENT HAVE GREATLY AIDED IN THEIR PREPARATION,

These Pages

ARE AFFECTIONATELY DEDICATED.

PREFACE.

This volume is devoted to those inquiries which now agitate the thinking world. It is committed to the care of the Christian Church. Its truths are God's, and will live forever. Its errors are the author's; they will be overruled, forgotten, and, he trusts, forgiven.

CONTENTS.

SUPERNATURAL BOOK.

SUPERNATURAL BEINGS.

SUPERNATURAL LIFE.

SUPERNATURAL DESTINY.

A SUPERNATURAL BOOK.

"Revealed religion is not of the nature of a progressive science." MACAULAY.

"For the prophecy came not in old time by the will of man; but holy men of God spake as they were moved by the Holy Ghost." 2 *Peter* i. 21.

"Also I heard the voice of the Lord, saying, Whom shall I send, and who will go for us? Then said I, Here am I; send me.

"And he said, Go, and tell this people, Hear ye indeed, but understand not; and see ye indeed, but perceive not.

"Then said I, Lord, how long? And he answered, Until the cities be wasted without inhabitant, and the houses without man, and the land be utterly desolate." *Isaiah* vi. 8, 9, 11.

"If a man says that God hath spoken to him supernaturally, I cannot perceive what argument he can produce to make me believe it." HOBBES.

"The prophetic element is not necessarily anything miraculous or exceptional." JAMES FREEMAN CLARKE.

"A single fact is worth a thousand arguments." FOX.

I.

PROPHETS AND PROPHECIES

RESPECTING ANCIENT CITIES AND COUNTRIES.

TWO inquiries are before us. First, Who and what were the Jewish Prophets? Second, Were they inspired — peculiarly and distinctively inspired — by Jehovah to speak and write the things contained in the prophetic books of the Bible? The question is not whether they were fanatics, speaking from a kind of oracular frenzy, or whether they were poetically inspired, or intellectually elevated; but were they in fact what they claimed to be, and what the Scriptures affirm they were — the voice of God to a sinful world? Were they moved by the Divine Spirit as no other men in any age of the world have been, and did they possess a power to disclose the mysteries of God, and point men upward and onward to that which otherwise would have been an impenetrable future?

The word *prophet*, in the original, means a "boiling over," and in the Hebrew never occurs in the active, but always in the passive voice. In a word, then, a

Bible prophet was a messenger of God, filled with the Holy Ghost, being himself merely a passive agent. Divine truth was placed in his soul to boil over, or bubble out of itself; or, extending the figure employed by our Lord, it was "as a well of water springing up" with divine life and truth.

We may divide the Prophetic Periods into four.

The first was the Patriarchal; during which God gave to his servants special communications, sometimes with his own voice, oftener by visiting angels. Such were the communications in Eden, the call of Abraham, the blessing obtained by Jacob, and the visions of Joseph. The truths thus communicated unto a few would be sufficient, even if not transmitted to writing, for the guidance of the race for a long time, when the families of the earth numbered but few, and when men lived a thousand years.

At the head of the second period stood Moses. With him were associated Aaron, Joshua, and Miriam. They were acknowledged by their countrymen as divinely-inspired prophets.

After the era of Moses, for upwards of six hundred years, the prophetic spirit appeared but once — the song of Deborah. The truths which had been spoken by Moses and his contemporaries were, in the mean time, carefully committed to writing, and guarded with the strictest religious veneration by a class whose sole business it was to preserve and teach them.

In the age of Samuel, the civil government of the Hebrews, which, from the time of Moses, had remained an unsettled theocracy, ruled by Jewish knights or crusaders, became a kingdom. During the period of this transition, old forms of Jewish society were broken up, and gave place to new ones. There was needed the utterance of divine truth to meet those changes and prepare the nation and the world for other and approaching events.

Consequently, after a silence of hundreds of years, the prophetic order was again revived. "The voice of the Lord came unto me, saying," and "Thus saith the Lord," were heard among the people. At the head of this new order stood the prophet Samuel. He is termed its father and founder.

This second prophetic period extended from 840 until 420 B. C., and presented an unbroken succession from Samuel to Malachi. It embraced the entire class of Major and Minor Prophets, among whom shine out those marvellous names — Isaiah, Jeremiah, Ezekiel, and Daniel — which have attracted, in all subsequent ages, the attention and admiration of every reader of the Bible. There can be no question that this order of prophets ceased with the reproving voice of Malachi. A host of legends, both Jewish and Mussulman, commemorate the extinction of the prophetic gift at his death.

A silence of four hundred years succeeded, during which the Jewish people remained in constant expectation of some new prophet. They looked, but they looked in vain. "Thus saith the Lord" was not heard, or heard only to be disregarded. To this place and that the expectant people journeyed. To this one and that they listened, only to find that the gift and spirit of prophecy had departed. Meanwhile, the Jewish church, as if moved by divine influence, appointed a special order of Scribes, who elected Ezra as their president. Under their sanction all the inspired books and prophetic rolls in its possession were united. In these writings the Jewish religion proper had been fully revealed and established. The New Dispensation had been described and promised. Until it dawned upon the nations, additional prophetic declarations and authority were unknown.

At length, in the days of Herod the king, the prophetic voice was again heard. The warning notes of John the Baptist, "Repent ye, for the kingdom of heaven is at hand," rang through the wilderness and plains of Judea.

The great and proud city of Jerusalem arose in one day, and went out to be baptized of John in Jordan. His name was a household word throughout their cities. The people felt that the word of God had come to John, the son of Zacharias, as it came to Isaiah, the son of Amoz, in the days of their fathers. So much did he resemble one of the old prophets, that some thought Elijah had revisited the earth in person to warn the nations of sin and danger. His real and predicted mission was that of a forerunner. "Prepare ye the way of the Lord!" he cried; by which he meant that the God-man was on his way to make a royal journey through the cities and villages of Judea, to teach the people the truth, and heal their diseases.

Suddenly the Prophet of Prophets was in their midst. He was the Word. He spoke from his own authority, as man never spake, but as God spoke to Adam. His ordinary discourses were prophecies.

He gathered about him a school of prophets, as Moses and Samuel had done before him. Through the disciples the sacred gift was continued for a season.

This fourth order of prophets lasted from John the Baptist until the death of the last apostle. With John, the son of Zebedee, on the Isle of Patmos, the name and spirit ceased, as it had ceased with the generation of Moses in Moab, and with Malachi in an unknown land. But now it ceased forever. The book and spirit of prophecy were then and there closed. Rome, through pope and priest, may assert the contrary; it will avail nothing. She may listen with open ear until doomsday, but will never hear prophetic word or syllable. New Lights may startle us with pretended disclosures from another world; but it is in vain.

During the past eighteen hundred years the world has not advanced one step in the actual revelation of supernatural truth. Despite all efforts, nothing new can be discovered. All things remain as they were since Christ and his apostles. Past revelations may be better arranged, systematized, and harmonized. Nothing essential can be added to or taken from them. The book of revelation is closed.

In the peculiar, biblical, Hebrew sense of the word, St. John was the last of the prophetic order. The patriarchs communed with God and his messengers until the time of Moses. Moses and those with him declared all the truth necessary for the people to know, and all that they would profit by until the days of the judges should end and those of the kings begin. Malachi and his immediate predecessors declared all that was needed for the direction and government of the nation until the old dispensation should end and the new begin. Lastly, Christ and his disciples proclaimed to the world all the truths requiring for their discovery divine inspiration, or essential for men's welfare until the heavens and the earth are no more. We shall need henceforth expounders and keepers of the sacred writings. We shall have them. The inspired Word will live forever. God has guarded the Scriptures in the past, and will guard them in the future, as the apple of his eye. They have suffered from no essential addition or diminution. They have been stereotyped by Providence. The history of their preservation is marvellous. The Jewish Church was their first divinely-commissioned guardian. While in its keeping they were so carefully preserved, for hundreds and hundreds of years, that the scribes and elders could tell the number of words they contained, the number of letters, the middle word, and the middle letter, of any given book, and of the entire Scriptures. Never in the history of the world have writings been kept with such scrupulous exactness, though they recorded the revolts of the nation and rebuked the sins of the people.

Later, and just at a time when the Jewish commonwealth would be the most strongly tempted to misinterpret and mar these prophetic declarations, they were taken from the Jews and committed to the care of the early Roman church, and it became a divinely appointed agent of preservation. Still later, and at a time when danger threatened them in the house of these professed friends, they were wrested from the

Catholic church, as they had been from the Jewish, and Evangelical Christianity became their body-guard. They were removed from the monasteries that had been built to protect them from fire and plunder through pagan and Jewish persecutions; they were taken from the hands of devoted monks, who had been commissioned to preserve them during the conflagrations of the world's literature accumulated in the libraries of Rome and Alexandria, and given, not to one church, but to the world. They were no longer to be locked in the embrace of dead languages, and read only by the learned, but were to be translated into every tongue, and become the light and joy of the whole earth. Tyndale, and after him the scholars of King James's court, were appointed to translate them; Luther was commissioned to thunder their truths in the Diets and cities of Germany; and in every age preachers have since been called, and will continue to be called, to declare their warnings against evil, and to comfort by their promises the hearts of God's people. Were the book supernatural, — as its friends claim it to be, — could we require a more remarkable preservation and history?

But, turning from the writings of these Hebrew and Jewish prophets, let us glance for a moment at their character and the peculiarities of their mission.

In some respects the Old and New Testament prophets were similar. They felt they were called to their work, not by the authority of the church, not by the exigencies of the times, but by the Voice of God and of Christ. They often shrank from entering upon their mission, and sometimes trembled and wept while uttering their prophecies.

Kings, priests, and ministers were ordained and consecrated; but not one of the prophets received such human ordinance. They went forth exclaiming, "Woe is me if I declare not the truth as I have heard it." They were called from no especial class of men, confined to no caste or rank of society, but were from every position and profession. "They discharged the ordinary duties of citizens." They were soldiers, kings, herdsmen, wandering Arabs, peasants, and fishermen. They lived among the people, in cottages, courts, in the halls of the temple, and on the summits of mountains. "They were," says an eminent scholar, "neither morose ascetics nor unlettered fanatics." They cultivated letters, and would have been ornaments to any society. To the poor, oppressed, and neglected they appeared as faithful friends; to the selfish, insolent, and frivolous, as implacable foes. They resisted the aggressions of the tyrant, and defended the rights of the subject. They were "watch dogs," says Stanley, "over every vice and crime, abuse and privilege, of society." They taught but one theology and one religion. It was equally free from fanaticism and formality. Beyond it modern civilization has not advanced one step. The Unity of God was their doctrine first and last. Among all the corruptions of the surrounding nations, the forty thousand deities of Egypt, the lords many and gods many of the Greeks and Romans, they declared that there was but one God; and the sublime declaration, "Ye believe in God, believe also in *me*," in the light of Evangelical Christianity, is but a confirmation of the same. A right life or a struggle towards it, a cross and every man on it or at its foot, was the burden of their religious creed. They cared little for the forms and ceremonies of religion, but everything for its life and spirit. Do right and live, Do wrong and die, were their constant exhortation and warning to the people. "To obey is better than sacrifice;" "The sacrifices of God are a broken spirit;" "What doth the Lord require of thee but to do justly, and to love mercy, and to walk humbly with thy God?" "Cease to do evil and learn to do well," — furnish a creed of practical Christianity, whose loftiness and purity silence all the vapid declamations of the New Lights of modern society against an antiquated Bible.

The teachings of the prophets are not, and never can be, antiquated. Truths which have ever flowed down into all the crevices of thought and society, and which have crystallized into gems, into gold, into diamonds, prove a most exalted authorship.

The Hebrew prophets were something more than mere protectors and educators of the people. "They were religious teachers," says an eminent English scholar,* "without the faults of religious teachers."

The palmiest days of Greece and Rome can furnish no higher examples of patriotism than does this entire class of disinterested champions of morality and virtue. The struggles of Moses in Egypt and on Mount Horeb, the wail of Jeremiah over the desolations of Judea, and the tears of Christ on the Mount of Olives over the sins of Jerusalem, tell the continued story

* A. P. Stanley, to whom we are not a little indebted.

of the love they bore their cherished country and kindred people.

As a class, they were independent and fearless men. They speak as if they had talked with God — rather as if God had talked with them. They felt the importance and authority of the commission with which they had been honored.

"Be not afraid," and "Speak my words unto them whether they will hear or forbear," incited them to reprove evil, whether met in the persons of kings, priests, or common people. They rarely turned to the right hand or the left, but frequently moved on to meet persecution and death in the discharge of duty.

They were not accustomed to ask, What is safe? What is prudent? or, What is expedient? but, What is true and right? Amid scenes of danger they stood as rocks against which the spray beats harmlessly. Moses before Pharaoh, Elijah before Ahab, Isaiah before Ahaz, Nathan before David, John before Herod, the greatest and divinest of all — nay, the Great and Divine One Himself — before the Pharisees in the temple, are examples of the sublimest heroism on record.

But the Hebrew prophets were something more than mere teachers, patriots, and heroes. In some instances they were literary men of the highest order, and in *every* instance of peculiar endowments. They have left "a literature unique in the history of the world."* Historians merely they were not; neither chronologists nor copyists, in the ordinary sense of

* Stanley.

these terms. They claimed that their disclosures were the ebullitions of a divine voice. No one of the prophets pretended to speak from personal knowledge or personal authority, from sagacity or clairvoyance, but by the supernatural revelation of truth from heaven. No modern political philosopher, though he has been able to predict future events accurately, has ever ventured to advance a claim like this as the ground of his knowledge and authority. Neither Burke, nor Webster, nor any of the politicians of 1812 or 1860 who saw with remarkable clearness beyond the visible political horizon, ever claimed that they were passive in their utterances. They confessed they knew of but one way of judging respecting the future; that is, from the past.

They reasoned, therefore, from the past to the future, from cause to effect; and there were, in most cases, visible causes operating to produce the fulfilment of what they predicted.

But the Hebrew prophets linked nothing with political or probable evidence, though they spoke of moral and spiritual issues. Their prophecies were based upon no arbitrary or fantastic accomplishments, though connected with moral and religious rectitude and dereliction. They present to the world but one assurance, — the "word of the Lord came unto me, saying," was the thrilling and inspiring introduction and conclusion of all their discourses. "Moved upon, they spake," is the only solution of what would otherwise be an inexplicable phenomenon.

The prophets also claimed that the very words they employed were not their own, but Jehovah's. In some instances their words seemed to be as much beyond their control as the thoughts they expressed. They were often left not fully to comprehend the facts they disclosed. We cannot doubt that the prophets believed in the existence of the strictest verbal inspiration. No one can doubt the *possibility* of such inspiration who is acquainted with the phenomena either of ancient or modern demoniacal possession. No one can doubt the *necessity* of such inspiration who imagines common peasants, as the prophets in some cases were, filled with the sublimest thoughts ever penned, and then left to express them as best they might. Such inspiration would be tantalizing beyond endurance; but if their lips were touched by the finger of God, *when necessary*, then they would not falter for word or expression. A miracle should be introduced only when and so far as is absolutely necessary in accounting for given phenomena. If the historic portions of the Scriptures and the simple narration of facts require that the writer be elevated merely and borne on by the Holy Spirit in his work, then verbal inspiration in these portions must give place to the infusion or impression of ideas. We do not decide. In either case, however, the writer must be inspired to such an extent as to be beyond the possibility of making a mistake both in the selection and statement of those facts which are in strictest accordance with the divine will.

From what has been said, does it not appear that the prophetic order of the Jewish church stands alone and unequalled in the history of the race? Are not those men who at the present time lay claim to similar inspiration, lunatics?

The second general inquiry proposed is concerning the direct evidence that the Hebrew and Jewish prophets were supernaturally aided in their disclosures of the future.

About twenty-five hundred years ago, the ancient capital of the Assyrian empire, situated on the eastern bank of the Tigris, six hundred miles from Jerusalem, rivalled, in internal wealth, extensive commerce, and splendid architecture, all existing cities of the world, save one. Jonah describes it as an "exceeding great city." Diodorus says that its circuit was somewhat more than fifty-four miles. Its walls contained fifteen hundred impregnable towers, were one hundred feet high, and sufficiently broad to admit of three chariots driven abreast. It was founded by the grandson of Noah, and was a nation's pride for nearly fifteen hundred years. Some idea of its extent may be gathered from Jonah's passage through its busy streets, when he was sent to warn its people and urge them to repentance. He journeyed on, everywhere raising his voice of alarm, from street to street, from square to square, past courts and temples, for twenty miles, even to the king's palace. He had then traversed but one third of the entire length of its principal thoroughfare. Infidels have laughed at the idea of a city then existing of such dimensions. They have said that prophets and historians wrote such descriptions from "their own puny ideas of extent and magnificence." Twenty years ago, a believer could not dispute them. Little was known of the city, save in prophecy and history

Later, a learned Frenchman and a wandering English scholar, Monsieur Botta and Mr. Layard, sought and found the site of this mighty Nineveh. They disentombed it. Beneath its shrouds of sand and ruin, they revealed to the astonished world the identical place where the captive tribes of Israel toiled and wept. They stood among its ruined temples and pillars, upon which, in the bloom of its greatness, the eyes of Jonah and Ezekiel looked as they passed through its lordly streets. Marble slabs have been excavated from its ruins, upon which was written the story of the existence and extent of Nineveh. Returning along the page of its history to the day of its splendor and power, when it could defy the world in wealth or arms, a hundred years before the fatal siege commenced, we hear one of the prophets of God, Nahum the Elkoshite,—who was sleeping with his fathers long before the siege was completed,—exclaiming, "Behold, I am against thee, saith the Lord." "I will make thy grave. . . . And it shall come to pass that they that look upon thee, shall flee from thee, and say, "Nineveh is laid waste." Nahum 5–7. Nahum claimed that he heard these words from the lips of the Almighty, upon whose authority he had pronounced the city's doom. There is no mistaking his language. It is simple and lucid. Do the facts of history confirm or contradict these lofty professions of inspiration? Lucian declared, sixteen hundred years ago, that in his time there was no vestige of the city remaining. So silent its grave, so heavy its shrouds, that none could mark even the spot of its interment. Upon its former greatness, its silence, and its tomb, as well as upon every slab and inscription transported from its disturbed ruins to Europe or America, sat the solemn and eternal genius of Prophecy. A few hundred miles to the south of Nineveh, and contemporaneous with it, arose another city of great size and magnificence. Its history runs back to a time not much later than the flood. The records of its early historians give dates two thousand years before the conquest of Alexander, and the Scriptures represent "the beginning of the kingdom" as belonging to the time of Nimrod, the grandson of Ham. Of its splendor under Nebuchadnezzar there can be no doubt. Pliny says, "It was the greatest city the sun ever shone upon." Isaiah called it the "Golden City." Its walls, three hundred feet in height, according to one of its historians, and seventy-five feet in breadth, appeared more like the bulwarks of nature than the workmanship of man. They were regarded by Strabo as one of the seven wonders of the world. The entire area within its massive walls, according to Herodotus and Ctesias, its chief historians, was two hundred square miles. Its temples, its palaces, its fortresses, its brazen gates, its enamelled brick, its plated pillars, its huge embankments along the shores of the Euphrates, its artificial mountains as high as the dome of St. Peter's, its ornamental architecture, its artificial lakes, and its lofty palaces, with its hanging gardens piled in successive terraces to the top of its walls, displayed more of the mighty works of mortals than have ever elsewhere been concentrated in one spot on the earth. Such was Babylon. And yet, while the city was in its glory, while royal power defended it, one hundred and sixty years before the foot of an enemy had entered its gates or menaced its walls, the prophets of God declared that the spearmen and the horsemen from the north should deluge the city in blood, and that the Almighty himself should sweep it with the besom of destruction. How improbable, nay, how impossible! on the very night of his overthrow, thought the king, who heeded neither the prophecies nor the power of God, the predicted name of Cyrus, nor the northern hosts encamped against him. Successive armies have moved against "The Mighty," the "Golden City," the "Hammer of the whole earth." Her silence is to-day broken by the cry of the bittern and the howl of wild beasts. "Thus saith the Lord of hosts," wrote Jeremiah, "The broad walls of Babylon shall be utterly broken." (Jer. li. 58.) This prophecy was not fulfilled before it was uttered. The walls were standing, as one of the seven wonders of the world, a thousand years after the words were spoken.

The city had been repeatedly conquered by Cyrus, Darius, Alexander, Demetrius, Trajan, Julian, and Omar, the successor of Mahomet, before the walls were utterly broken. St. Jerome states that they were standing as late as his time. But in the sixteenth century they were last seen by any European traveller. The word had been spoken. Siege after siege, the storms of a thousand years, the annual overflow of the Euphrates, the sand from the parched desert, and the removal of the stones to build other towns and villages, have been appointed agents in the hand of God, and have left nothing by which those ancient and renowned walls can now be traced.

The words of Isaiah concerning this city were, that the wild beasts of the desert should lie there. (Is. xiii. 21.) "As I approached the ruins of the great temple of Belus," writes Sir Robert Ker Porter, "I saw two majestic lions." The kings of the forest in the king's palaces! "Babylon shall become heaps," said Jeremiah. (Jer. li. 37.) "She shall be cast out of her grave," wrote Isaiah. (Is. xiv. 19.) "The rapacity of the Turks has led them, in searching for treasures, to dig up the earth in every direction, leaving it in heaps," says Porter. (Porter's *Travels.*) "Neither shall the Arabian pitch his tent there," was the voice of Isaiah. (Is. xiii. 20.) "No Arab," says Keith, "however well armed, can be persuaded to remain overnight among these ruins, through dread of their being the abode of spirits. They traverse them by day, but never by night." Captain Mignan says, "It is impossible to eradicate these superstitious ideas from the minds of these people. I saw the sun sink behind the Mujelibah, and obeyed, with infinite regret, the summons of my guides, — Arabs completely armed, — and could not persuade them to remain longer, from the apprehension of evil spirits." (Mignan's *Travels.*) "It shall never be inhabited," "Nor dwelt in from generation to generation," are the united predictions of Jeremiah and Isaiah. (Is. xiii. 20. Jer. l. 13.) Porter, who carefully inspected the entire region, says that "ruins composed, like those of Babylon, of heaps of rubbish, impregnated with nitre, doom it to lasting sterility." Rich, in his Memoirs, says, "The ruins of Babylon can never be cultivated." In the sixteenth century, we are informed that not a house was to be seen upon the original site of Babylon. In the nineteenth century it is tenantless. "Babylon shall be an astonishment" (Jer. l. 13) was the voice of prophecy; and Babylon has become an astonishment, is the voice of all those who have stood among its desolations, and remembered its history. The majestic stream of the Euphrates wanders in silent solitude, like an aged pilgrim, through its lonely ruins. Upon its banks are the river-weeds, and the gray willows on which the captives of Israel hung their harps, and refused to be comforted while their beloved Jerusalem was not. These remain; but not one thing which the prophets declared should be destroyed, from outer wall to inner court, can now be seen in that ancient and mighty metropolis of the world. From its palaces, its arches, and its terraces, broken and fallen; from this throne of the kingdom sitting in the dust; from its active life, the thronging of its busy feet, now clad in silence, and buried in the grave, — do we not seem to hear ascending in solemn grandeur the response, "The Lord God Almighty hath spoken it"?

Less than a thousand miles to the south-west of Babylon was Egypt, one of the most civilized of the ancient kingdoms. Its learning was proverbial. It was the great university of ancient sciences. In it astronomy and astrology, chemistry and the art of working metals, were more thoroughly studied than anywhere else on the globe. Here, also, the industrial arts flourished, and the "fine linen of Egypt" found its way into Palestine, while its delightful climate and fertile soil made it the granary of the world.

Other countries might suffer from drought; there

would be corn in Egypt. It was renowned for its august burials, its impressive ceremonies, its extended catalogue of mighty kings, and its majestic pyramids; standing under whose imposing shadows, it is not surprising that Napoleon thrilled his troops when he exclaimed, "Soldiers, forty centuries are now looking down upon you!" While at the height of its prosperity, predictions were uttered against this country; not, as against Nineveh and Babylon, that her monuments and walls should find their grave, but that the waters of its seas should fail, that its former enterprising spirit should forsake it, and that it should become a base and despicable kingdom. The exact predictions from the prophet Isaiah were these: "The Lord shall utterly destroy the tongue of the Egyptian sea." (Is. xi. 15.) "The waters shall fail from the sea." Poole R. Stewart, of the British Museum, says that "an important geological change has, in the course of centuries, raised the country near the head of the Gulf of Suez. Since the Christian era, even, the head of the Gulf has retired considerably southward." "The spirit of Egypt shall fail in the midst thereof." (Is. xix. 3.) "Egypt, smitten and accursed," continues Mr. Stewart, "has lost all strength and energy. . . . Long oppression has taken from her the power and the will to advance." "The paper reeds by the brooks . . . shall wither, and be no more." (Is. xix. 7.) Anciently, the papyrus was a common and important plant in Egypt, and of its leaves the famous paper was manufactured. "But now," says the author above quoted, "it is there almost, or quite, unknown." Isaiah and Ezekiel both predicted that Egypt should become "the basest of kingdoms." "In Egypt," says Gibbon, "there is no middle class, nobility, clergy, merchants, nor landlords. The inhabitants live in mud-walled huts, on the ground once occupied by the far-famed palaces of the Pharaohs."

"There shall be no more a prince from the land of Egypt," was a prediction of Ezekiel. (Ezek. xxx. 13.) Three hundred and fifty years before Christ Egypt became subject to the Persians. It was subdued by several other powers, until the Mamelukes usurped control in 1250. Since that period, a mode of government the most singular and surprising that has ever existed was established, and has since been maintained. Each successive ruler has been raised to supreme authority from being a stranger or a vassal. From the second Persian conquest until our own day, not one native ruler of royal blood has occupied its throne. The prophecies against Egypt were spoken in language easy to be understood, and the facts concerning its history are before us. Was it merely scientific knowledge which foretold those geological changes? Was it merely political sagacity which foresaw and foretold that ages should pass with no native prince to sit upon the throne of a country which previously had not been deprived of a prince in regular line of succession for more than two thousand years? Do such prophecies, accomplished in such a manner, uttered without qualification or comment, dependent upon a thousand contingencies, a few of which would have rendered the whole abortive, require anything less than a divine agency in their disclosure or their fulfilment?

From Egypt looking towards the North East was

another country, which included the most hallowed and sacred spot on earth. This now claims our at tention. Eighty years ago, a French infidel, by name Count de Volney, left his home in Paris to visit the East with the avowed purpose of testing, by every means at his command, the truthfulness and accuracy of the statements that had been made by former travellers and explorers. His merits as an accurate delineator of the countries he visited have placed him in the front rank of this class of writers. "As a sceptic," says Keith, "he was one of the most zealous partisans and successful promoters of infidelity." "He took every occasion," says the British Encyclopædia, "to hold up the contents of the Scriptures to the mockery and derision of mankind." Such the man and his mission. The results of his patient and critical investigations are before us, and we pause to compare them with the words of ancient prophecy.*

Concerning Syria, fifteen hundred years before Christ, Moses declared that "the stranger that shall come from a far land, even all nations, shall say, Wherefore hath the Lord done this unto this land? What meaneth the heat of this great anger?" (Deut. xxix. 22–24.) Speaking of his journey through this region, Volney says, "I wandered over the country. Great God! from whence proceed such melancholy revolutions? Why are so many cities destroyed? Why is not their ancient population reproduced and perpetuated?" Says the prophecy of Ezekiel, "Rob-

* For the selection and translation of the parallelisms here given, and for many other valuable thoughts on prophecy, we are chiefly indebted to the works of Dr. Alexander Keith.

pers shall enter into it and defile it." (Ezek. vii. 7-22.) "The government," says Volney, "is far from disapproving a system of robbery and plunder." In Jeremiah we read, "Every one that passeth by shall be astonished." (Jer. xviii. 16.) "So feeble a population in so excellent a country," writes Volney, "may well excite our astonishment." "Your highways shall be desolate." (Lev. xxvi. 22.) "There are neither great roads (or highways) nor bridges," writes Volney. "It is remarkable that we never saw a wagon nor a cart in all Syria." "The wayfaring man shall cease." (Is. xxxiii. 8.) "Nobody travels alone." (Volney.) "All the merry-hearted shall sigh." (Isa. xxiv. 8.) "To hear their plaintive strains it is almost impossible to refrain from tears." (Volney.) "The joy of the harp shall cease." (Isa. xxiv. 8.) "Such instruments as they have are detestable." (Volney.) "The mirth of the land shall depart." (Isa. xxiv. 11.) "The inhabitants never laugh." (Volney.) "Upon the land of my people shall come up thorns and briers." (Isa. xxxii. 13.) "The earth produces only briers and wormwood." (Volney.) "Because they have transgressed the law, shall the curse devour the earth." (Isa. xxiv. 5, 6.) "God has doubtless pronounced a secret malediction against the earth." (Volney.) "I will bring your sanctuaries into desolation." (Amos vii. 9.) "The temples are thrown down." (Volney.) "The palaces shall be forsaken." (Isa. xxxii. 14.) "The palaces are demolished." (Volney.) "I will destroy the remnant of the sea-coast." (Ezek. xxv. 16.) "The ports are filled up." (Volney.) "I will make your cities waste."

(Lev. xxvi. 31.) "The towns are destroyed." (Volney.) "Few men are left." (Isa. xxiv. 6.) "The earth is stripped of inhabitants." (Volney.) "I will make the land desolate." (Isa. xxiv. 1.) "It seems a dreary, burning place." (Volney.) In this one sentence from Volney, beginning with "the temples are thrown down," without the necessary addition or alteration of a single word, he has clearly, though unconsciously, shown the fulfilment of no less than six definite and distinct predictions. Though he entered Palestine without a pilgrim's spirit, have not his long sojourn in it, his careful researches, and his published works made him of more value to the church than would have been the journey thither of a thousand ordinary though sincere pilgrims? "This infidel chief," Keith well remarks, "contends like an indomitable hero, and reasons like an irrefutable philosopher in our behalf." Like Gibbon in some of his statements, seemingly self-forgetful, he is borne on to conclusions utterly subversive of his own principles, reiterating, almost word for word, the prophecies with which he is not familiar, knowing of them only to hate them. How blind are the wilfully blinded! A man in a rayless dungeon may doubt the shining of the stars. But unless he bandage his eyes, can he go forth in a cloudless night, when the heavens are throbbing with beauty, and say there are no stars? Can any one familiar with the facts before us fail to see that history is prophecy fulfilled? As we enlarge the circle of our observation, can we remain destitute of humble veneration for the sacred Scriptures? See! Zion is "ploughed as a field." The great city of Samaria is occupied as "a vineyard." The princely Tyre is "a plain" in part, in part a sea bottom on which "fishermen spread their nets." The cots of shepherds have supplanted the royal palaces of the lords of the Philistines. Ammon has become "a stable for camels." The temple of ancient Petra is "a court for owls." Askelon has become "a desolation." Ishmael is "a wild man." The Jews are "wanderers." The inhabitants of Moab are "dwellers among the rocks" which border on the Dead Sea.

Where shall we pause? All things come to our aid. Sceptics are our allies. As they continue to write the Progressive History of Man and Nations, the Rise and Fall of Empires,— as they weigh the natural sciences against revelation, accumulating evidence and piling up the results of their erudite researches into what they think and declare will be dark and formidable pyramids in the Christian world, — have we not ample reason to believe that, as in the past, so in the future, they will continue unwittingly to render the church effective aid? Is not the day hastening when all these lofty pyramids are to be taken down by the believer, and by him reconsecrated and transferred to the foundation which standeth sure, and reconstructed into the sublime temple of God's truth and prophecy?

"The grass withereth, the flower fadeth; but the word of our God shall stand forever."

PROPHECIES

RESPECTING EXISTING NATIONALITIES.

"Remember the former things of old: for I am God, and there is none else; I am God, and there is none like me; declaring the end from the beginning, and from ancient times the things that are not yet done, saying, My counsel shall stand, and I will do all my pleasure." *Isaiah* xlvi. 9, 10.

"Then the Lord put forth his hand, and touched my mouth. And the Lord said unto me, Behold, I have put my words in thy mouth.

"See, I have this day set thee over the nations and over the kingdoms, to root out, and to pull down, and to destroy, and to throw down, to build, and to plant." *Jeremiah* i. 5, 9, 10.

"Now I tell you before it come, that when it is come to pass, ye may believe that I am he." *John* xiii. 19.

"The perfection of reason calls the mind to a living observation of living facts." *The Reasoner, Oct.* 5, 1853.

"A wise man proportions his belief to the evidence."

HUME.

II.

PROPHECIES

RESPECTING EXISTING NATIONALITIES.

AN amount of prescience sufficient to disclose a future transaction seems the more wonderful in an economy not of absolute predestination, but of perfect freedom. The cursing or blessing of prophecy, whether immediate or remote, is subject, in every instance, to the voluntary choice of the individual, or the nation. Men can occasion or prevent, hasten or retard, any given moral or spiritual event. They can hasten the millennium, or defer it; accelerate the coming of Christ, or postpone it. Hence, if a prophet is able to foretell the future fate of a nation or an individual, in a world where events happen, not because they are foretold, but because it was known that they would happen in accordance with the free volition of men, he must, beyond question, be assisted supernaturally.

Though God could as easily have foretold the dates of prophetic events as the events themselves, yet he has, for the best of reasons, remained the sole possessor of the precise time when events are to transpire. He has not revealed to the prophets, nor to the angels in heaven, "the day or the hour." When the prophet received his message from the spirit or mouth of God, the dates were not only withheld, but even the chronological order of the events. It was as if the prophet had been permitted to look at the landscape, without being able to tell which object was nearest or most remote. There were the picture and the terms to be employed. Over them or under them the dates were not engraved. These were left to be inscribed by the free agent himself; left to take us by surprise, like the coming of the Son of Man, or like a thief in the night. God seems to have said to his prophets, as Christ did to his disciples, "It is not for you to know the times or the seasons which the Father hath put in his own power." This thought, it is hoped, will relieve the perplexity existing in some minds respecting the apparent confusion in the order of events as prophesied and as fulfilled.

The three principal races of mankind, though they have intermingled one with another, and have undergone many revolutions, remain comparatively distinct.

The descendants of Shem — the Mongolians — include the Persians, Assyrians, Arabs, Israelites, Chinese, Mexicans, and North American Indians. The descendants of Japhet — the Caucasians — include the Greeks, Romans, Germans, Spaniards, and Anglo-Saxons. And the descendants of Ham — the Africans — find their leading and living representative in the Negro, the native inhabitant of that region of Africa lying south of the Atlas Mountains. Four thousand years ago, coeval with the deluge, when the members of a single household included the entire race of mankind, a prediction was uttered by a servant of God, and recorded in sacred history, respecting these three great divisions of the human family. The unnatural conduct of Ham, the respectful behavior of his brothers Shem and Japhet towards their aged father on a certain occasion, gave rise to it, and "Cursed be Canaan; a servant of servants shall he be;" "Blessed be the Lord God of Shem; Canaan shall be his servant;" "God shall enlarge Japhet, and Canaan shall be his servant," was the prophecy that awaited fulfilment. (Gen. ix. 25, 27.)

Thomas Paine once observed, "If there are prophets of God, we should expect them to foretell future events in such terms as could be understood." The terms employed in the present instance are unmistakable, and answer his condition. The evident meaning respecting Ham and his descendants is, that they were to become slaves. It is true that they have not always been such; for a part of his descendants once disputed with the Romans the empire of the world, and all of them were once as free from slavery as the rest of mankind. The prophecies rolled on to their accomplishment. Tyre fell before the arms of Alexander; Carthage yielded to Roman conquerors; and Canaan became, as predicted, the servant of Japhet, as the earlier Canaan had been to Shem, his brother. Since that time, Africa has been distinguished above all countries of the globe as the land and home of slavery. It seems natural to enslave its people. Slaves at home, they have been transported to other countries for slaves. The bondmen of the West Indies, of Brazil, Arabia, and America have been, and are, from this unfortunate and inthralled race. The nations of the earth have seemed to vie with one another in fulfilling prophecy, and in making the descendants of Ham the "slave of slaves and servant of servants." But, if this be true, it is sometimes asked, Is it not right to enslave them? A false view of this question having blinded many sincere Christian people, it calls for a passing remark.

It is one thing to reveal an evil, and quite another to sanction it. "The wrath of man shall praise God;" but it has nothing of righteousness on that account. Nebuchadnezzar was the instrument of divine judgment, but was none the less guilty. He was sent to find his dwelling among the beasts of the field. Pharaoh was likewise employed to work for God. For his sins he was drowned in the sea. Christ was delivered into the hands of his enemies They were none the less "wicked hands that slew him."

God is not an accomplice in iniquity because he foreknows it, nor were the prophets because they foretold it. They foretold the sins of the people, and at the same time deplored them. The principle is simply this: The foreknowledge or the foretelling of a future event has nothing to do with its moral character.

God has *permitted* nations to enslave the African people. He never willed it. He has opposed it. He let fall, in consequence, an almost crushing blow on the American people, and holds another in suspense above them; for he will not regard any people guiltless who follow other than the Golden Rule.

Returning, we are met by this question: Unless God communicated the events of the future to his people directly, or through his prophets, how was it possible that it should have been foreknown and foretold, ages beforehand, that the descendants of Ham would become the slaves of the world? Or, if it is true, as some have said, that they became bondmen because they were peculiarly adapted to such a condition, — so constituted as to be satisfied with the slave cabin and banjo, — how was that continued adaptation foreknown? Or, knowing it, how ventured the prophets to utter other prophecies of golden hue, which mark the conclusion of the long servitude of this people? By what means was it known, in those dark ages, that every yoke should be broken, that the oppressed should go free, and that they should take their places among the rulers of the nations in which they had dwelt? Such authority comes from Heaven. We await other inevitable issues. A wonderful transformation, and a reconciliation of broken fraternal relations throughout the world, will soon take place, such as history has not yet recorded. Otherwise the prophets had not spoken. The once "accursed African" will take his seat, by the suffrages of the people, in the halls of state and national legislation. One of the future presidents of the American republic may be a black man, who will not perhaps disgrace the position as it has been disgraced by *Japhet*, his brother. We await, in sure confidence, the accomplishment, concerning this people, of all unfulfilled prophecy.

We pass to other nationalities. It was announced that Shem and his descendants were to be a blessing to the world. Accordingly, from them have sprung the Hebrew Commonwealth, the Jewish Church, the Patriarchs, the Prophets, the Sacred Scriptures, Christ, and Christianity. The man must be blind, indeed, to the weal of humanity, who does not pronounce that family signally blessed of God which was chosen to purify the religions of the world, advance its civilization, and give to it the only faultless life that ever breathed its air or walked its surface. It was announced that Japhet and his descendants should enlarge their borders. What shore has not echoed to the conquering tread of the lordly Caucasian?

These several prophecies, in some respects, are the most remarkable on record. They were delivered in the infancy of the post-diluvian world, and their undeniable fulfilment has reached down through forty centuries to the present time. The mind almost staggers under such weighty facts. As the African, bending under his burden, passes before us; as Christianity, from its Mongolian home, presses onward to the redemption of the world; and as the Caucasian extends his conquests over the whole earth, — how can we fail to hear the repeated echo of the voice of Jehovah, which was spoken to the survivors of the flood?

But later prophecies concerning two branches of the family of Shem, the Arabian and Jewish, now claim our attention. They constituted, with the Egyptians, the three most distinguished nations of remote antiquity embraced in the Mongolian division. Of the Arabians, there are, and always have been, two classes

— the fixed, or agricultural, who inhabit villages, and the nomadic, or wandering tribes, who are the modern Bedouins. The early history of both classes is somewhat involved in myth and mystery. Their language and ancient inscriptions indicate that the fixed tribes are mixed in their progeniture, while the Bedouins have remained distinct, and are more properly and purely the descendants of Ishmael. When we speak of the Ishmaelites, we must refer to the Bedouins especially, and not indiscriminately to all the inhabitants of Arabia.

A thousand years after the date of the prophecies spoken concerning the sons of Noah, and while the bond-woman of Egypt, the consort-wife of Abraham, Hagar, the mother of Ishmael, was wandering from the threshold of her home into the wilderness, more than three thousand years ago, she was met by a mysterious angel-prophet, who told her that the son she bore should be called Ishmael; that he should be a wild man; that his hand should be against every man, and every man's hand against him; that his seed should be multiplied exceedingly, and that he should become a great nation. (Gen. xvi. 10–12.) Have the Ishmaelites become such a people? Their history and present condition furnish our answer. They have always been recognized as the dreaded enemies of mankind. Their hospitality is found only in exaggerated and questionable fables. Their plundering and belligerent propensities are the same, whether we encounter them in the past or in the present, in the land of Shinar, in the valleys of Spain, on the banks of the Tigris, in Araby the Blessed, or Araby the Barren. Give them the desert for their home, the horse and spear for their companions, murder and rapine for their recreation, and they will envy no man his wealth, and no monarch his throne. Though surrounded for ages by flourishing and polished nations, they have maintained their unchanged, unsubdued, and predicted character. They have not only retained their original characteristics, but have remained through the past, and still are in the present, a great and powerful nation. As a body, they have escaped the yoke of the most victorious monarchies surrounding them. The armies of Sesostris and Cyrus. of Pompey and Trajan, were repeatedly sent against, but never subdued them. The power of Great Britain, which has established a residence in almost every country, has been able to enter their territories only to accomplish the predetermined destruction of some fortified place, and then retire without securing a foothold. The Sultan of Turkey, their nominal ruler, has been compelled to pay them a yearly tax, or be refused permission to transport his caravans across their plains to Mecca. Their conquests in the past have included the greater part of the temperate zone. They are found to-day in force throughout Northern Africa, on the continental shores of the Persian Gulf, and in the plains of Syria and Mesopotamia. Their empire extends from India to the Atlantic Ocean, and embraces a wider range of territory than was possessed by the Romans at the time they were styled "the lords of the world." No nationality on earth can with such manifest propriety wear the double prophetic epithet of "wild and mighty." How was it possible for that poor bond-woman Hagar, as she sat houseless and disconsolate by the fountain in the wilderness, to have discovered and foretold this remarkable fate of her descendants, unless the angel-prophet, commissioned of Jehovah, according to the Scriptures, had first come to her, and made the announcement?

We turn to other and later prophecies, which concern the kin of Ishmael, the Israelite.

The commonwealth of Israel, from its establishment to its dissolution, existed more than fifteen hundred years. It ended with the fall of Samaria under the power of Assyria. At that time the kingdom of Judea alone remained erect, and gathered into itself the whole spirit and life of the Hebrew nationality. It became the representative of the covenant people. Other titles gave place to the terms "Jew" and "Jewish."

It was not far from three thousand two hundred years ago, while the ancestors of this people were wandering in the wilderness, without a city and without a home, that their great leader and prophet foretold their sins and destiny. "Thus saith the Lord," was his authority, and these the words that he spake and recorded: "I will scatter you among the heathen." (Lev. xxvi. 33.) "Ye shall flee as fleeing from the sword." (Lev. xxvi. 36.) "Ye shall have no power to stand before your enemies." (Lev. xxvi. 37.) "Yet for all that I will not cast them away, neither will I destroy them utterly." (Lev. xxvi. 44.) "The Lord shall bring thee into a nation which neither thou nor thy fathers have known." (Deut. xxviii. 36.) "Thou shalt become an astonishment, and a proverb, and a by-word among all the nations whither the Lord shall lead thee." (Deut. xxviii. 37). "And all these plagues shall be upon thee for a *sign* and a *wonder*, and upon thy seed forever." (Deut. xxviii. 46.) "And thou shalt be plucked off the land that thou goest to possess." (Deut. xxviii. 63.) "And the Lord shall scatter thee among all people, from one end of the earth even unto the other." (Deut. xxviii. 64.) "Neither shall the sole of thy foot have rest." (Deut. xxviii. 65.)

The voice of the third prophetic age did not contradict that of the second. While Jerusalem was surrounded with its sacred attractions, Isaiah, Jeremiah, and others, who possessed all the Jewish characteristics, pointed down the path of history to the day when God was to blast the people and their city as with mildew. They declared that their marked and national exclusiveness should not shield them from utter dispersion; that their patriotism, which was never surpassed, should not secure to them a city or a country; that their theocracy, which had been "festooned with the garlands of centuries," should be superseded, and their temple-worship, which had been observed for so many ages, should be forever obliterated.

Those prophets, one after another, declared and recorded the blindness of the people, their ceaseless wanderings, their impenitence, avarice, pusillanimity, spoliation, and unextinguishable existence.

Later, one of the fourth order of prophets, the Great Prophet Himself, appeared in the temple, and confirmed the declarations of the second and third orders. With mingled entreaty and warning, he announced that the sufferings of this people should be such as had never been heard of. "There shall be great tribulation," was his language, "such as was not from the beginning of the world to this time, — no, nor ever shall be." (Matt. xxiv. 21.) "Jerusalem shall be trodden down of the Gentiles until the time of the Gentiles be fulfilled." (Luke xxi. 24.) Here, then, we have this vast array of prophecy concerning the Jews clearly stated, repeated, and intensified. Our questions are brief. Have the persecutions and sufferings predicted of this doomed race befallen them? Have they been dispersed among the nations of the earth? Have they remained, amid their dispersions, a distinct and peculiar people?

Beginning with the Passover a few years after the death of Christ, we are informed that, while two or three million Jews were assembled in Jerusalem, they were suddenly surrounded by the Romans. Three different factions within the city began to murder one another. The unburied dead produced a pestilence. Starvation drove the people to cannibalism. Their temple was fired, and six thousand fell beneath its ruins. Probably not less than one million one hundred thousand perished during a siege of only six months. We are also informed that the whole extent of Jerusalem, except three towers and a small part of the wall, was levelled to the ground. The ploughshare has sin e torn up the very foundations of the sacred city.

All this was but the prelude of their mournful sufferings. Trace their history through the reign of the emperors. Adrian slew five hundred and eighty thousand Jews in battle. Constantine regarded them as "the most hateful of all nations;" and, after having suppressed one of their revolts, he commanded their ears to be cut off, and then dispersed them as vagabonds throughout different countries. Adrian forbade them under penalty of death to approach within three miles of the walls of Jerusalem. Justinian destroyed all their synagogues and abolished their public worship. The Triumphal Arch at Rome and the Coliseum, built by them as slaves, within whose walls they were the first victims slain, bespeak alike their early bondage and misfortunes. So bitter was this spirit of persecution, that had it continued, the extinction of the Jewish race must soon have followed. A change was for some reason providentially inaugurated.

Succeeding the emperors, especially during the reign of Charlemagne, there was a period of Jewish prosperity. The storm that had raged so long and fiercely, cleared away. The troubled waters on which they had been tossed were soothed to rest. It seemed as if the world, by universal consent, had resolved to give this oppressed people time and opportunity to replenish their treasures and recuperate their wasted strength. Throughout the domains of the caliphs, in the East, in Africa, in Spain, and in the Byzantium Empire, the Jews were not only allowed to pursue unmolested their lucrative and enterprising traffic, they were not only merchants of splendor and opulence, but they suddenly arose into offices of dignity and trust. They administered the finances of Christian and Mohammedan kingdoms. They were the ambassadors of the mightiest kings and sovereigns. It was not their religion, their nationality, their genius alone, that had given occasion, under the emperors, for their peculiar treatment, but a Heaven-permitted and Heaven-foretold punishment for a sin involving no ordinary degree of guilt. It is true that Christians have also been persecuted. This was foretold. They suffered, however, not for guilt, as in the case of the Jews, but for the glory of God. The period of Jewish prosper ity, of which we were speaking, was not of long continuance; of different duration in different parts of the world. In the East it was soon interrupted by their own civil dissensions, and by the persecutions of the Moslemite sovereigns. In the west of Europe it was soon succeeded by the age of iron. In Spain the sunlight remained longest, but at length set in a total night of storms. Mahomet announced to the world his doctrine: "There is but one God, and Mahomet is his prophet." The triumphal battle-cries of his followers, "The Koran or death!" "Islamism or war!" echoed through the valleys of Arabia. The Jews were the first whom this pretended prophet endeavored to proselyte. That "God is one" was their own creed; but that a prophet to them had sprung from the seed of Hagar the bond-woman, they proudly denied. They shrank back from him in sullen unbelief. There was no alternative: The Jews of the Arabian peninsula were sold as slaves, were massacred or banished, until none remained. The edict went forth, that the sacred land which had given Mahomet birth should no longer be profaned by the unclean footsteps of an unbeliever. The same bitter spirit of persecution thereupon swept westward. Kingdom after kingdom, people after people, tribe after tribe, followed the dreadful example of the Arabian monarch. "Hep! Hep! Hep!"— the initials of the words "*Hierosolyma est perdita*," "Jerusalem is destroyed," which was the actual cry throughout Germany,— became in spirit well nigh universal. Mohammedanism, Catholicism, and nominal Christianity vied with one another in calling the people to the work of Jewish persecution; each strove to be first in pealing the death-knell of the descendants of Israel. The most unreasonable and unjust accusations were brought forward upon which to condemn them. They were physicians: if they healed their patients, they were charged with employing satanic influence; if their patients died, they were accused of administering poison. They were the advisers of kings: if their advice succeeded, they were charged with receiving their knowledge from Beelzebub; if it proved detrimental, they were arraigned for conspiracy against the realm. If they chanced to be poor, they were charged with being cursed of God; if rich, with being unlawful extortioners. On the most trivial complaints they were arrested and condemned. Hundreds suffered death for the single — real or imaginary — offence of one. The plagues of Northern Europe, the choleras of France, the leprosy and epidemics of the East and West, North and South, were attributed to them. The poor pillaged them; the clergy denounced them; the rich repudiated their loans, and monarchs gained the right of entire confiscation. No political or religious movement sought their weal. The feudal system gave neither place nor advantage to the Jews. They could not be lords, they were not serfs; they could make no claims for protection from any source; there was scarcely a city of continental Europe where they were not brutally massacred by the crusaders. Chivalry, the mother of so much good to others, was a system of oppression and of almost unmitigated evil to them. Hallam's account of their condition in the middle ages is short, but significant. "They were everywhere the objects of popular insult and oppression. A time of festivity to others was usually to them a season of mockery or massacre." They were left without appeal or protection. Every passion in every grade of society was let loose upon them.

Passing westward, we are informed by history that the cry which became popular throughout England was, "Destroy these enemies of Christ!" At the coronation of Richard I. they were hunted out that they might be butchered. In York they resolved to die by their own hands. Fathers with razors cut the throats of wives and children, and then committed suicide or employed their domestics to kill them.

In 1277, hundreds were hanged and quartered on charge of clipping the coin, of which they were, no doubt, guilty, having been driven to it by exorbitant taxation.

In 1287, all the Jews of the realm were ordered to be apprehended in a single day. Their goods were confiscated to the king, and they, to the number of fifteen thousand six hundred and sixty, were banished from the country. If one remained after a fixed day, he was to be hanged without mercy.

A similar fate awaited them a century later in France. Under the Capet dynasty they were all banished, and every debt due them was declared null and void. Subsequently they re-entered France, and were a second time expelled, though they could command by deed and mortgage one half the wealth of Paris.

Under Philip the Fair, in 1300, their synagogues were converted into churches, and their gravestones dug up to furnish building materials for the city. In 1394, they were for the third time expelled from the kingdom.

Thus, by repeated persecutions and banishments, France and England were purified, as it was deemed, from the infections of the Jewish race and infidelity. But Spain still remained their asylum. The Jews of that country had become far nobler in rank than those of Germany, England, or France. They were the most enlightened and influential class in Spain. Elsewhere they had been reduced to sordid occupations and debasing means of extorting riches as best they could; but in Spain they were cultivators of the soil, ministers of finances, judges in supreme courts, and stood at the head of educational, commercial, and political affairs.

Their golden age, in that country, remained bright and resplendent for centuries. A Jewish writer thus speaks of Spain and the condition of the Jews in it during their persecutions elsewhere: "Spain might be looked on as our happy land and earthly paradise. Party madness has not disturbed our sweet domestic peace. Every one can worship God in his own manner, without, on that account, being hated or despised. Even Israel, the oppressed and persecuted people elsewhere find in happy Spain a haven of freedom, and here can sing thanksgiving to the mighty God of Israel, who has given his people a rest so long unknown." But, at length, the same spirit that had swept over the continent, over England and France, fell upon Spain — the more fatal from its long delay. Ferdinand and Isabella determined that the air of their prosperous domains should no longer be breathed by any one who did not profess the Catholic faith. Their fatal edict commanding all unbaptized Jews to abandon the kingdom was published in 1492. Thus the most industrious and successful population that Spain ever knew — under no charge of recent conspiracy, on account of no disloyal demeanor — were driven from their homes. The formal charges brought against them were centuries old. Four months only were allowed them to depart. If found on Spanish shores after that time, inevitable death was the penalty.

The number of exiles is variously estimated, the highest figures reaching eight hundred thousand. They left this country of their fathers, which had been fertilized by their labor, enriched with their wealth, and adorned with their learning. They left their synagogues, their schools, the sacred tombs of their ancestors, and the newly-excavated graves of their friends and kindred. With a resolute spirit of devotion, which challenges our admiration, they resolved to relinquish everything rather than desert their ancient religion. They were wanderers, with no hospitable shore on the face of the globe to welcome them. It makes one's blood run cold to read their fate after this expulsion from Spain. They were enslaved; they were killed and torn open by the Turks, who believed that they had swallowed their gold on their departure from Spain; some were landed on desolate islands, there to perish; others were drowned in the sea; some reached the coast of Genoa, bearing with them famine and plague; while others found their way to lonely places in Asia and Africa. A few were admitted into Rome, but were afterwards treated with such severe inhospitality, that they were compelled to sell their children for bread. In different places they were bonded, bequeathed, pawned, bought and sold, plundered and murdered.

What a catalogue of misfortunes to be meted out to one people! Can history show another such record? Arabia, England, France, and Spain, with the hills of all Europe and plains of all Asia, stained with Jewish blood, and echoing with Jewish groans, indicate what no other people could bear and live. Every heart must yield a response to the beautiful song of one who could appreciate their condition.

"O, weep for those that wept by Babel's stream,
Whose shrines are desolate, whose land a dream;
Weep for the harp of Judah's broken shell;
Mourn — where their God hath dwelt the godless dwell.

"Tribes of the wandering foot and weary breast,
How shall ye flee away and be at rest?
The wild dove hath her nest, the fox his cave,
Mankind their country — Israel but the grave!"

"And there shall be great tribulation, such as was not from the beginning of the world to this time; no, nor ever shall be. Behold, I have told you before." (Matt. xxiv. 21, 25.) We pause at this point for a moment, to fix the exact relation of prophecy to the misfortunes we have recounted. The relation was not arbitrary. The punishments were inflicted in consequence of the violation of law, and not for the purpose of fulfilling prophecy. These events, being foreknown supernaturally, were foretold that we might believe. God did not command Ferdinand and Isabella to banish the Jews, though he knew they would do it. He did not hold Spain guiltless for he act, but has shrouded her prosperity from that day to this. Jewish history presents not an instance of the punishment of the sins of the fathers visited upon the children of successive generations, but of each generation bearing the punishment of its own sin. The Jews, since the Christian era, have been committing a definite sin (and the blackest sin possible when committed under the revelations of the Holy Ghost) — the avowed rejection of Christ. When the Jews stood amid the scenes of the crucifixion, shouting, "His blood be upon us and our children!" they uttered a terrible imprecation. They were almost guilty of a second apostasy. The same infatuated cry has broken from the lips of every Jew, in every age. Until those lips are closed, their disgrace and punishment will continue. There will be years of respite, but years of proscription will follow. The present is a golden age in Jewish history; but it will end — end either in their renewed persecutions or their conversion to Christ.

The Lord hath spoken concerning it. Such an avowed rejection of Christ cannot long be passed in silence. The day they shall look upon Him whom they have pierced, and mourn, that day shall witness an end of their sufferings and dispersion.

But again: Have the Jews, as predicted, been in a peculiar sense a wandering people? Have they, as foretold by Ezekiel, been "scattered into all the winds"? (Ezek. xvii. 21.) Have they been "wanderers among the nations," as predicted by Hosea? (Hos. ix. 17) — a prediction which has been reiterated by major and minor, Old and New Testament prophets. Their history is so well known in this respect, that we hardly need pause to answer. Take up a volume of the history of any country, at any age since the fall of Jerusalem, and this strange figure encounters you. You find the Jews there just as we now find them — dwelling in the seclusion of their own communities. When Denham and Clapperton, the first travellers who ventured across the great Sahara, reached the banks of Lake Tchad, there they found that the "Wandering Jew" had preceded them. When the Portuguese settled in the Indian Peninsula, and when the English took possession of Aden, in South Arabia, they found the Jews were there before them. The missionary Gobat found them on the elevated plains of Abyssinia; and the European traveller, in his distant and dangerous migrations, always hears of their existence in places which are beyond his reach. As it has been in the past, so is it in the present. "The restless feet" of this ancient people of God are pressing every inhabitable region of the world. They are met in every port, in every city, in every mart of business, in every climate, among people of every language, from the freezing snows of Siberia to the burning sands of Sahara. From Morocco to Lisbon, from Japan to Britain, from Borneo to Archangel, from

Hindostan to Honduras, no other inhabitant of the earth is so well known as the Jew. He is found everywhere, but everywhere felt to be, not a traveller, but a stranger. He bears about with him continually the unmistakable image and reflection of Hebrew prophecy. What is more remarkable is this: Amid all their sufferings and wanderings, in harmony with prophecy, they have remained a distinct and peculiar people. With neither a country nor a nation that could be called their own, they have uniformly preserved a distinct nationality. A rapid glance at history will show us that such a condition has fallen to the lot of no people excepting the descendants of Israel. Though they have looked upon the mightiest revolutions among the Gentiles; though they have been moving among extensive migrations, from east to west, and from north to south; though they have been dwellers in different empires while in their ascendant, supremacy, and decline; though we have seen them passing through all those political and civil convulsions which have destroyed every nation around Judea, except the Persians alone, who restored them from their Babylonish captivity,—yet, for eighteen centuries they have remained, in all essential features, the same. The learned Egyptians, the warlike Assyrians, the ancient Babylonians, and the proud Romans, who have formed some of the most powerful monarchies of earth, cannot now point to a single living representative. But these Jews, of still greater antiquity, who have been among and a part of the most distinctive changes, are numbered by millions. Though they have been oppressed, vanquished, and enslaved, yet, like the "Wandering Jew" of the legend, they have been the ordained witnesses and survivors of all the revolutions of ages. It is true that ukase and edict have compelled them at one time to adopt peculiar clothing, at another the dress of the common people; that different observances have been, from time to time, forced upon them; but it is also true that these avowed enemies of Jesus of Nazareth have remained *Jews*. Emperors and kings have learned that, while they may make slaves or noblemen of them, they cannot transform them into Russians or Europeans. They have been isolated in their nationality as by divine command.

They maintain the same laws, and number about twice as many, as when Moses led them out from the land of Egypt. They have continued to preserve their own and their old identity. Living in the present, they are a prophetic thing of the past. All who have read their history, and have had acquaintance with them, know that they possess to-day nearly the same spirit of national pride and boasted superiority as when David occupied the throne of Israel.

Into the meanest streets of Europe, Asia, or America, the beggarly-looking Jewish hawker carries with him the conviction that he is a representative of the nation chosen to stand at the head of the world. Whatever his losses, the dream of past and future glory never deserts him. Point to his meanness, and his pride will instantly raise him above your contempt. Though banished from the world, he is haughty as a Roman. He continually throws back the sentence of banishment when passed, and retreats under the lofty conviction that his race is not excluded as unworthy, but merely kept apart as sacred. He owns it is humiliated, but claims that it is hallowed and reserved for the sure, though tardy, fulfilment of God's prophecies. "The fear of man" is constantly before his eyes. The same timid, cautious watchfulness is stamped upon each. Every one is a Shylock of Venice or an Isaac of York. Their conduct up to nearly the present year has been such as to inspire that hate against them which resulted in their persecutions centuries ago. The instincts of the world have been to pass them by, unless some selfish advantage could be gained.

Until but recently, the companionship of an emigrant fresh from the peat bogs of Ireland, and the presence of an ebony slave from the Sea Islands of the South, would have been less objectionable than Jewish associations, though rich, intelligent, and powerful. However much we desired their spiritual weal, we could not help hating that sullen pride, that expression of ruined greatness, which in their person everywhere met our eyes. That thirst to extort from us, because we are "Gentile dogs," the pound sterling, or the "pound of flesh," though nearest the heart, bespeak their continued intolerance, and the source of the excessive dislike we have borne them.

They retain their ancient looks, as well as character. Meet almost any one of these mysterious strangers in the crowded streets of London, in a Parisian square, on the Rialto of Venice, in one of the quarters of the Eternal City, on the sun-burnt coasts of Africa, amid the traffic of New York, or in the romantic gold regions of California, you would know him. There is no mistaking that peculiar countenance, which bears the lineaments of the descendants of Abraham, as reflected from the exhumed slabs of Nineveh. His receding forehead, his full eye and quick glance, proclaim his lineage as unmistakably as if we saw him weeping over the ruins of his beloved but fallen Jerusalem.

Is there nothing in all this to arrest our attention? The continued existence of this people; the wandering and wondering suspense with which they move among us while awaiting the consummation of their history; their non-coalescence, though mingling with all the nations on earth for sixty generations, and each event of their history set forth in so many prophecies; the recent change in their conduct, and in the sentiments of the world towards them, — have all these things no meaning or cause? Yes; chance. What a marvellous God, then, is Chance! Let us fall down and worship him.

A discussion of the Jewish people and prophecy cannot pass a certain question in silence which is frequently asked: *Will the Jews return to Palestine?*

The climate and soil of Palestine have been frequently misrepresented in books of travel. Many travellers are "*highwaymen*" rather than explorers. Let us quote from some of the more accurate observers. "Palestine," says Volney, "unites different climates under the same sky; and, with its numerous advantages of soil and climate, it is not surprising that the Greeks and Romans ranked it among the most beautiful of their provinces. The land in the plains is fat and loamy, and exhibits every sign of the greatest fecundity; and, were nature assisted by art, the fruits of the most distant countries might be produced within the distance of twenty leagues." "Galilee," says Malte Brun, "would be a Paradise, were it inhabited by an industrious people, and ruled by a beneficent government. Vine-stocks are to be seen here a foot and a half in diameter." Gibbon also speaks respecting both the climate and soil of these regions in the highest terms. "Under a good government," says Dr. Clarke, "the produce of the Holy Land would exceed all calculation. Its perennial harvests, the salubrity of its climate, its matchless plains, hills, and vales, prove it to be a garden of the Lord." "Palestine," says Isaac Taylor, "in the age of its wealth, was a samplar of the world; it was a museum counting many lands in one; the tread of the camel, in two or three hours, may now give the traveller a recollection of his own home, come whence he may, from any country between the torrid zone and our northern latitudes. Every spring its hill-sides are gay with the embroidery of flowers — the resplendent crocus, the scented hyacinth, the anemone, the narcissus, the daffodil, the florid poppy, and the ranunculus, the tulip, the lily, and the rose. These jewels of the spring morning, these children of the dew, bedded in divans of sweet thyme, invite millions of bees, and the most showy of the insect orders: flowers, perfumes, butterflies, birds of song, — all things humble and beautiful here flourish, and are safe; for man seldom intrudes upon this smiling wilderness."

Moses predicted that the soil should rest from culti

vation while the Jews dwelt in the land of strangers. (Lev. xxvi. 33–45.) The eagle eye of prophecy continues to watch it closely. Its native countryman is to-day obliged to sow its fields, musket in hand. The prophet declared that "the substance should remain in the soil." There it is stored, as for future use. There exists a feeling of secret sympathy between this country and its exiled people. The very earth seems to feel that its true children are absent, and will come home again. That land stubbornly refuses to yield to other possessors the rich harvests which lie concealed within its bosom. But what of all this? Nothing, replies the sceptic.

The Jews are rich. "Rich as a Jew" has passed into a proverb. Generally speaking, they are the bankers, the brokers, the merchants, and the traders of all countries; but, since their expulsion from Spain, the agriculturists of none. It has been remarked that the gold of all Europe is so much in their hands that they can make a monetary crisis at pleasure. The passion of the most orthodox Jews is to put themselves in position to turn, at short notice, all their possessions into ready money and movables, as if they ever had their eyes upon the words of Isaiah — "to bring their sons from far, their silver and gold with them." No seats in parliaments, or cabinets, or chairs of learning, no political ties to thrones or republics, no lapse of time, no witchery of music or song, can soothe, or lull to rest, certain inherited desires, or inspire within them love for any country but their own. Their deposits of silver and gold, which stretch their commercial and golden links across land and sea over almost the entire circle of Gentile rule, gravitate nowhere else with such an irresistible tendency, if not destiny, as towards the Promised Land. Thither the people look and thither they long to turn their weary footsteps. They have, in every age, clung with fondest love and devotion to the thoughts of their father-land. Heathens, Christians, and Mohammedans have alternately possessed Judea; the Saracens have preyed upon it, and the descendants of Ishmael have repeatedly overrun it; the children of Israel have alone been denied the right to occupy it, though their hearts have ever been on fire for its possession.

When the crusaders were seized with a temporary fever to conquer the Holy Land, in order that they might become masters of the sepulchre of the crucified Saviour, the Jews everywhere beheld their preparations with dismay. They felt, in every instinct of their soul, that that land was their own, and that no other race, or nation, or religion on the globe had any right whatever to make such a crusade, or rebuild its tombs.

When Julian issued his edict for rebuilding the temple and for the restoration of the Jewish worship to its original splendor, Milman represents that the whole Jewish world was in commotion.

The following, in substance, is his account: The Jews felt that their time and day of deliverance had come. They called Julian their Messiah. They came from the most distant places to be present and assist at the great national work. Those who were unable to come envied their more fortunate brothers as they set out upon their glorious pilgrimage, and waited in anxious hope for the first intelligence that they could again send their offerings, or make, their journey, to the temple of the God of Abraham in his holy place. Their wealth was poured forth in lavish profusion. All who were near the spot, and could not contribute so amply, offered their personal exertions. Blessed were the hands that toiled in such a work. Unworthy the blood of Israel was he who did not unlock, at such a call, his most secret and sacred hoards. Men cheerfully surrendered the hard-won treasures of their avarice; women offered up their jewelled ornaments; the very tools to be employed were thought to be sanctified by the service. They were made, in some cases, of the most costly metals. Some had shovels and baskets of silver. Women were seen carrying materials in robes of velvet and mantles of silk. Men blind from birth groped among the ruins to lend their embarrassing aid; the aged tottered along the way bowed beneath the weight of a burden such as they had not carried since the days of their vigorous manhood. The confidence and triumph of the Jews were unbounded. The Christian world looked on in amazement, and wondered if the murderers of the Son of God would actually be permitted to rebuild their ancient city, and raise their temple again from "the abomination of desolation" while they rejected Christ.

Materials accumulated from all quarters; the work commenced. They had dug down to a considerable depth, and were preparing to lay the foundations, when suddenly flames of fire came bursting from the centre of the hill with terrific explosions. The affrighted workmen fled on all sides The project dear to every Jewish heart was abandoned. The occurrence may have been natural or supernatural; we think it natural: the Jews thought otherwise. It matters not. In consequence of it, and in the sudden death of the remarkable man and apostate, Julian, who led the enterprise, the Christian world thought it saw the vengeance of God, and the Jewish world saw the extinction of the long and fondly-cherished hopes of a *speedy* return to Jerusalem.

Notwithstanding this signal defeat of their plans, Jerusalem has never been forgotten. To-day they are alert to catch any word that comes from the land of their fathers. Though they have spoken every dialect, wandered on the banks of every river and sea, their attachment for the sacred soil is undiminished. Their patriotism is the same as when they were in Babylonish bondage, and their earnestness the same as when they set about rebuilding the temple. Their reverence for the ancient metropolis is stronger than the most ardent patriotism on record. Cheerfully they make long and weary pilgrimages to lay their hand upon some relic of its past glory, or to weep over the tombs of their ancestors. Let but the leading Jews in different countries announce the intention of purchasing Jerusalem, or of returning to the land of Palestine, and the thought would fire the race with an enthusiasm that would astonish the world. There, they feel, is their home. Nowhere else on earth can the ordinances of their religion be celebrated. Does not this unquenchable thirst, this undying ardor, point to the inevitable fulfilment of prophecy? What thinking man is not compelled to acknowledge that it is now morally certain that the waste places of Judea shall again blossom as the rose? Do not the natural and the supernatural unite in a common horizon, near which is seen this peculiar people going back to the Promised Land, from their long Gentile dispersion, as they went back from their Egyptian and Babylonian captivity? Can they much longer reject Christ? Can we not almost hear the touching and poetic exhortation of Isaiah, "Ye can speak comfortably to Jerusalem, and cry unto her that her warfare is accomplished, that her iniquity is pardoned"? (Is. xl. 2.) Then shall they come with rejoicing, and it shall be their last return and their final restoration.

"The king of France complacently announced to the French Chambers on the 4th day of December, 1841, that he had concluded a connection with the King of Prussia and the Queen of England for the consolidation and repose of the Ottoman empire. The repose of a part of it will, beyond question, be secured, but not, however, by human, connections." * When that consolidated repose does take place, it will be sweet and lasting. When that day comes, it will come to all — to Jew and Gentile alike. The millennium is only another name for the consummation of the spiritual blessings promised to Abraham and reaffirmed by the Messiah.

The world is moving rapidly towards thrilling events. The Jews, as a body, are on the verge of acknowledging that Jesus was the Messiah. The great obstacle is, that they fear one another, and their ecclesiastical rulers. Let Christ be acknowledged in a civil

* Stanley.

capacity by them, and evangelical Christianity will have made its sublimest conquest. The Jews cannot become Roman Catholics, for they can never worship the virgin Mary; they cannot become radical Unitarians, for their Christ will be divine. They can become, and will become, the soundest evangelical Trinitarians on earth. What a foreign missionary society they could organize! Hereditary zeal, immense wealth, and a familiarity with every tongue on the globe, give them advantages over all other nationalities in the evangelization of the world. The morning dawns!

In wandering through this wonderful field of history, imposing as the truth of God and strange as the most stupendous miracle, we may for a moment have seemed to lose sight of the main question at issue — that of prophetic inspiration and a supernatural book. It is in appearance only. The return is natural and easy. The philosophical Hume asserted that "a wise man should proportion his belief to the evidence." Grant it. Do these things constitute a chapter of accidents? Are they the "fortuitous concurrence of incidents"? Could arms, genius, climate, politics, nationality, or religion have suggested those far-off scenes of suffering, depression, and preservation of the Jewish people?

Silent all as the hammers that reared their sublime temple. We have D. D.'s among us without number, and many of them without merit. We have M. D.'s, and LL. D.'s. Can any of them predict minutely, and without qualification or alternative, the fate of an existing city or nation two thousand years hence — a fate which shall be entirely dependent upon the sins or virtues of the people? All sane men feel that such things are dark as death to mortal ken. These Hebrew prophets have given us, however, fact upon fact and prophecy upon prophecy, extending through many generations, involving the most complicated and hair-breadth predictions, as well as those of more general application. They have been fulfilled to the letter, by responsible and absolutely free agents. Let the wise man proportion his belief to the evidence. Will he longer reject the sacred volume?

PROPHECIES

RESPECTING CHRIST AND CHRISTIANITY.

"God, who at sundry times and in divers manners spake in time past unto the fathers by the prophets, hath in these last days spoken unto us by his Son, whom he hath appointed heir of all things, by whom also he made the worlds." *Hebrews* i. 1, 2.

"I saw in the night visions, and behold, one like the Son of man came with the clouds of heaven, and came to the Ancient of days, and they brought him near before him. And there was given him dominion, and glory, and a kingdom, that all people, nations, and languages should serve him: his dominion is an everlasting dominion, which shall not pass away, and his kingdom that which shall not be destroyed." *Daniel* vii. 13, 14.

"And the seventh angel sounded; and there were great voices in heaven, saying, The kingdoms of this world are become the kingdoms of our Lord and of his Christ; and he shall reign forever and ever." *Revelation* xi. 15.

"And John, calling unto him two of his disciples, sent them to Jesus, saying, Art thou he that should come? or look we for another? When the men were come unto him, they said, John the Baptist hath sent us unto thee, saying, Art thou he that should come? or look we for another? And in that same hour he cured many of their infirmities and plagues, and of evil spirits, and unto many that were blind he gave sight. Then Jesus, answering, said unto them, Go your way, and tell John what things ye have seen and heard; how that the blind see, the lame walk, the lepers are cleansed, the deaf hear, the dead are raised, to the poor the gospel is preached. *Luke* vii. 19–22.

"O, who shall paint Him? Let the sweetest tone
That ever trembled on the harps of heaven
Be discord; let the chanting seraphim,
Whose anthem is eternity, be dumb;
For praise and wonder, adoration, all
Melt into muteness, ere they soar to thee,
Thou sole perfection! theme of countless worlds!"

ROBERT MONTGOMERY.

III.

PROPHECIES

RESPECTING CHRIST AND CHRISTIANITY.

IT is the tendency of mankind to dwell upon the glories of antiquity. It finds an iron age in the present, but a golden one in the past. We throw the wreath of distinction about the head of some sage, hero, or king who has already appeared. No heroes are concealed in the future. The Jewish nationality forms a complete exception to this general rule. The entire Hebrew commonwealth was established upon a most vivid view of the future. In its days of greatest power and splendor, under the reigns of David and Solomon, future events furnished its inspiring themes. We need express no surprise, much less refer the cause to climate, laws, or national peculiarities. The reiterated promises of the prophets respecting a coming King, and the establishment of his empire over the whole world, are explanatory. This great and thrilling thought had been the burden of nearly every prophecy. We hear it in the communications of God to the fallen race in Genesis. We hear it in the thundering of the final judgments of Malachi. Though the prophetic books were composed in the centre of Asia, amid the sands of Arabia, in the deserts of Judea, in the four courts of the temple of the Jews, in the rustic schools of the prophets of Bethel and Jericho, in the stately palaces of Babylon, and wherever else the nation wandered,—though their composition extended from the time that Moses held his pen in the wilderness, four hundred years before the war of Troy, and nine hundred before the publication of the writings of Thales and Confucius, down to the last page of Jewish inspiration,—the writers never varied the theme of their discourse. They never lost sight of that bright, rising, glorious star of the future, which symbolized a kingdom suited to the weary and disappointed hearts of men. Remove the thought of Christ and his work from the Bible, and its sublimest prophecies lose their charm. Recognize Christ, and not only every prophecy, but every type and figure, every promise and word of comfort to nations and individuals, is lit up as with sunlight. All their united and concentrated rays of light point calmly and steadily to Bethlehem. Every thing else is eclipsed. The Jewish golden age is not Adam's abode in Eden, not the period of patriarchal rule, but the kingdom of the Messiah.

The date of the earthly appearance of Christ claims our attention. There was a time, above every other in Jewish history, when the people were aroused with unusual excitement and expectation. Multitudes who had been residents in distant parts of the world now took up their abode in or near their great metropolis. Every startling event was noted. As soon as the voice of the Baptist was heard, the people flocked to the banks of the Jordan. Publican and Pharisee received his preliminary baptism. They were not filled with idle curiosity, but they believed those were the days of the promised Messiah. The whole Eastern world was alert with eye and ear. It was believed at Rome, while Pompey held Jerusalem, that Judea, or, according to Suetonius, that nature, was to bring forth a king. The senate decreed that no child born during the year of the conquest should be permitted to live. Every family in Rome thought it saw in its own child the universal monarch. The decree could not be enforced. There was no doubt in the Jewish mind that the time of Herod and Pilate would witness the advent of the One of whom all the prophets had spoken. Let us examine the ground of this expectation. Beginning with the patriarchal age we find that the last blessing of Jacob to his sons contains the following prediction: "The sceptre shall not depart from Judah, nor a lawgiver from between his feet, until Shiloh come; and unto him shall the gathering of the people be." (Gen. xlix. 10.) We read also in Malachi the following prediction: "Behold, I will send my messenger, and he shall prepare the way before me; and the Lord, whom ye seek, shall suddenly come to his temple, even the messenger of the covenant, whom ye delight in; behold, he shall come, saith the Lord of Hosts." (Mal. iii. 1.) The prophet Daniel is still more definite, and seems to depart from the general rule laid down, that God holds the times and seasons of events in his own councils. The importance of the event may have required this singular departure. "Seventy weeks are determined upon thy people, and upon thy holy city, to finish the transgression, and to make an end of sins, and to make reconciliation for iniquity, and to bring in everlasting righteousness, and to seal up the vision and prophecy, and to anoint the most Holy. Know therefore and understand, that from the going forth of the commandment to restore and to build Jerusalem, unto the Messiah the Prince, shall be seven weeks, and threescore and two weeks: the street shall be built again, and the wall, even in troublous times. And after threescore and two weeks shall Messiah be cut off, but not for himself: and the people of the prince that shall come shall destroy the city and the sanctuary; and the end thereof shall be with a flood, and unto the end of the war desolations are determined. And he shall confirm the covenant with many for one week: and in the midst of the week he shall cause the sacrifice and the oblation to cease, and for the overspreading of abominations he shall make it desolate, even until the consummation, and that determined shall be poured upon the desolate." (Dan. ix. 24–27.) It was a common practice among the Jews to compute time by weeks of years. In this particular instance the Jews would have misunderstood Daniel, had he meant ordinary weeks. Uniting these different prophecies and facts, we can approximately fix upon the time at which the Messiah must appear, in order to fulfil the prophecies. The limits are these: He must come, according to the first prediction, before the national offerings and sacrifices of the Jews should finally cease, — before their theocracy should fall in all its departments into neglect and disuse, — before the sceptre should be smitten from Judah's hand, the crown fall from his head, the law giver depart from between his feet, and before the house of David should be found to possess no descendant to maintain its name and authority. He must make his first *public appearance*, being, at least, twelve years of age (the age at which a Jewish child became "a child of the law"), before Archelaus, the Jewish king, should be dethroned and banished.

According to the prediction from Malachi, he must come while the temple of the Jews was yet standing; and the public work of his life could not commence until the prophetic silence which had succeeded Malachi, should be broken by the voice of one like Elias.

According to the prophecy of Daniel, he must appear four hundred and eighty-three years after the command of Cyrus to rebuild Jerusalem, or after Ezra went up from Babylon to Jerusalem bearing a commission to restore the government to the Jews. Let the eye scan the horizon. Does one appear within the prescribed limits who answers our expectations? Is not the Kingdom of Jesus Christ subduing all others? "When therefore the angel says to Daniel, 'Seventy weeks are determined upon thy people,' &c., was this written after the event? Or can it reasonably be ascribed to chance, that from the seventh year of Artaxerxes the king (when Ezra went up from Babylon unto Jerusalem with a commission to restore the government of the Jews) to the death of Christ (from ann. Nabon. 290 to ann. Nabon.

780) should be precisely 490 (seventy weeks of) years? Or can it reasonably be ascribed to chance, that from the twenty-eighth year of Ataxerxes, when the walls of Jerusalem were finished, to the birth of Christ (from ann. Nabon. 311 to 745), should be precisely 434 (sixty-two weeks of) years? When Daniel further says, 'And he shall confirm (or, nevertheless he shall confirm) the covenant with many for one week,' was this written after the event? Or can it reasonably be ascribed to chance, that, from the death of Christ (ann. Dom. 33) to the command given first to Peter to preach to Cornelius and the Gentiles (ann. Dom. 40), should be exactly seven (one week of) years?" *

The coincidences multiply upon examination, until they are overwhelming. That Being, whose name has become the inspiring watchword of all nations, did not commence his public ministry until after the warning voice of John the Baptist had been heard in the wilderness. He made his first public appearance in the temple of the Jews, and confounded the learned doctors of the nation, when twelve years of age — on the very year that the Jewish king Archelaus was banished. Coponius was then appointed procurator, and the kingdom of Judea, the last remnant of the greatness of Israel, was debased into a part of the province of Syria.

Devout Jews throughout the world acknowledge that the Messiah ought to have followed John the Baptist.

* Inquiries of Dr. Samuel Clarke, suggested by Sir Isaac Newton

A distinguished modern Jew has remarked, that if he thought Jesus of Nazareth were the Messiah, he should kill himself by shouting his praises. Coincidences so overwhelming cannot be ignored. They demand the world's investigation.

But other prophecies relating to the place and family line in which Christ should appear arrest our attention. We read in Genesis that an angel of the Lord called unto Abraham out of heaven, and said, "By myself have I sworn, saith the Lord, for because thou hast done this thing, and hast not withheld thy son, thine only son, that in blessing I will bless thee, and in multiplying I will multiply thy seed as the stars of the heaven, and as the sand which is upon the sea-shore; and thy seed shall possess the gate of his enemies; and in thy seed shall all the nations of the earth be blessed; because thou hast obeyed my voice." (Gen. xxii. 16–18.)

Moses, of the second order of prophets, thus speaks to the children of Israel: "The Lord thy God will raise up unto thee a Prophet from the midst of thee, of thy brethren, like unto me; unto him ye shall hearken; according to all that thou desiredst of the Lord thy God in Horeb, in the day of the assembly, saying, Let me not hear again the voice of the Lord my God, neither let me see this great fire any more, that I die not. And the Lord said unto me, They have well spoken that which they have spoken. I will raise them up a Prophet from among their brethren, like unto thee, and will put my words in his mouth; and he shall speak unto them all that I shall command him. And it shall come to pass, that whosoever will not hearken unto my words, which he shall speak in my name, I will require it of him." (Deut. xviii. 15–19.) Isaiah, speaking of the age of the Messiah, says, "And in that day there shall be a root of Jesse, which shall stand for an ensign of the people; to it shall the Gentiles seek: and his rest shall be glorious." (Isaiah xi. 10.) Micah, speaking of the place of his birth, says, "But thou, Bethlehem Ephratah, though thou be little among the thousands of Judah, yet out of thee shall he come forth unto me that is to be Ruler in Israel; whose goings forth have been from of old, from everlasting." (Micah v. 2.) After the visit of the Magi of the East to Jerusalem, in the days of Herod, we read that, "When Herod the king had heard these things, he was troubled, and all Jerusalem with him. And when he had gathered all the chief priests and scribes of the people together, he demanded of them where Christ should be born. And they said unto him, In Bethlehem of Judea: for thus it is written by the prophet, And thou Bethlehem, in the land of Judah, art not the least among the princes of Judah: for out of thee shall come a Governor, that shall rule my people Israel." (Matt. ii. 2–6.)

Gathering up these various prophecies, we discover that, in order to secure their fulfilment, the predicted One must come, not from the ancient Babylonian or Assyrian empire, not from classical Greece, or imperial Rome, where the world would have looked for him, but he must be an Israelite, of the tribe of Judah, of the family line of David, and from the town of Bethlehem. The spot of his birth must not be near, but remote from, the scenes of his childhood. The place where he begins his ministry is not to be the place of his birth, but elsewhere. He must come from Egypt, but be called a Nazarene. On all these points the prophets leave no alternative. Violence in exposition is the only escape. Our thoughts are fastened to the hills of Bethlehem, and to the family line of David, as inevitably as the north fastens and holds to itself the needle.

The predicted character of the Messiah must not be overlooked.

Some of the wisest and best of the ancients had represented what they thought embodied the highest types of excellence. They had been in possession of sublime dreams, which had been excited, perhaps, by the voice heard in Eden, and reported through tradition, or, perhaps, by the words of prophecy which had found their way beyond the boundaries of Judea. They were but dreams. No one had exemplified them. No one was expected to. The best of the ancient heathen were trying to steer their barks and shape their course towards some ideal, instead of towards some real personage, who, they believed, would come on earth. The nations at large felt that they needed something which they did not possess. They desired a new order of things — a new king, or a new kingdom. The most devoted devotees of every religion in the world, before the coming of Jesus, felt, and in most cases expressed, a craving for divine revelations. Brahminism, tired of itself, demanded a living and divine intelligence, which should hold converse with men. The Buddhist desired a living and divine intelligence *in man*. The old Persian expressed his want of an infinite and absolute being, called "Illimitable Time." The Egyptian, weary of dead monotony, asked for a living intelligence, a witness of the hidden and silent God. The Greek was distressed that his mythology did not furnish him with an embodiment of fate and power, something real and not abstract. The Goth demanded an Odin, who could travel from city to city, and heal the diseases of the people. The Roman felt he must have something more for a God supreme than the one visible in the marble statuary of Jupiter at the Capitol. All the gods of Rome were collected in a single temple. They stood there as objects of the mockery of humanity, which had become tired and disgusted with idols. Then rose from the city a distressed cry, which was echoed back from every part of the world, for a new and better manifestation of the Deity. Mankind took no pleasure in the radiance that had been thrown over a distant past. It mourned a degenerate present, and looked forward to a dark and uncertain future. Thus ended the revelations to the heathen world.

Turn to the obscure Hebrew nationality. Listen to the voice of its teachers and prophets. They announced that a distinguished personage would arise, and accomplish for the world a most extraordinary work, and leave to the race a faultless system of morality and religion. They announced that his teachings should be rejected by the Jews, received by the Gentiles, and be by them extended in subsequent ages throughout the whole world. They predicted that his reign would diffuse universal happiness, and furnish to the race the most perfect conditions of peace and consolation ever enjoyed by mankind. They did not merely express dissatisfaction with the national religion as then practised; they did not merely fail to find among their countrymen a national leader who was faultless in life and character; they did not merely give an indifferent account of a future Reformer and Saviour; but besides designating the date and place of his appearance, and the character of his mission, with remarkable uniformity, they laid great stress, first and last, upon certain qualities which were to adorn him — qualities which, if actually possessed, would distinguish their possessor from all others who have lived, and make him the most inexplicable personage of all times and of all nations. The Hebrew prophets retained in the promised Messiah the most brilliant and thrilling hopes, whilst the hopes of all others were shrouded in darkness. They declared that his life should combine every virtue, and be a model of every excellence. Isaiah draws characteristic after characteristic of this divine personage, until One stands before us attractive and marvellous beyond comparison. He represents him as divine and human; as God-begotten and man-born; whose humanity is temporal, whose kingdom and nature are eternal. He is said to be rich and poor, a master and a slave, a king and a subject, a lion and lamb, religious and yet an upbraider of religion. Sometimes he is named, sometimes unnamed. Sometimes he is represented as near, sometimes as receding into distant ages. Who could have believed that such a one would actually come to the earth — one whom the fondest and purest desires of the whole world find to be "all in all"? The Hindoo would then find the divine intelligence conversing with men; the Buddhist, the divine intelligence in man; the old Persian, a being properly called Illimitable Time; the Egyptian, a witness of the silent God; the Greek, the embodiment of fate and power; the Roman, something more than the marble statuary in the Pantheon; and the Goth, a physician travelling from city to city, and healing the people of their diseases. The sublimest ideals of the most exalted minds, and the noblest aspirations ever breathed by the race, or dared to be hoped for, would suffer no disappointment at his coming. Listen to the blended song of those prophets while contemplating the future glory of this Prince and kingdom: — "I behold him, but not now: I see him, but not nigh. He shall have dominion from sea to sea, and from the river unto the ends of the earth. Break forth into singing, and cry aloud. The Lord of Hosts is thy name. The Lord of the whole earth shall he be called. The wilderness and the solitary place shall be glad, and the desert shall rejoice and blossom as the rose." These prophecies need not be — indeed they are not — matters of controversy, but simple fact. The time, place, character, and mission of the coming One are plainly stated. Are the statements confirmed? Does history furnish a character which unquestionably answers the various and apparently contradictory conditions imposed by this variety of complicated predictions? How naturally and inevitably our eyes again turn to Jesus of Nazareth and the hills of Judea!

For it is admitted beyond question that the mysterious Being who arose eighteen hundred years ago out of the Jewish nation and from the house of David possessed a character which stands forth in solemn and sublime pre-eminence above all others. By universal consent he is the boldest relief on the page of history, and as remarkable as the expectation which preceded him. There is a general harmony in the confessions of Germans and Frenchmen, of Englishmen and Americans, of critics and sceptics, as well as of theologians and ecclesiastics. Says Byron, in view of the faultless life of the Redeemer, "If ever man was God, or God man, Jesus Christ was both." Says Rousseau, "Can it be possible that the personage whose history the gospel contains should be a mere man? What sublimity in his maxims! What profound wisdom in his discourses! If the life and death of Socrates are those of a sage, the life and death of Jesus are those of a God." Fichte, the noblest representative of recent pantheistic speculation in Germany, bore Christ the highest testimony it was possible for one man to bear another, making him the propounder of his philosophy. Goethe, the universal genius of modern Germany, speaking of Christ, says, "He is the Divine Man — the Holy One." Mr. Carlyle ever refers to Christ in terms of profoundest reverence. "The greatest of all heroes," he says, "is One whom we do not name here. Let sacred silence meditate that sacred matter." Said Mr. Parker, in one of his most rigid discourses against evangelical religion, "Try Christ as we try other teachers: how soon *their* pupils, though humble men, go beyond them!

Eighteen centuries have passed; but what man or sect has mastered His thought? He pours out to the world a doctrine beautiful as the light, sublime as heaven, and true as God." And then, after arguing for some length that, though the Bible itself were destroyed, its great precepts would live, he falls into this strain: "But we should lose (O, irreparable loss!) the example of that character, so beautiful, so divine, that no human genius could have conceived, as none, after all the progress and refinement of eighteen centuries, seems fully to have comprehended, its lustrous life." Renan, in his Life of Jesus, says, "Jesus is without equal; his glory remains complete, and will be revered forever. The memory of his life has been like the perfume of another world, and all history is incomprehensive without him. . . . Jesus was more than a reformer. . . . Between him and God there will no longer be any distinction. His sermon on the mount is unequalled, and whatever be the surprises of the future, Jesus will never be surpassed."

How much these men acknowledge! They feel and confess that the world at Jesus' birth dated a new epoch, and that the Christian era sprang from no myth or fable, but from vital changes in the condition of things. These men have caught sight of the outside brilliancy of his coming and adornings. What if they had partaken of his divine life! If the blade yields such fruit, what of the full corn in the ear! If unbelievers laud him to the skies, may he not be praised in the house of his friends? Is he not entitled to a place above all mankind? Measure his work. As the story and influence of his life have reached the darkest heathen realms, they have grown instantly light under their touch. As ships laden with his treasures have landed upon savage shores, the rude inhabitants have bent their knees to welcome this Lord of Glory. The men of the North Pole have grown warm while leaning upon the glowing heart of this great and faithful Shepherd. When the Prince of Peace has once entered their iceberg homes, they have bloomed like the garden of Paradise. The distant isles of the sea daily lift up their songs of praise, and answer back, that God is in the midst of them. The song of church bells, beginning in the far East, Sabbath by Sabbath, goes round the world. The echo of a great and mysterious Voice is heard, saying, "It is done. Amen. And the kingdoms of this world are become the kingdoms of our Lord, and of His Christ."

> "O, scenes surpassing fable!
> One song employs all nations, and all cry,
> 'Worthy the Lamb, for he was slain for us!'
> The dwellers in the vales and on the rocks
> Shout to each other, and the mountain-tops
> From distant mountains catch the flying joy;
> Till, nation after nation taught the strain,
> Earth rolls the rapturous hosanna round."

When we see the predicted mission of the Messiah so faithfully fulfilled, — when we see the great world's history bending itself to the birth of Jesus, in the "Anno Domini" of its dates and superscriptions, — when we see that the world has moved as in deepest sympathy with the humble Nazarene, working ever in his behalf, — when we behold all events marching onwards through the centuries to the beat of time, preserving, as Napoleon thought, "a celestial order," to accomplish one given result — the universal and final ascendency of the Son of David, — when we see that all opposing systems can no longer hold comparison with the religion given to the world by him, than can the pale, thin, extended crescent ring of the setting moon hold comparison to the full blaze of the unclouded noonday sun, — when we discover that this mighty one issued from the house of David before its fall, and from Bethlehem in the days of Herod, must we not acknowledge that He is the Being whom the prophets declared to be one with the Father Almighty?

As we follow his mysterious footsteps, and take note of his humble birth, his mortal lineage, his divine nature, his heavenly life, his unsullied purity, his invincible courage, and his more than human resolution, — as we behold him moving among men, the example of the child-like, the companion of publicans, and the friend of sinners, — as we witness his chivalric devotion, the mildness of his conversation, his tears over Jerusalem, his forgiveness to enemies, and his provision for the world's redemption, — as we behold him calming the waves of the sea by a word, and restoring to life the dead by a touch, — as we see him standing alone among the millions of the race, "the only pattern of absolute perfection, whose entire life, without inclining a hair's breadth to either side, pointed straight upward to heaven," — as we behold him breaking completely the monotony of the world, and concentrating in himself all the glowing and glorious attributes of the King of earth and heaven, — as we behold him lifted on the cross, almost in sight of his birthplace, and hear him cry, "It is finished," — as all the separate and wandering rays of prophecy that had sparkled through the divine word are combined and concentrated, and rest as with a sacred halo on his head, how can we do otherwise than spread our palms and robes in his pathway, shout over hill and valley his hosannas, and proclaim our convictions in that prophetic, startling, and sublime word, "Immanuel"! — God with us. Yes, God himself has been in the world. Fortunate world! you can ask no more. You have seen the brightness of God's glory, "and the express image of his person." In him the dreams of wise and good men of all ages are satisfied. Whoever has embraced him has found him to be all the prophets declared he should be. No man who has given him his heart, and taken hold of his hand, has been in the least disappointed: he has said, as Philip did to Nathanael, "We have found him of whom Moses in the law and the prophets did write — Jesus of Nazareth, the son of Joseph."

As intelligent observers, what shall we say to these things? Must not the prophets have known of what they spoke? Could they have spoken at random? Can we possibly explain the prophecies without introducing a supernatural element? Recall for a moment the entire ground passed over. Stand by the silent but prophetic graves of Nineveh and Babylon, and remember that the cities of China and Japan, of almost equal antiquity, remain in undiminished extent and with enduring foundations. Visit the great national graves of other people, into whose d ep abyss the gigantic forms of predicted empires have fallen, in some cases with a sudden crash, in others with the lingering death of deserted walls; in some instances with conflagration and bloodshed, in others with the abandonment of national life and spirit, but in every instance in the exact manner prescribed long beforehand. Listen to the tragic chorus of these inspired seers, as it "breaks forth in sublime funereal anthems" over the greatness and prosperity of Moab and Ammon, of Damascus and Tyre. Hear the song of universal freedom, rising at first in the sad dirge of bondmen under the yoke, but afterwards in the thrilling anthem of the yoke broken and bondmen free. Follow the wild Arab, who continues to love his desert home, and ever contends in his independent warfare against mankind. Observe the Jewish people shattered in pieces like a vessel in a mighty storm, and for eighteen centuries the prophetic wreck afloat. Stand under the refreshing shadow of the mysterious stone cut out of the mountain, but filling the whole earth. What! were all these events — concerning any one of which an uninspired man would have fluctuated in absolute uncertainty — foretold solely through mortal agency? Impossible!

Examine the marvellous volume in other respects. Is there not discovered upon every page, whenever, wherever, and by whomsoever written, the same protest for truth, justice, and mercy; the same message of wrath for the oppressor, the cruel, and the impious; the same righteous care for the widow, the fatherless, and the stranger? Are there not, throughout the Scriptures, the elements of all true theology, which, as a system, "is so entire," says Taylor, "that after ages of painful cogitation on the part of the most profound and the most exact minds, — whether philosophers or divines, whether ancient or modern, — nothing that is profitable, nothing that is deep and affecting, which has been educed and taught, or is at this moment extant and patent, in books classical or in books recent, can surpass the glorious truths declared?" Is not the prophet, if we take him as the chief of his own order, after two thousand years, our master in the school of the highest reason and truth? Do we not inevitably come to the same conclusion as that reached by a recent reviewer, that "the Bible is a unit; it is *a* Bible, as well as *the* Bible — one book no less than the *only* one: a collection of books, and yet a single book; the fruit of many pens, yet written as if by one alone;" the inseparable expression of the prophets, of Christ, of the apostles, and of the Holy Ghost?

Though we disregard the idle ripple of a single wave among the pebbles, do we not, when every wave moves in the same direction, when the tide is at work on all shores and continents, seek a law, and find it in the sky?

Must not the Bible, especially if we *exclude* the supernatural element, be regarded as the most stupendous miracle ever conceived?

Should not the believer and the non-believer exchange names and places? Ought the man who can believe, with these facts before him, that God did not in a special manner inspire his prophets, be known as a sceptic? We protest! His powers of belief exceed those of the believer.

"In the beginning God created the heaven and the earth. And the earth was without form, and void; and darkness was upon the face of the deep; and the Spirit of God moved upon the face of the waters." *Genesis* i. 1, 2.

"The grand old book of God will stand, and this old earth, the more its leaves are turned over and pondered, the more will it sustain and illustrate the Sacred Word." PROF. DANA.

"It is now thirty-five years since my attention was turned to these considerations. It was then the fashion of science, and, for a large part of the educated and inquisitive world, to rush into a disbelief of all written revelation, and several geological speculations were directed against the Bible. But I have lived to see the most hostile of these destroyed."

SHARON TURNER.

IV.

THE EARTH AND THE BIBLE.

A STATEMENT of the evidences of a supernatural book would hardly be complete without some allusion to the department of science, as well as to that of history. We now compare the statements of the Bible with the modern developments of geology. In selecting this particular science, we would not convey the impression that it is a field more interesting or convincing than that of astronomy, physical geography, law, philology, archæology, or psychology. We examine the science of geology because the greatest recent battles between belief and unbelief have here been waged, and because the infidel world is still active in this branch of science, and apparently confident of its ability thereby to overthrow the statements of revelation.

The Mosaic Account of Creation.— The opening chapters of Genesis have always been justly celebrated for their simplicity and sublimity. Though the subject treated is one of unparalleled grandeur, the writer makes no effort at rhetorical embellishment

His language is simple and common, his account brief and explicit; like all such accounts, it gives occasion for explanation and discussion. "In the beginning God created the heaven and the earth." How much that passage involves! It breaks the silence of a past eternity; it points to and embraces all subsequent communications, of every kind, concerning the kingdom of nature, and of God's relation to it. It is a blow at almost every false religion and physical error of the world.* It denies Atheism, for it assumes the existence, eternity, and omnipotence of God. It denies Polytheism and Dualism, for it assumes that there is but one Creator, and he a being of supreme goodness, who did not suffer a work to pass from his hands until he could pronounce it *good.* It denies Materialism, for it asserts the creation of matter. It denies Pantheism, for it assumes the existence of God before all things, and separate from them. It denies Fatalism, for it involves the freedom of the Eternal Being, who willed and spoke before matter and objective order appeared. And it constitutes one of the strong pillars that support all Christian theology. "In the beginning God created the heavens and the earth," and "In the beginning was the Word," and "without him was not anything made that was made," are the morning and evening psalms which echo through the universe forever, and which forever unite as in one the Old and New Testament dispensations.

When Moses uttered this passage, he spoke of that which the most thorough acquaintance with every

* See Murphy's Commentary on Genesis.

branch of modern science would fail to disclose. Natural science takes cognizance only of things existing — not of their beginnings. He spoke not of the universe at large, but of the earth, and of man, its rational inhabitant and appointed king.

He assigns no date for the creation. "In the beginning" means not six, nor sixty, nor six hundred thousand years ago, but in the beginning of time, when the earth was not, and when matter was not. After a great amount of discussion and investigation, men have settled upon one of these two suppositions: either that the materials of which the earth is composed have always existed, or else that God, at a given time, and in the *beginning* of time, created them. On this question physical science is silent. We are left to revelation and reason. As matter has none of the properties of a necessary, and therefore of an eternal existence, and as there is not one chance in a billion for it to happen to occupy its present limits in space, we seem forced to the conclusion that matter has not always existed, but was at some indefinitely early period created.

The literal rendering of the second verse is; "And the earth *had become* a waste and a void, and darkness was upon the face of the roaring deep, and the Spirit of God was brooding upon the face of the waters." Connecting this passage with the account of the creation of the different orders of existing flora and fauna, the obvious meaning must be, that after the earth had been created, after it had existed a countless number of ages, during which it may have been governed by natural laws, may have met with change and vicissitude, have laid up in storehouses the geological deposits of granite and clay, of coal and oil, of salt and lime, of silver and gold, then it became a waste. So far as the region first inhabited by man is concerned, not a living thing moved on its surface, or burrowed in its soil. The earth as a whole was covered with roaring waters and thick darkness. Harmonizing the date of this condition with biblical and secular chronology, the most natural interpretation of the passage before us is, that God, about six thousand years ago, bade the darkness become light, rolled the waters back into the seas, and in six literal days clothed the barren waste with the verdure which now decks it, and gave to a scene of death, the life that now breathes its air and walks its surface.

Geological Account of Creation.—The materials of the earth are so arranged that we can read its history, much as we read the published history of secular events. There is one leaf above another; one page follows another, written, engraved, and illustrated. We wish to ascertain whether the account of creation given us by the Hebrew prophet agrees with this book of earth. Beginning with the foundation, upon which the vast structure rests, we find that it is granite and the different ingredients of granite. Had not this formation been washed bare by the action of water, and lifted from its deep bed into mountain ranges and peaks by the natural agencies at work in the bosom of the earth, it would nowhere meet the eye. It would be concealed by subsequent formations. Examining this underlying rock, we discover no evidences of life during its formation. There are no remains of plants or animals of any kind. How long the matter of the globe remained after its creation before it took this form, even, we cannot tell. How long it remained bare, naked granite, we are totally ignorant. It must have been age upon age; for "of old he laid the foundations."

The formation next above this is called the Silurian. It is the first story of the building above the foundation — the second page in the world's history. The rocks of this period are, chiefly, the sandstones, slates, and limestones. Including the older and newer formations, they are not less than thirty thousand feet in thickness. An examination of this layer will disclose fossil plants, and the fossil remains of the four great branches of the animal kingdom — the Radiates, typified in the star-fish and sun-fish; the Mollusks, in the clam and land-snail; the Articulates, represented by worms and insects; and the Vertebrates, by fishes, birds, and mammals. The fish, however, is the only vertebrate which then existed. Search ever so carefully among the ruins of that ancient era, and not the bone of a bird nor mammal can be found. What is still more remarkable is, that, though we find more than a thousand different fossil species, and though there are three hundred thousand living species of the same classes now in the waters, yet not *one* can be found among those which at present swim the sea, or creep across the earth, that does not differ in its species from every one of those that lived, died, and were buried in the great Silurian Period. How long it had taken these thirty thousand feet to form, how many of those ancient inhabitants had lived and died, none but God can tell.

The next page in this wonderful book is called the Old Red Sandstone. In the State of New York it is fourteen thousand feet thick. In it we find the remains of numerous plants, and the four branches of the animal kingdom, as in the last; but, though there are a thousand different species, though the remains are such as to show that the waters of this period must have swarmed with life, still it may be safely stated that but *few*, if any, species of animal or plant found in the preceding, and that *none* found in the present, age existed during the formation of the old red sandstone.

Next above this formation, we reach the age in which the coal we use to warm and light our dwellings was formed and deposited. It is called the Carboniferous Period. The growth of vegetation in this age transcends all calculation. Immense forests sprang up as in a day. The exuding sap, i. e., petroleum, flowed down into the limestone and iron-cased vats or basins, and was there preserved. The undergrowth of the forests consisted of at least three hundred different varieties of fern. The atmosphere was charged with carbonic acid, loaded with all the mephitic gases, with moisture and miasms. This is indicated both by the wonderful growth of vegetation, and by portions of the gaseous atmosphere of that old world, which, for our instruction, were caught, and have been imprisoned through the ages in the deep coal caverns of earth. The sunlight was excluded from all those forests. The geologist, the chemist, and the botanist tell us they were never touched by an illuminating sunbeam. More than tropical heat extended to the polar regions. These are conditions the most perfectly adapted for vegetable development, but the most fatal to animal life. As we should expect, though the limestone and iron which constitute the introduction of this period abound in the remains of a great variety of land insects and reptiles, not one of any kind or class of air-breathing animals or insects can be found in the coal formation proper. Not a bird warbled its song or built its nest among those mighty forests. Not an insect — not so much, even, as a worm — fed upon the leaves, or spun its thread from the branches. Says Lyell, "In the United States, five million tons of coal are annually extracted; and no fossil insect has yet been met with in the carboniferous rocks of North America. . . . In like manner, no land shell, no aquatic mollusk, is recorded to have come from the coal of Europe, worked for centuries before America was discovered."

"We have ransacked," he continues, "hundreds of soils, have dug out hundreds of stumps, and carboniferous trunks and roots; and after all we continue almost as much in the dark respecting the invertebrated air-breathers of this epoch as if the coal had been thrown down in mid-ocean."

But when the supplies had been stored up in vast quantities, when the carbon and poisons had been taken up from the atmosphere by the development of vegetation, to which, indeed, it owed its growth, then those ancient forests were suddenly checked in their development. Perhaps they withered in a day, under some atmospheric or climatic change. Soon after this they fell into the abyss of subsequent ages, never to rise again with life and beauty. They were sunk beneath the ocean, and stratum after stratum of sandstone and limestone were piled over that forgotten vegetation, hiding it for centuries, and pressing it, like a modern peat-press, into solid rock. That rock is our coal.

The next deposit above the coal is the New Red Sandstone. In this, as we should expect, the poisons of the atmosphere having been absorbed, we again find the remains of air-breathing animals. The birds of the period especially claim our attention. They were found in such abundance that we may term it the Bird Epoch. They consisted of at least thirty-five different species. They were, in some cases, of enormous size. Birds from twelve to fifteen feet in height, whose footprints are twenty-two inches in length, stalked for thousands of years along the shores of the Connecticut River, from the northern part of Massachusetts to New Haven. In New Zealand their bones are found, the thigh-bone being larger than that of an ox. Fragments of their egg-shells, which are found in Madagascar, indicate that they were six times larger than any living ostrich. They were the giant rulers of the hills and vales of earth for centuries; but, like every other race that had preceded them, they at length perished. Not a spot can now furnish a solitary living example like them. These extinct species never return.

The next period is very properly called the Reptilian Age. Reptiles flourished at this date as vigorously as plants had in the coal period, and as the birds had in the age just preceding. There were at this time gigantic reptiles, seventy feet in length, which could walk the earth, swim the sea, or fly the air, equally well. Think of a flying lizard sixty feet long, and of a frog larger than an ox! Such were once the inhabitants of the earth. More than forty species of the lizard have been discovered belonging to this period. These monsters might have been seen flying through the air, sporting in the fens, devouring their prey, or rolling and frolicking in the waters, where now is the solid earth of the British Isles. But, having lorded it over the earth, sea, and air, for an allotted time, they met, at length, a sudden and total extinction. They left only their skeletons to acquaint us with the facts of their existence and nature.

Ages again pass, and new orders appear. They constitute what is called the Chalk or Cretaceous formation. If we could have visited the earth during the period of these deposits, we should have found it inhabited, century after century, by the minutest shell animals, many species of which are imperceptible without the aid of the microscope. It may properly be called the Shell-insect Age. How unlike the age of monster birds and reptiles which preceded! Where is the development theory? *

But after these little animals had done their work, — after their accumulated remains had provided the

* The leading facts of geology are so utterly at variance with the theory of "transmutation of species," that no additional refutation is necessary.

The more recent scientific inquiries furnish no evidence whatever in support of Mr. Darwin's theory of the "formation of species by natural selection." The Mosaic account of creation rests upon an undisturbed basis.

Egyptians with the materials for building their pyramids, — after they had built Northern Europe, Western Asia, and Mount Lebanon, — after they had furnished our western prairies with their rich and productive soils, — after having supplied the world with its chalk, its marble, and the different varieties of carbonate of lime, — then their age and reign ceased. They and their work were sunk beneath the seas, and subsequently buried under other and later formations.

We now approach comparatively near the earth's surface, and may begin to talk of *modern* times. Above the Cretaceous, lies the last of the Tertiary, or the Mammal deposits. Visiting the earth at this stage of its construction, we should have entered magnificent forests of oak, hickory, and magnolia, whose branches were covered with the richest foliage. We should have seen the stately palm, decking in clusters every hill and valley, while flowering plants and shrubs of every hue and form would have entangled our pathway. The race of mammals would especially have attracted our attention and excited our surprise. "They agreed," says Cuvier, "neither specifically, nor even for the most part generically, with any hitherto discovered in the living creation." Gigantic elephants, of twice the bulk of those which now exist in Ceylon and Africa, roamed in herds over the plains; two-horned rhinoceroses, of immense proportions, forced their way through the forests, wallowed in the swamps, and plunged into the stagnant waters, from the River Altamaha to the polar regions, and from Siberia to the south of Europe; wild oxen, of colossal strength, found subsistence in the plains and on the hill-sides; tigers, larger and more savage than those of Bengal, lay in wait for their prey, and sprang upon it, with savage roar, from their lairs; troops of hyenas, larger and fiercer than the hyena crocuta of Southern Africa, repeated nightly their hideous howlings; they thronged the valleys and crushed the bones of their prey in the dark caverns of earth. There were monstrous camels and reindeer; there were bears larger than the grizzly bear of the Rocky Mountains, and whales of equal bulk with those which now swim the ocean. But, during this entire age of magnificent forests and mighty mammals, we are to bear in mind that the earth at no time, and in no place, echoed to the voice of man, or felt the impress of his footfall. All these orders disappeared before his arrival. They were destroyed, not by the advancing civilization of man, but by the command of God. Some of the species, and even genera, of this period, seemed to have suffered an earlier extinction than others. They remained also in some localities much longer than in others. Many perished by natural death; others were destroyed by bursting volcanoes. At length, amid some of the most terrible convulsions that have ever shaken the earth, these races expired, with as sudden death as that of the savage monsters of an earlier age. The temperature seems to have fallen suddenly to a freezing point, where had formerly existed tropical heat. Masses of ice were formed among the northern mountains, which will not melt until the end of time, and which may some day fill the ice-houses of the world.

Animals were in some cases so suddenly overtaken

that they were frozen in the mud of Siberia, and within a few years have been excavated, the flesh in so perfect state of preservation as to be greedily eaten by dogs. What a refrigerator! "The disruption of the earth's crust, extending W. 16° S., and E. 16° N., through which the chain of the great Alps was forced up to its present elevation, which, according to M. D'Orbigny, was simultaneous with that which forced up the Chilian Andes, — a chain which extends over a length of three thousand miles of the western continent, — terminated the Tertiary Age, and preceded immediately the creation of the human race and its concomitant tribes. The waters of the seas and oceans, lifted up from their beds by this immense perturbation, swept over the continents with irresistible force, destroying instantaneously the entire flora and fauna of the last tertiary period, and burying its ruins in the sedimentary deposits which ensued." *

Soon after this, the old gray burial-ground of earth, which had witnessed at least twenty-seven different exterminations and re-creations, was itself buried under the freezing waters of the glacial and drift period. This constitutes the first formation of the last geological layer — the Diluvian. Ice and snow, except, perhaps, under the tropics, were at that time the lords of the world. The moisture of the atmosphere was condensed; howling winds, loaded with stinging frosts, struck upon this surging ocean, and were the only visitants to the few mountain peaks of

* Lardner's Popular Geology.

all the middle and northern latitudes which remained above the coagulated waters; frozen vapors shut out the light of the sun, and "darkness was upon the face of the deep." How far, infinitely far, does this history of earth, in its astonishing surprises, transcend all the poetry and romance of mortals!

We were speaking of the drift period. Scarcely a voyage is made across the Atlantic without encountering huge icebergs. They are found in all high latitudes. These floating monsters have sealed the fate of many a ship. They have been stranded upon the shores of islands, and produced winter in mid-summer. They have been seen standing out of the water five hundred feet, which would make their entire altitude upwards of four thousand feet. Captain D'Urville met with one in the Southern Ocean which was thirteen miles in length, and stood out of the water, with perpendicular walls, one hundred feet. They are often loaded with thousands of tons of rocks and soil, which, becoming detached, fall through the waters upon the ocean's bottom. Here is the "drift" in miniature. We need no better explanation of the presence of those large and disconnected boulders which are met everywhere in fields and on hill-sides. During the drift and the modified drift periods, the earth *must have been* submerged. North America, to the depth of two or three thousand feet, was covered with the sea. The peak of Mount Washington was the only visible land of New England.

Professor Ramsey says that the submergence of the British Isles is beyond question. The earth was at that time swept with oceanic currents, loaded with icebergs which had been wrenched off from the mountain peaks. A boulder, containing one hundred and sixty-one thousand cubic feet, was moved a distance of thirty-two miles from Jura, one of the Alps. By careful measurement the exact place from which it was taken among the mountains has been found. Northern Germany, Poland, and Russia are overspread with boulders from Sweden, Lapland, and Finland. Granite rocks, from some source, have been thrown down upon Iceland, though the island itself was formed from lava. These boulders, disconnected from the ice-floats to which they had been attached, sank through the flood of waters, and were anchored where they now remain.

Do such things seem incredible? They are facts, and it would be as impossible to blot them out as it would be to obliterate the sun from the heavens. That the whole earth, at one time or another, has been under water, is the uniform testimony of science. Says Humboldt, "The highest peaks of the Alps were once beneath the ocean's surface." "All land," says Lyell, "has been under water." "It seems," says Hitchcock, "that the surface of the globe has been a shoreless ocean." "The highest mountains," says Tenney, "have once been the ocean's bottom." The same sublime and startling record is inscribed upon every mountain peak and range around the globe, east and west, north and south, far and near. But whence came the waters? No matter whence: there are the facts. The land may have been depressed; if not, there is water enough in reserve to drown the world at any time.

Were the moisture in the forty miles of atmosphere above us condensed by the proper climatic changes, or were the electricity discharged from it to the earth, there would be an amount of water, which, in connection with that in the fifty miles of the earth's crust beneath us, could easily produce, without a miracle of creation, the drift-flood or the flood of Noah. Or, in the language of Scripture, "if the windows of heaven should be opened," "and the fountains of the great deep be broken up," by the simple passage of electricity from the atmosphere to the earth for forty days and forty nights, there would be water enough, as the result, to flood the world to the mountain tops.

It is because of God's mercy, and because he has promised to hold these elements suspended, and because the beautiful bow spans the heavens after a summer shower, that we have not every reason to fear lest the earth be again deluged in water.

Before passing from the drift period, let us reflect for a moment upon the lapse of time which must have intervened after the earth had received its present configuration, and even after it had become the abode of animal and vegetable life, before reaching this Ice epoch.

Investigation proves that the Rivers Rhine and Connecticut must have been in existence not less than twenty thousand years. They were flowing all this time through nearly the same configuration of country as that along which they now wander to the sea. The one looked upon its romantic and limestone, the other its picturesque and red sandstone banks

The Niagara, with six hundred thousand tons of water passing a given point every minute, judging from its present rate of retrocession, had been wearing its channel back from Queenstown for not less than thirty-six thousand years. But the sublimity of its fall and the beauty of its arch of light were seen through all that period by no human eye. Its majestic voice fell only upon the ear of the beasts that denned among the adjacent mountains or wandered upon its trembling shores. The Mississippi, which, with its present rate of deposit, must have been flowing at least fourteen thousand years, had found its way to the Gulf, and was forming with its sediment the State of Louisiana.

Back of these dates the ages roll up almost beyond conception. Mountain ranges were rising, valleys were sinking, oceans becoming dry land, and dry land becoming oceans, demanding ages and ages for their transitions to take place. The embalmed fossil subjects of the past, though in as perfect a state of preservation as the mummies of Egypt, have been handed down, in some instances, through millions and millions of centuries. But why is revelation silent as to these things? Why, it might as well be asked, is it silent as to almost everything, save our duties and relation to God? Why silent as to so much secular history, — dwelling almost exclusively upon those events which point forward and backward to the Christ of God and of Calvary? If the Bible contained a full report and history of the universe, who could read it? It was important that man should know how he came upon the earth, and who was the author of his being; but was it important that he should know the number of the planets, or the number of convulsions through which the earth has passed in its long history.? Concerning these things the Bible is silent: an impostor would not have been.

But how compare and harmonize the accounts of science with those of revelation? This is the vital question. We must admit that if revelation, when properly interpreted, and science, when rightly understood, are two opposing citadels, frowning defiance upon each other, then Moses was not inspired, the book is not supernatural, and must fall to the ground. If, on the other hand, each has its own separate foundation, and both together prove themselves compartments of one great fabric, reared to the glory of God, then would it not appear that the Mosaic account of creation is supernatural?

The test question is before us. Is the first chapter of Genesis ancient *or* modern? Is it ancient *and* modern? Can we claim that there is no language or speech at human command which more perfectly or more exactly expresses the condition of the earth after these mighty vicissitudes of which we have been speaking had taken place, and during the drift, when the world was ingulfed in dark, turbid, and frozen waters, than the original text of the old Hebrew prophet? Is it true that "the earth *had become* a waste and a void, that darkness was upon the face of the roaring deep, and that the soul of God was brooding upon the face of the waters"? Can we evade the evidence of inspiration, if the Bible and science agree at this point? And do they not agree? Is it not true that long after the creation of matter, "in the beginning," long after the sandstones, coal, limestones, and animal remains of earth had been formed and deposited, long after the ancient river courses, the Rhine, Niagara, and Mississippi, had found the sea, that then, all things were ingulfed under the waters of the drift, which were laden with ice-floats and which bore upon their bosoms the ruins of past generations? Do not the surface boulders and erratic stones found in every country confirm the statement that this was the condition of the world, and that it occurred *just before* the present, or the human era?

Says Lyell, — and his testimony is of peculiar value, as he never makes an attempt to reconcile revelation and science, — "Some parts of the Mississippi valley show that it has been excavated, then filled up, and subsequently re-excavated." Of this last submergence, taking his observations from Europe, as well as America, he says, "The retreat of the waters may have left no monument, in some cases, of the event; but from those existing we must infer that it was an event of times comparatively modern." Neither will Lyell, nor any other geologist, deny the statement that the world has not been above the waters of that period in its present condition for much, if any more, than six thousand years. Is not the book ancient *and* modern? But test the question still more rigidly. Examine the Mosaic days of creation, granting that the previous flora must have been destroyed by the drift, that man had nowhere been seen, and that most of the old fauna had perished, may we not ask, whence the present life and beauty of the world? Was there anything in the apparently insane and boisterous play of the great physical catastrophe of the nine distinct and long-continued eras we have been considering, anything in the turbulence and mighty clamor of the drift period, which could repeople the earth with living inhabitants? Of course there was nothing. Had not the voice of God been heard above the waters, they had remained as they were.

But at length the Spirit of God, the energizing power of all things, brooded upon the face of the deep. The world's temperature was changed. A warm breath floated over the seas. The condensed vapors gave way somewhat. The gaseous medium, which had been produced perhaps by plutonic action, was penetrated by light. The surface of the abyss was visited by struggling rays so far illuminating it that the interchange of day and night became discernible, though the heavenly bodies were still excluded from view. "Then was evening, then was morning, day one." Thus ended the first day of the last creation, a day of twenty-four hours.

At the dawning of the next morning an element was introduced into the atmosphere, by which the murky and aqueous fogs were lifted to the higher regions of the sky, or became invisible vapor. Heavy, dark, and dripping clouds still overspread the sky; but there was a space of pellucid air mantling the earth, suitable for the respiration of flora and fauna. "Then was evening, then was morning, day second."

As the third day approached, the waters might have been seen receding. They were absorbed into the atmosphere, They flowed down from the heights. They sank into new-made gulfs, and places that had been prepared for them. The gray mountains and the shaded dells rose from their watery beds, greeting the new-born light, and the ancient rivers resumed their former channels to the sea. The description of the Psalmist for beauty of representation cannot be surpassed. "Thou coveredst it with the deep as with a garment; the waters stood above the mountains. At thy rebuke they fled: at the voice of thy thunder they hasted away. They go up by the mountains; they go down by the valleys unto the place which thou hast founded for them. Thou hast set a bound that they may not pass over; that they turn not again to cover the earth." (Ps. civ. 6–10.) Near the close of this day God also covered the hills and valleys with full-grown grass, herbs, and fruit trees; "and formed every plant of the field before it was in the earth, and every herb of the field before it grew." (Gen. ii. 5.) "Then was evening, then was morning, day third."

The darkness of that third night was followed by a sublime morning. The leaden clouds were broken through by the sunbeams. They glistened upon the mountain peaks, they kissed the vales, they tipped the waves of the sea with silver. The new-made flora felt their influences. The life-giving sap circulated through trunk and limb, and the leaves nodded to the breeze.

After this followed naturally the appointments of those indispensable heavenly measures of time, to be "for signs, and for seasons, and for days, and years," according to which are meted out the eras of human history and the cycles of natural science; according to which the mariner has learned to mark the latitude and longitude of his ship; according to which the astronomer determines the place, as well as the time, of the planetary orbs of heaven; and according to which the laborer shall ever go to his labor, and seek his repose. In the inimitable language of Mr. Everett, "But for all the kindreds and tribes and tongues of men, — each upon their own meridian, — from the Arctic pole to the equator, from the equator to the Antarctic pole, the eternal sun strikes twelve at noon, and the glorious constellations, far up in the everlasting belfries of the skies, chime twelve at midnight; twelve for the pale student over his flickering lamp; twelve amid the flaming wonders of Orion's belt, if he crosses the meridian at that fated hour; twelve by the weary couch of languishing humanity; twelve in the star-paved courts of the empyrean; twelve for the heaving tides of the ocean; twelve for the weary arm of labor; twelve for the toiling brain; twelve for the watching, waking, broken heart; twelve for the meteor which blazes for a moment and expires; twelve for the comet whose period is measured by centuries; twelve for every substantial, for every imaginary thing, which exists in the sense, the intellect, or the fancy, and which the speech or thought of man, at the given meridian, refers to the lapse of time." "Then was evening, then was morning, day fourth."

On the fifth day the lower orders of the existing species of animals were created, with the possible exception of a few survivors of the drift, which may have remained in the seas and on the mountains of the tropics, — such as the red-deer, wild-cat, bear, wild-boar, wolf, weasel, hedge-hog, mole, dor-mouse, field-mouse, water-rat, and shrew. This class of animals might have subsisted upon tropical mountains, under the conditions imposed by the drift.

On the sixth day, the higher orders of mammals were created. Then, when all else was completed on earth; when the volcanic fires had fused and crystallized its granite, and piled it up in lofty mountain ranges; when the flowing and returning waters had selected and borne down into distant vales the vegetable soils; when electric shocks had interlaced the earth with metallic veins; when the ancient forests had hardened into coal, and were stored up by the cubic mile, having yielded also their vast reservoirs of petroleum; when the deposits of primeval waters had become iron and crystal salt; when successive races of animals had become a multitude of useful materials; after reptiles had cleared the waters of impurities; after birds had devoured the animal remains, and enriched the soil, and after the monster mammals had removed the rubbish from the earth's surface; after the great flood had rolled back, and "the star-spangled dome had been lit up," and the earth's surface had been carpeted with delicate and soft green; after the rich profusion of natural scenery had been prepared, the flowers filled with fragrance, the trees hung with delicious fruit, — "then created God the man, in his image; in the image of God created he him; male and female created he them." "Then was evening, then was morning, day sixth."

Sceptics have occasionally startled the world with

an announcement of the alleged discovery of human remains and stone instruments among geological deposits of much earlier date than the Alluvium. All, however, agree that none are found earlier than the mammal age. All agree that great uncertainty attends chronological conclusions based upon two consecutive periods. It can be proved with equal satisfaction, from coins found in the conglomerates at Tisbury, England, that the reign of Edward I. was thousands of years earlier than it actually was. Egyptian monuments show similar results. Bricks dug from the shores of the Nile, which must have been embedded there not more than three or four thousand years B. C., appear, by the same evidence which carries the antiquity of man beyond the alluvium, to have been left there from twelve to thirty thousand years ago. Such errors are not uncommon. We admit that human remains of bones and stone instruments may be found in close proximity to animals of the Mammal age, some species of which may have existed early in the Post-Pliocene. They *ought* to be in such neighborhood, for the Drift only intervened. But we may unhesitatingly affirm that Adam was the only living type of his kind on earth at the time of his creation, and that it remains to be satisfactorily proved, so far as any discoveries have yet been made, that any human being appeared on the earth earlier than six thousand years ago. How near these thoughts bring the present race to the Infinite Mind! We seem to feel the touch of his hand upon us. We seem to hear his voice, as in the garden, and feel his sustaining agency at every step of our pilgrimage. Being so near us, is it to be thought improbable that communion is still open between God and the race of the fallen?

The world was prepared; man was created; the seventh period dawned; God rested. Search in the air, over the land, or through the seas, to find one new species, created since the appearance of man, and you will search in vain. Six thousand years ago the work of creation was completed; and, as connected with this world, completed never again to be resumed, until the Sabbath of His repose shall be broken by the display of the new manifestations which await the consummation of human history. But, in the mean time, what ought the world to say respecting the coincidences between revelation and science? Is the wisdom displayed by that old Hebrew prophet, almost in advance of the accumulated discoveries of four thousand years, of no account? Was all he said the result of unaided human wisdom? Was the language which so wonderfully embodies the world's history from the beginning — its creation and development — accidental? Adding to this account the prophetic character of the book, its poetry, its morals, and its religion, may we not well concur with the admission of Sir Walter Scott, "There is but one book"? May we not verily pity the man whose numb and icy fingers handle this sacred word without perceiving that in kind there is none like it? Is it not supernatural?

SUPERNATURAL BEINGS

"This Jesus hath God raised up, whereof we are all witnesses." *Acts* ii. 32.

"And if Christ be not risen, then is our preaching vain, and your faith is also vain.

"Yea, and we are found false witnesses of God; because we have testified of God that he raised up Christ; whom he raised not up, if so be that the dead rise not.

"And if Christ be not raised, your faith is vain: ye are yet in your sins.

"Then they also which are fallen asleep in Christ are perished.

"If in this life only we have hope in Christ, we are of all men most miserable." 1 *Cor*. xv. 14, 15, 17–19.

"The resurrection of Christ is a true *Shibboleth*, distinguishing opposing world views." STRAUSS.

"The words 'Christ is risen from the dead' should be well marked, and written with great letters. Each letter should be as large as a town, yea, even as high as heaven and broad as the earth, so that we see nothing, hear nothing, think nothing, know nothing beyond it." MARTIN LUTHER

"I *will not* believe a miracle." VOLTAIRE.

I.

THE RESURRECTION OF THE LORD JESUS.

DID that person who called himself Jesus, who is known by that name both in sacred and profane history, actually die? and afterwards did he rise from the dead? Concerning this remarkable event we have in existence the written testimony of four different persons, for whom especial inspiration is claimed; also the statements of certain other writers, for whom inspiration is not claimed. The first step in the discussion will be an examination into the character and competency of the witnesses, their relation to the person of Christ, their knowledge of his life, and the substance of their testimony.

The Inspired Witnesses.— Following the order of the Gospels, the first writer and witness we notice is Matthew, the publican. Before his conversion this evangelist was a collector of customs at the port of Capernaum, a city situated upon the great commercial thoroughfare between Damascus, Babylon, and Southern Palestine. During an early visit of Jesus of Nazareth to this city, Matthew was awakened by his teachings, obeyed a great and gracious call, forsook a highly remunerative employment, and became a disciple. His Gospel was, probably, the first written. Irenæus states that it was composed while Peter and Paul were preaching and founding a church at Rome. It was written first in the Hebrew, subsequently in the Greek language. The statements of Matthew concerning the life, death, and resurrection of his Master are the happy embodiment of a joyous and vigorous faith. It was based upon the facts of Christ's history, and a personal connection therewith. His acquaintance with Jesus commenced before the sermon on the mount, and continued until the ascension.

The Holy Spirit directed Matthew, as an inspired writer, to record the things *done* and *said* by his Master, rather than to give the precise order in which they took place. He recalls and delivers to the world the narratives of the Gospel and the sermons of his Teacher with the strictest verbal exactness, irrespective of special logical connection.

The second witness and writer is Mark. This evangelist was a native of Jerusalem. He is sometimes called John Mark. He was a friend and occasional fellow-laborer with Paul, a convert and companion of Peter, a nephew of Barnabas, and the son of a certain Mary, a woman of influence, wealth, and piety, whose residence, we have reason to believe, was the usual place of entertainment for our Lord while in the city of Jerusalem. Her house seems to have been a common resort for early Christians; to it Peter naturally directed his steps upon his deliverance from prison. She was also proprietress of an estate in the suburbs of Jerusalem, near or in the garden of Gethsemane. John Mark, her son, though not a disciple, was, at an early age, made an acquaintance and friend of Jesus. He was undoubtedly the young man his Gospel mentions who followed Christ on the night of his betrayal and arrest. Admitting the inspiration of this writer, it seems that the peculiar work assigned to him by the Holy Spirit was, in a fresh, peculiar, and lively narrative, to set before the world a history of the official mission of Christ, rather than his verbal teachings. He recounts, with striking clearness, his Master's glorious achievements in a warfare against sin and Satan. We have from his pen the highest example of heroism on record. Mark was not, as some have supposed, a mere secretary, or penman, of the apostle Peter. The evidence is entirely satisfactory that he wrote his Gospel by the revelation of the Holy Spirit to himself. Of this fact, tradition informs us, Peter was fully cognizant. Mark writes with the peculiar minuteness, freshness, and circumstantial ease of an independent eye-witness. He described the looks, gestures, and tones, employed on different occasions, so graphically as almost to transform us into eye-witnesses. This phenomenon goes very far in proving that he wrote independently, except as directed by the Holy Ghost.

The third writer whose testimony we have is the evangelist Luke. This witness was a liberally-educated man. He was a physician by profession. He was born in Syria. He passed his early life in the polished city of Antioch. Later, he became a faithful friend and companion of the apostle Paul. Just before his martyrdom, writing from his Roman prison to Timothy, Paul gave this touching testimonial of the faithfulness of this evangelist and friend: "Only Luke is with me." On turning from the Gospels of Matthew and Mark to that of Luke, we are conscious of receiving a peculiar impression, as of one passing into another atmosphere. It is a Gospel upon the same theme, but different in form, different and fuller in its narratives. The composition and style plainly indicate that the writer was not brought up at the receipt of customs, or among the nets of the fishermen of Galilee, but convey upon the surface the strongest possible evidence of refinement and scholarship. Luke was not an eye-witness from the beginning of our Lord's ministry, but was an eye-witness of the most important events of his life, especially of those occurring amid the scenes of his death and resurrection. In some respects the most interesting appearance of Christ after his resurrection was granted to this disciple and Cleopas, while journeying to Emmaus.

Admitting the inspiration of Luke, the particular work assigned to him by the Holy Spirit was, to make the most careful researches from all reliable sources into the facts of the life of the Lord Jesus, from the beginning, and to represent him as practising in that profession to which his own life had been previously dedicated. We have from his pen a picture of Christ as the great Physician of the world. In his Gospel the Saviour is seen "going about doing good," healing, by his touch or his word, difficult and long-standing diseases, and implanting hope and joy in the troubled hearts of humanity.

The fourth and last inspired witness, whose complete record we have, is John, the brother of James.

This writer was the son of pious Jewish parents, who took rank, not among the higher and professional, but among the middle, though respectable, classes of society. John was, at first, a disciple of the Baptist bearing the same name. He was one of the first to follow our Saviour. His Gospel and style are peculiar. Gibbon says, "He is the most sublime of all the evangelists." There is no writer in the world with whom it is not difficult to compare him. His opening chapter bears the most overwhelming evidence that he wrote as moved upon by the Spirit of God. He was directed to give us a deep and inspiring insight into the divine and eternal nature of that Being whom he loved and worshipped. There is something melancholy, something inspiring, something sublime, and something which often implies more than language can express, in much that he says. But behind these fleecy clouds which occasionally arise, we are ever confident there is shining the full, clear, glorious Sun of Righteousness. Of the death and resurrection of Christ this evangelist speaks with remarkable force and clearness. He tells the world that he was an eye-witness. He says he saw his Master when dead, and when risen, and on no less than five different occasions. He is confident. He knows what he affirms. He was on the spot. He must be impeached or believed.

Such, in brief, are the four inspired witnesses of the risen Saviour whose testimony has been recorded and handed down to us. They are men of different natures. They give especial prominence to different events. They were *chosen* to give us these records *because* different, and because they could thus meet and better satisfy the wants of the world.

Two objections are frequently urged against their inspiration. First, that their accounts do not, in all points, agree. Second, that the individual peculiarities of the writers everywhere appear in the Gospels, which would not need be the case if the men were inspired, especially if they were verbally inspired.

If by non-agreement is meant that the different accounts of the death and resurrection of Christ are not in *unison*, we admit their non-agreement. But if it is meant that the accounts do not *harmonize*, the objection is groundless. There is not *unison*, but there is *perfect harmony*, from the first passage of Matthew to the last of John. As in music, so among these writers, the effect from harmony is far deeper and purer than that from simple unison.

Again: If the objector means that the Scriptures are not written in a manner which is best calculated to convince the world of the truth of verbal inspiration, independent of every other consideration, the objection is valid. God's purpose has not been to give signs to men, but to disclose truth. For the most part he avoids the appearance of supernatural agencies, both in nature and revelation; always, except when such displays are peculiarly necessary, or when an assertion is required in order to establish authority. The proof of inspiration, plenary as well as verbal, must, in God's economy, be largely incidental.

But, on the other hand, if it is meant that the Scriptures are not written in a manner which is best calcula ed to convince mankind of the truthfulness of the facts recorded (which was doubtless the object of the Holy Spirit), then the believer denies the force of the objection. The manner and style of the Gospel narratives are the best possible for such a purpose. Strike out the individual peculiarities from the records, and the unbeliever would disregard entirely the ordinary arguments for inspiration, and would admit only the evidence of forgery and connivance.

These positions may be illustrated. If we desired to give society the best account of some distinguished preacher of our own day, we would not select one witness, but three or four. We would not choose men who are as nearly alike as possible, but who are unlike, respecting age, culture, and character. In making their announcements, we would not have them employ the same, but different language, in presenting the same incident. We would not have them copy, or *seem to copy*, one another's statements. We would have them write, in fact and in appearance, independently of each other. We would have one selected who would be adapted to give a careful survey of the preacher's entire discourse, — the occasion, text, course of thought, and subject matter, — and who would give it in an orderly and business-like manner. This is what has been done, in the case of our Saviour, by Matthew, and, in certain respects, by Matthew alone.

Another critic would be selected, who, from choice, would describe the preacher's manner in the pulpit, and who would be able to give a graphic description of the effect of his discourse upon his hearers. This is what has been done, in case of our Saviour, by

Mark, and, in certain respects, by Mark alone. Another would be selected who would naturally give a reliable account of the past history of the preacher in question, his deportment among the poor and sinful, and who could appreciate his remarkable sayings, and who could select notes from his pulpit, his beauties, his gems of thought, without being confined to any given order, or plan of sermon. This is what has been done, in the case of our Saviour, by the evangelist Luke, as by no other witness.

Lastly, we would select one who could appreciate the spirit of the preacher, his hidden and devotional life, the deep and inspiring motives of his soul, and his communion with the Invisible. The presentation of this peculiar phase of Christ's life and character has been given us by the apostle John, and by him alone. The Gospels present to the world a model in respect both to the fulness and the truthfulness of the facts recorded. Look at these witnesses. Two were members of Christ's church — Matthew and John. Two were members of his congregation — Mark and Luke. One was a business man; another was a young man, who witnessed the daily life of our Saviour, and whose mother's house was his customary home during his visits to the city. One was a professional man, an educated physician; and the other was for three years a most intimate companion. By what possible choice or concurrence could a better selection have been made? Upon what possible arrangement of testimony could one more securely stand while cherishing the sublimest truths that can ever greet our ears?

Uninspired Witnesses. — The first from this class is Ignatius. He was a devoted Christian, a contemporary of our Saviour, and a martyr to his belief in his Lord's divinity. In his letter to the Philadelphians he employs the following language: "Christ truly suffered, as he also truly raised up himself. I *know* that after the resurrection he was in the flesh, and I *believe* him to be so still. And when he came to those who were with Peter, he said to them, Take, handle me, and see that I am not an incorporeal phantom."

The genuineness of this letter remains undisputed. The writer claims to have had convincing evidence of Christ's resurrection, either from eye-sight or from the testimony of those who had seen him after he had risen. Another early writer was Polycarp. He was a personal friend of Ignatius, and a convert and disciple of the apostle John. In a letter written to the church at Philippi, he exhorts the converts to believe in Christ, "whom," he says, "God did certainly raise from the dead." Surely the dogma of Christ's resurrection was not a late invention of the church!

One of the most celebrated writers of the early Christian church was Tertullian. According to Eusebius, he was highly distinguished among the most eminent men of Rome. In one of his works — the "Apologeticus" — he says that "the fame of our Lord's remarkable resurrection and ascension being now spread abroad, Pontius Pilate, according to an ancient custom of communicating novel occurrences to the emperor, that nothing might escape him, transmitted to Tiberius, Emperor of Rome, an account of the resurrection of our Lord from the dead." In this account Pilate intimated that Christ was believed to be a God, after his resurrection, by the great mass of the people. "Tiberius," continues the writer, "referred the whole matter to the senate, who, being unacquainted with the facts, rejected it."

The integrity of this passage is not questioned by the most sceptical critics. But for the destruction of the Alexandrian and Roman libraries, we have every reason to believe that there would be found in them to-day the account of Christ's resurrection, which was written by Pilate to the Roman senate, together with the record of their action respecting it. Those libraries have been destroyed. That of Alexandria, containing seven hundred thousand volumes, was consumed by fire, its entire destruction occupying six months. Those of Rome were destroyed during the reign of Gregory the Great, about the close of the sixth century. Fortunately for the world, however, providence had taken care to preserve the most important records of the most important events in history. Few to-day can be found who are not ready to acknowledge, however much they may regret the spoliations of Khaleefeh' Omar and Gregory, that the loss of the Sacred Scriptures would have been more serious to the world than has been the loss of all the libraries of Rome and Alexandria.

An examination of the facts which the evangelists have stated concerning the death and resurrection of our Saviour.

On the evening of the day preceding his trial, Jesus and his disciples, according to the united testimony of the evangelists, partook of their last meal together.

(Matt. xxvi. 20. Mark xiv. 17. Luke xxii. 14.) The day is not stated. It has been generally supposed that it was Thursday. There are many forcible considerations which decide in favor of Wednesday. Later the same evening, probably between eleven and twelve o'clock, they left the banquet-hall for a retired garden, or park, situated to the east of the city. (Matt. xxvi. 30–46. Mark xiv. 26–42. Luke xxii. 39–46. John xviii. 1.) On the following morning the Saviour was betrayed, and suffered a voluntary arrest. (Matt. xxvi. 47–56. Mark xiv. 43–52. Luke xxii. 47–53. John xviii. 2–12.) The various trials were then instituted, and occupied until daylight. (Matt. xxvii. 1. Mark xv. 1. Luke xxii. 63–71. John xviii. 28.) The preliminaries of the crucifixion followed, and were completed some time before nine o'clock the same morning. From that hour until noon, the multitudes stood by beholding. (Luke xxiii. 35.) The priests and rulers, followed by some of the people, meanwhile insulted and mocked him. (Matt. xxvii. 39–44. Mark xv. 29–32.) From twelve o'clock, noon, until three in the afternoon, a thick darkness veiled the heavens. (Matt. xxvii. 45, 46. Mark xv. 33, 34. Luke xxiii. 44–46.) A fact stated both by contemporaneous Christian and pagan writers. Says Phlegon, a pagan, and the compiler of "The Olympiads," "There was, at this time, an eclipse of the sun, the greatest of any ever previously known." Celsus also alludes to the same phenomenon, but regards it only as something very wonderful. It is worthy of remark that this could not have been a natural eclipse of the sun; for the passover was always held at the time of full moon, which precludes the possibility of a solar eclipse. During this darkness, Christ expired. (Matt. xxvii. 50. Mark xv. 37. Luke xxiii. 46. John xix. 30.) The darkness which had continued for three hours gave place again to sunlight. Shortly after this, a soldier, in the faithful discharge of his duty, as he supposed, but that the Scriptures might be fulfilled, pierced the Saviour to the heart with a spear. (John xix. 33.) John, who says he was present, states that blood and water followed the removal of the spear. (John xix. 35.) From this statement the world may know that Christ was dead, and not in a swoon. It is possible that his spiritual sufferings had been so intense for several months as to result in an affection of the heart, which at length, in a paroxysm of excessive grief, burst, resulting in instant death. On this supposition, the flowing of both blood and water from the wound of the spear can be easily accounted for. "And Joseph of Arimathea, a counsellor, went unto Pilate, and begged the body of Jesus." (Matt. xxvii. 57, 58. Mark xv. 42, 43. Luke xxiii. 50–52. John xix. 38, 39.) "And Pilate marvelled if he were already dead." (Mark xv. 44.) He died not from crucifixion; his death was too sudden for that; but the Saviour of the world had died from a *grief-burdened* and literally *broken heart.* Permission being granted by Pilate, the corpse was taken from the cross, and placed in a new tomb, by two secret friends of Jesus. These men were not numbered among his disciples. They were both members of the great national council of the Jews, which had condemned him. (Matt. xxvii. 59, 60. Mark xv. 45, 46. Luke xxiii. 53. John xix.

40–42.) At the instigation of his enemies, a strong guard was subsequently despatched to the place of interment. The language is very explicit — "The chief priests and Pharisees came together unto Pilate, saying, Sir, we remember that that deceiver said, while he was yet alive, after three days I will rise again. Command therefore that the sepulchre be made sure until the third day, lest his disciples come by night, and steal him away, and say unto the people, He is risen from the dead: so the last error shall be worse than the first. Pilate said unto them, ye have a watch; go your way, make it as sure as ye can. So they went, and made the sepulchre sure, sealing the stone and setting a watch." (Matt. xxvii. 62–66.) The strong guard, the large stone, the governor's seal, show what ample precautions were taken to guard against deception.

Such, in brief, is the narration of the death and burial of Jesus Christ. Applying whatever historical tests we choose to these accounts, must we not concede that he actually died at the time, in the place and under the circumstances here narrated? Would not a denial reduce all history, ancient and recent, to a myth?

The Account of the Resurrection.—Certain women, friends of Jesus, had gathered in Jerusalem on Friday afternoon, and by contribution and purchase were collecting various kinds of spices for the purpose of embalming the body. They did not know that this had been attended to by Joseph and Nicodemus. Six o'clock Friday evening was upon them, and further arrangements must be deferred. At that time the Jewish Sabbath began, and all preparations of the kind, by custom and law, must cease. They remained in the city, however, and observed the following day, according to the commandment. (Luke xxiii. 56.) On the succeeding morning (our Sunday), before light, they started for the sepulchre in the garden of Gethsemane. While on the way an earthquake of unusual power and extent occurred; it is the one, undoubtedly, to which Phlegon refers, and which he says "was felt in distant Bithynia, overthrowing some of the houses." This, and certain other unnatural phenomena, so terrified the guard that they fled, fearing less to encounter death than to remain and witness the strange scenes that confronted them. (Matt. xxviii. 2, 4.) The women were also terrified. They paused in their steps, and gazed in silence upon each other's faces. The effects of the heavy shock soon passed away. There was again the wonted calm of early dawn; the earth ceased to tremble; the disturbed atmosphere was again in repose; the flashing light faded away; the native birds broke forth in their early songs; the fingers of the morning were seen pointing steadily up from the eastern sky; and the women, filled only with desires of honoring their divine Master, and anxious only to know who should roll away the stone, continued their journey. (Mark xvi. 3.) They seem not to have heard of the last order to guard the tomb, or else, not understanding what was the import of the "governor's seal," they looked for no opposition to their effort; and they met with none. The guard had fled; the seal was broken, the stone removed; but the body they sought was not there. (Mark xv. 4. Luke xxiv. 2, 3.) This discovery filled them with disappointment. "And it came to pass, as they were much perplexed thereabout, behold, two men stood by them in shining garments" (Luke xxiv. 4), and said unto them, "Go your way, tell his disciples and Peter that he goeth before you into Galilee: there shall ye see him, as he said unto you." (Mark xvi. 7.)

Peter and John had remained during the night at some place near the tomb; so near, they could pass the entire distance at a single run. The other disciples had fled, perhaps through fear, to some more distant place, probably Bethany, beyond the Mount of Olives. The mission of informing the disciples was then arranged by the women, as follows: Mary was to make the announcement to Peter and John, which she did in the mournful words, "They have taken away the Lord out of the sepulchre, and *we* know not where they have laid him." (John xx. 2.) The rest of the women were to depart quickly for Bethany, and announce what they had seen and heard to the other disciples. (Mark xvi. 8.) Peter and John, informed by Mary, were soon on their way to Gethsemane. They went in haste, leaving Mary behind them. John, the younger, outran Peter, and, reaching the tomb first, looked in, but did not enter. "Then cometh Simon Peter, and went into the sepulchre, and saw the linen clothes and napkin," properly laid and folded. The resurrection had taken place quietly, and with all the composure of divinity. After these examinations had been made, Peter and John retired, going "unto their own home." (John xx. 10.) The tomb was again left without guard, or visitor. The distressed Mary could not long remain away from the sacred spot, and soon after the departure of the disciples, she revisited the tomb, this time alone. The other women were on their way to Bethany.

Why should she *return* to the sepulchre! — Where else would she be likely to go? The best friend she had ever known — the one who had saved her from a terrible malady, and instructed her in the way of eternal life — was dead. As she sought alone the entrance of the empty tomb, she simply followed the natural instincts, not of a "distracted," but of a *devoted* woman's heart. While she lingered there, the vision of angels was repeated — "And they say unto her, Woman, why weepest thou?" She, in her reply, offered the same artless language as that employed to Peter and John, with the exception that this time she made use of the singular, "*I*," instead of the plural, "*we*." And "they have taken him away," was the bitter thought that haunted her troubled soul. Mary, they have not taken him away! "She turned herself back, and saw Jesus standing, and knew not that it was Jesus;" but, "supposing him to be the gardener, saith unto him, Sir, if thou have borne him hence, tell me where thou hast laid him, and I will take him away." (John xx. 15.) "Jesus saith unto her, Mary." (John xx. 16.) Belief, hope, conviction, and amazement burst upon her soul at the sound of that familiar voice speaking her own name. In the excess of her joy her native Hebrew dialect came first to her lips in the honored expression, "Rabboni!" (John xx. 17.) And Mary Magdalene, once a sinful woman, by virtue of her subsequent zeal and devotion, became the first mortal preacher of the risen Saviour. (Mark xvi. 9.) Christ bade her not delay at the tomb, but go and announce his resurrection to his brethren. After this he appeared to the other women, probably while on the way to Bethany, and bade them also make the same announcement. They hastened to the house where the disciples were met, and related that, while they were on their way, Jesus had met them, saying, "All hail!" (Matt. xxviii. 9, 10.) "And they returned," says Luke, "and told all these things unto the eleven, and to all the rest. And their words seemed to them as idle tales, and they believed them not." (Luke xxiv. 9, 11.) The disciples concluded that the sleepless night, the early walk, and the perplexing scenes through which the women had passed, had produced an hallucination in their minds.

Later in the afternoon of the same day, Christ appeared, in the form of a Jewish traveller, to Luke and Cleopas. The name of Cleopas only is given, Luke modestly withholding his own, but describing the scene with all the minuteness and accuracy of an eye-witness. After journeying and conversing together for some time, these men represent that their eyes, hitherto veiled, were suddenly opened. They knew him, and he vanished out of their sight. "And they rose up the same hour, and returned to Jerusalem, and found the eleven gathered together, and told them what things were done by the way." (Luke xxiv. 13–35.)

Not far from this time, the apostle Peter, having separated himself from the rest of the company, in order to obtain some clew to these strange events, or, perhaps, to grieve over his own sad fall, was met by his Master, who bound up his bleeding heart. Afterwards they separated. Peter, returning to the company of the disciples, made his report. (Luke xxiv. 34. 1 Cor. xv. 5.) "All these went," says Mark, "and told it unto the residue." "Neither believed they them." (Mark xvi. 13.) The whole account they looked upon as a child's ghost story.

Before proceeding with the testimony, we pause to gather up the evidence, both direct and circumstantial, thus far deduced. We note especially these two facts: First, that, after this accumulation of testimony from Mary and the several other women, from Luke, Cleopas, and Simon Peter, the great body of the disciples were still incredulous. They desired that the facts stated might be true, but doubted the possibility. Second, that the rulers of Jerusalem believed in Christ's resurrection sooner than his disciples. "Now when they were going," says Matthew, "some of the watch came unto the city, and showed unto the chief priests all the things that were done. And when they were assembled with the elders, and had taken counsel, they gave large sums of money unto the soldiers, saying, Say ye, His disciples came by night, and stole him away while we slept. And if this come to the governor's ears, we will persuade him, and secure you. And this saying is commonly reported among the Jews until this day." (Matt. xxviii. 11–15.) Thus, while the disciples and friends of Jesus disbelieved, the Sanhedrim, believing, were deliberately and maliciously fabricating a falsehood for the terrified and bribed soldiers. This fact Justin Martyr publicly charges upon the Jews of his own day.

"You sent," he says, "chosen men for the especial purpose of circulating this falsehood."

Return to the assembly of the disciples. While they were still listening to the testimony given, while discussing, doubting, and cross-questioning, having barred the doors and fastened the windows, "for fear of the Jews" (John xx. 19), "behold, Jesus himself," says Luke, "stood in the midst of them, and saith unto them, Peace be unto you." (Luke xxiv. 36.) Not a door had been opened. Not a window-bolt had been loosened. He was before them! So mysterious was his coming, that "they were terrified and affrighted, and supposed that they had seen a spirit." (Luke xxiv. 37.) "And he upbraided them," says Mark, "for their unbelief and hardness of heart." (Mark xvi. 14.) Luke, a physician, whose attention would more naturally be called to the fact, adds, "And he said unto them, Why are ye troubled? and why do thoughts arise in your hearts? Behold my hands and my feet, that it is I myself; handle me, and see; for a spirit hath not flesh and bones, as ye see me have. And when he had thus spoken, he showed them his hands and his feet. And while they yet believed not for joy, and wondered, he said unto them, Have ye here any meat?" (Luke xxiv. 38–42.) And he partook of it; not that he must eat to support life, but that he might convince them that he was something more than a spirit. After this he disappeared, and the company of disciples dispersed. "But Thomas, one of the twelve, called Didymus," says John, "was not with them when Jesus came." (John xx. 24.) And he, we are told, could not be prevailed upon to believe that Christ had risen, or that they had seen him.

Seven days passed, and the disciples were again met, and Thomas with them; and to him, on this occasion, was granted the most overwhelming evidence that the Christ risen was identical with the Christ dead. (John xx. 26–31.) The remaining appearances, as given by the evangelists, are these: to the disciples by the Lake of Tiberius (John xxi. 1–24); to the multitude on a mountain in Galilee (Matt. xxviii. 15–17. 1 Cor. xv. 6.); to the disciples, singly or in company, through a space of forty days (Acts i. 3); and, lastly, to the disciples, near Jerusalem, on the road to Bethany, at the descent of the Mount of Olives. It was on this occasion that he unfolded, in their hearing, the prophetic Scriptures, and gave them transcendent promises, bidding them no longer expect an earthly, but to prepare themselves for a heavenly kingdom. And that road, which had witnessed his triumphal entry into the sacred city of the Jews, then witnessed his triumphal entry into the sacred city of God, which is in heaven. (Luke xxiv. 50, 51.) "And it came to pass, while he blessed them, he was parted from them, and carried up into heaven." "And while they looked steadfastly toward heaven," a voice addressed to them these words of mingled consolation and prophecy: "Ye men of Galilee, why stand ye gazing up into heaven? This same Jesus which is taken up from you into heaven shall so come in like manner as ye have seen him go into heaven. Then returned they unto Jerusalem from the Mount of Olives, which is from Jerusalem a Sabbath day's journey." (Acts i. 9–12.) Such is the wonderful story of Christ's resurrection from the dead. He was seen first by Mary Magdalene; second, by the other friendly women;

third, by the disciples, journeying to Emmaus; fourth, by Simon Peter; fifth, by the ten apostles, and other friends; sixth, by the eleven apostles, and friends; seventh, by the apostle on the shore of the Sea of Tiberias; eighth, by the apostles and the multitude on the mount; ninth, by the disciples and friends at his ascension; and we may add a tenth especial appearance granted to James (1 Cor. xv. 7); and, lastly, to Paul himself. (1 Cor. xv. 8.) The accounts of these events, excepting the one in 1 Corinthians, have come to us from a fourfold source. They differ, but not conflict. They are an artless and honest narration of facts. The language used is not in the least mystical, the thoughts not in the least sublimated. "The inventor of the Gospels," Rousseau once exclaimed, "if they were invented, would have been a greater hero than Christ himself, even if all that has been said of him were true." Daniel Webster, who possessed a wonderful faculty for detecting, both from the substance-matter and manner of expression, what was true and false in testimony, after examining the statements of the evangelists, was so strongly convinced of the truthfulness of the events stated, that he believed them, and contemplated the preparation of a work on the evidences of Christianity. A multiplicity of professional and public duties compelled him to relinquish the undertaking. What a bright and redeeming chapter that might have been in Mr. Webster's brilliant but tarnished life! How humanity is healed by touching the hem of His garment!

Not only are the style and manner of the writers convincing, but the substance of their testimony is also convincing. To be sure, they do not make

Christ appear very publicly, nor yet exclusively to a few. According to their testimony, he disputed no more in the temple, attended no more weddings in Cana or elsewhere, fed no more the multitude in the fields or on the mountains; but he appeared, not to a limited number of his disciples in every instance, but on one occasion, at least, to a promiscuous assemblage of more than five hundred persons. He did not show himself to the Sadducees, who denied the possibility of the resurrection; for they would have said, "He is not dead," or, "The disciples have stolen him away." He did not appear to the rulers; for they would have said, as in the case of Lazarus, "He is raised by Beelzebub, the prince of devils." He showed himself to his friends. He repeated to them his promises. He gave them instruction and encouragement, which they were commissioned to hand down to subsequent ages, as the solemn yet beneficent benediction and support of all his followers. He did not come again in his humility. One such appearance was enough. He did not come in the splendor and pomp of an earthly king. He was neither to establish the theocracy, nor suffer defeat at the hands of the Romans. He came in a manner more sublime and impressive than either. He had the same body, but new endowments. He could transport himself instantly from one place to another. He was sometimes visible, sometimes invisible. He bore at one time unmistakable evidences of his former condition; at another he appeared as a stranger. On one occasion he resembled a common gardener, on another a Jewish traveller. He came, walked among and conversed with his disciples in an organized body, but with power to clothe it in his accustomed garments and expression, or otherwise. He had a body, but not one which was then glorified.

His appearances differed. At one time he flashed before them like a vision of the night, at another as the soft shining of the morning. At one time he slowly hovered near them, like an appearance from another world; again he came as the King of the whole earth, sending his ambassadors to all nations and kindreds. His appearance to Mary was the most tender; he spoke and she recognized him. That before the Emmaus travellers was the most human; he walked with them sixty stadia, until the evening hour; he interpreted to them the Scriptures, until their hearts burned within them. His appearance before the body of the disciples was the most composed — calculated to relieve their anxiety; that before Thomas the most convincing; that on the shores of Tiberias the most mysterious; and that on the mountains of Bethany the most sublime. What a wonderful diversity in appearance! how solemnly impressive! All this the invention of men? What! were these witnesses, who had received testimony at first with such extreme caution, deceived? Did these honest-spoken men really fabricate such unheard-of falsehoods, and publish them to the world? Dr. South, after reviewing this class of evidence, once exclaimed, "A man who will not believe the resurrection of Christ, upon a statement of these facts, would not believe it if he himself should rise from the dead." The statements of the evangelists embody the most startling, eternal, and glorious truths ever published, or the most audacious, *miraculous*, and monstrous lies ever perpetrated.

From direct testimony respecting Christ's resurrection we pass to other evidence, noticing, first, —

The Conduct of the Disciples. — Up to the hour of Christ's death the disciples clung to the fond expectation that he had come to restore Israel; they believed that he was to throw down the Roman Eagle, and trample her proud banners under his feet. This thought filled them with enthusiasm. All their hopes were now extinguished in the apparently disgraceful death of their Leader. "He has ended," said Celsus, the earliest, if not a contemporaneous sceptic, — "he has ended a miserable life by a wretched death." The disciples were confounded. The entire transaction was so unaccountable and perplexing that upon the arrest of Christ they fled. No ordinary event could have rallied them. But in two months from that date, on the occasion of another national feast, these men were again in Jerusalem. They were in the midst of all that had opposed Christ — where the faces of the priests, and rulers, fifty days before, had been pale with hate, and their hands stained with blood. The events of the former Passover were fresh in the minds of all. Under circumstances which precluded the possibility of practising deception, these disciples of Christ, in the presence of a large assemblage of rulers, resident Jews, and foreigners (who had been called together by the report noised through the city that the Holy Ghost had made his appearance), boldly declared that they had seen Christ, and that he had risen from the dead. Simon Peter, who, at the feast two months before, denied his Master, now stood up and addressed the assemblage. His confession was not, as formerly, that he did not know the man. He did not ask public forgiveness for having caused the present disturbance. He did not say that Jesus was only a man; that he had deceived the people, and was not risen from the dead; but he declared that this speaking with tongues which they heard was the fulfilment of prophecy. He lifted his voice in a clear and full declaration of the truths he believed. "Ye men of Israel, hear these words: Jesus of Nazareth, a man approved of God among you, . . . ye have taken, and by wicked hands have crucified and slain, . . . whom God hath raised up, having loosed the pains of death, because it was not possible that he should be holden of it." (Acts i. 22–24.) What had changed this man and his companions? What had made of them, in this short space, such bold champions of truth? How dared they breathe defiance so calmly, in the face of deadly opposition, and expose themselves, if false, alike to public death and the wrath of Heaven? They had recourse to no clandestine whispers. They recommended no blind faith. They appealed to no unheard-of transactions, but spoke of public and well-known events. They provoked the people and the world to examine their statements and confute them. They referred to the wonders which had taken place in the heavens and on the earth, — the sun darkened as never before, the moon veiled as in blood, the earth quaking to its centre, the stone rolled away from the tomb, and the guard fleeing in terror. If these things had not thus occurred, if the disciples had not been in possession of facts, would they, without authority, have silenced men of authority? Would their simple story, if false, have baffled subtlest policy, and their rude speech persuade sooner than national learning and rhetoric? Would these men, standing upon falsehood, have dared impeach a nation, arraign its justice, and charge its rulers with the murder of innocence? Does it not look as though the disciples believed in their Lord's resurrection? Had he not appeared to them? Had he not removed their doubts, comforted their hearts, and implanted within them immovable and immortal hopes? Had those forty days been less important in their training than had been the previous three years of his active life? Was their belief the result of a few weeks' cogitation? Was it a mere idea with them, as Renan claims? "The shadow created by the delicate sensibility of Magdalene?" Such stupidity from such a pen seems unpardonable.

The Conduct of the Rulers and People of Jerusalem. — If there had not been a public belief respecting the facts stated by the apostles on the day in question, why did the Jewish rulers fear to arrest them? Why did they stand like criminals at the bar of justice, conscience-smitten and unable to say why sentence of death should not be passed upon them? The city abounded in public and detective police, the authorities were alive and sensitive to this question. Why so inactive, unless public sentiment and well-known facts overawed them? Did they not know that the tomb had been secured beyond possibility of robbery? Why so restless and excited, unless they felt that the "discomforted and disembodied spirit of the Jewish religion" was wandering about Christ's grave, calling for another guard and seal, the one having been put to flight, the other broken? The rulers and police of Jerusalem were *terrified:* that explains it. What! terrified because they had murdered a common malefactor? All Jerusalem thrown into an uproar by a random ghost story! Offer large sums of money to the Roman soldiers to say that the disciples had stolen him, when they had only offered the paltry sum of fifteen dollars to Judas, for his betrayal, and at last forced to the humiliating expedient of accounting for his disappearance by asserting that a handful of his disciples had robbed the graveyard, removing the stone and breaking the seal, in the presence of the best-disciplined troops in the world — death being the inevitable penalty of their sleeping at their post! Surely, "whom the gods wish to destroy, they first make mad."

But the people — why are they alarmed, and why so strange their conduct? They repented, and smote their breasts; multitudes suddenly professed faith in a risen Christ, and became Christians; they departed from the city. Their reports through the countries were electrical. All writers have noticed the rapid spread of Christianity during the first centuries.

Pliny the Younger, at that time Consul and Governor of Pontus, in a letter to the Emperor Trajan, inquiring what course to pursue with the Christians under arrest, said, "Suspending all judicial proceeding, I have recourse to you for advice. It has appeared unto me a matter highly deserving consideration, especially for the great number of persons condemned. There are many, of all ages, and every rank, and of both sexes likewise; nor has the contagion of this superstition seized cities only, but the lesser towns also, and the open country. Neverthe less, it seems to me that it may be restrained." Of his own time, Tertullian says, "If the laws against Christians were enforced, Carthage would be desolate." Does it not look as though the multitudes at Jerusalem had been converted by witnessing some strange and inexplicable phenomena? Would they otherwise have gone forth from the city like flaming torches of God's truth and Christ's divinity?

Between two and three millions of people were assembled in and around Jerusalem at the feast during which Christ was executed. These things had not been done in a corner. The events of the trial and death of Jesus had become, for some reason, a question of universal agitation. As far as the hills and the plains of Calvary furnished room, they were crowded on the day of the crucifixion with anxious spectators. The disciples on the road to Emmaus were astonished that even a stranger in the city, one there only for a day, had not heard of these events. Does it not look as though an hour of awakening from the national intoxication and bewilderment, which had thrust upon the people this deed, had come?

That night after Christ's death was a night of terror in Jerusalem, and that morning of his :esurrection was to the people a morning of terror, and of conviction also. Does not the lingering pallor of death upon so many countenances, does not that cry of despair from the multitude, "Men and brethren, what shall we do?" bear appalling and overwhelming evidence to the divinity and resurrection of the dead Christ?

The Institution of the Christian Sabbath.—Saturday is now, as then, the Sabbath of the Jews throughout the world; their shops are closed, their synagogues opened. Why do not Christians observe it? Hear the fathers of the church. Ignatius, shortly after the death of John, says, "Let every one that loves Christ keep holy the Lord's day, the queen of days, the resurrection day." Theophilus, about sixty years later, says, "Both custom and reason challenge us that we honor the Lord's day, seeing that on that day it was that our Lord Jesus completed his resurrection from the dead." Says Clement of Alexandria, thirty years later, "Christians, according to the command of the Gospels, observe the Lord's day, thereby glorifying the resurrection of the Lord." Was it a small undertaking for a few men, without authority or influence, without occasion to warrant it, and with no particular motive or reason, to begin and accomplish so important a change of days as this? Nay, Bunker Hill Monument is a far less enduring witness than the Christian Sabbath. It presents no surer evidence that a battle was there fought on the 17th of June, 1775, between the American and British troops, than the existence of the Sabbath is evidence that it was instituted in commemoration of our Saviour's resurrection, and would not have been instituted without it.

Why should his resurrection have ever been thought incredible? His life, in many respects, was exceptional. It is true that his birth and parentage, the low garb and dim lustre of his earthly career, his hunger and thirst at the well, his weary body, tear ful eyes, and sad death, disclose his humanity. But his resurrection, that "power to lay down life and to take it again," discloses as unmistakably the majesty of his divine omnipotence. Carlyle at times does not venture even to speak the name of this mysterious Being. He prefers "to meditate upon that sacred matter in sacred silence." Rousseau, Renan, Emerson, and others like them, pronounce Him indefectible. All men confess that he lived as no other being has ever lived. We believe, therefore, though he was once dead, as he did not live like other men, so he did not lie in the grave like other men. But he arose, was seen, and was heard to speak. He bore about with him a mysterious body. Afterwards he ascended to "the right hand of the glory of God." He is now there, "the express image of God," the sole and only visible personal manifestation of deity that will ever greet our eyes. His entire life on earth was a part of another and eternal life. It was the visible section of a divine and illuminated orbit, appearing at Bethlehem, and disappearing on the Mount of Olives. He was the sudden appearing and disappearing to the world of a brilliant and glorious star, which shines in heaven forever and ever.

But all this is miraculous. True. A miracle is possible. To deny it is atheism. If God exists, he is a supernatural being. If he is a supernatural being, he can act in a supernatural (miraculous) as well as in a natural manner. The most stupendous of miracles is the resurrection of Christ. Its historical evidence is the most overwhelming. It is the most sublime of facts. It affords the happiest of hopes. "*Christos aneste, alethos aneste!*" "*Christ is risen, is risen indeed!*" is destined to become the most frequent and fragrant greeting among men, gracing their conversation and cheering their lives. Christ's resurrection is the crowning passage of his doctrine, the seal of truth upon all he promised, and the potent argument to the race that he was not a natural, but a Supernatural Being.

"Hear, O Israel; the Lord our God is one Lord." *Deuteronomy*, vi. 4.

"As ye have therefore received Christ Jesus the Lord, so walk ye in him.

"For in him dwelleth all the fulness of the Godhead bodily." *Colossians* ii. 6, 9.

"And now, O Father, glorify thou me with thine own self, with the glory which I had with thee before the world was." *John* xvii. 5.

"But the Comforter, which is the Holy Ghost, whom the Father will send in my name, he shall teach you, and bring all things to your remembrance, whatsoever I have said unto you." *John* xiv. 26.

"Go ye therefore, and teach all nations, baptizing them in the name of the Father, and of the Son, and of the Holy Ghost." *Matthew* xxviii. 19.

"O thou Eternal One! whose presence bright
All space doth occupy, all motion guide!
Embracing all, supporting, ruling o'er!
Being whom we call God, and know no more!

From the Russian of DERZHAVIN.

"Begotten Son, divine Similitude,
In whose conspicuous countenance, without cloud
Made visible, the Almighty Father shines,
Whom else no creature can behold!
Transfused in thee his ample spirit rests."

MILTON.

"The Spirit of God,
From heaven descending, dwells in domes of clay;
In mode far passing human thought, he guides
Us in such gentle murmurs, that to know
His heavenly voice we must have done his will."

JOHN HEY.

"In those Three Persons the One God was shown,
Each First in place, each Last, — not one alone;
Of Siva, Vishnu, Brahma, each may be
First, Second, Third, among the Blessed Three."

Kalidâsa the Brahman.

II.

THE THREE-ONE.

BY the term "Trinity," the evangelical church means a union in one Godhead of the Father, Son, and Spirit. It does not teach that there are three persons in one person, if we use in both cases the term "person" in one and the same sense. Employing the word "person" in its ordinary sense, there is but one, and there can be but one, personal and manifest agent in the Trinity; employing it in the sense of personation, there may be an indefinite number of persons in one and the same person. No one has ever believed that there are three personal existences in the Trinity, and at the same time but one existence of *the same kind* If our eternal salvation depended upon it, we could not believe it. It would be a stupendous make-believe. God does not require us to believe anything of this kind more than he requires a man to believe that the communion bread is Christ's body in fact, rather than a symbol of it. If we try to make our fellow-men believe such a dogma, we are more like deluded Roman Catholics than intelligent Christians.

To no other revealed truth in revelation is more prominence given than to the unity and oneness of God. The expression "the Lord is one God," or its equivalent, is iterated time and again. That God has no equal is taught in upwards of fifty passages. The Divine Unity is no more clearly pronounced throughout the material universe than it is throughout the Bible. It is the introduction and conclusion of all scientific researches. Any other representation contradicts both creation and revelation. Its denial is a proper object for the ridicule of every thinking man, and of the disbelief of every Orthodox Christian. Let this, then, be our first and necessary conclusion — that Deity, whether creating, inspiring, or otherwise manifesting itself, is one God; one, and no more. But, as we investigate the inspired word, we meet with three distinct personalities. To each of the three, divine ascriptions are paid with equal consideration and uniformity. The distinctions are represented by the terms "Father," "Son," and "Holy Ghost," or "Spirit." From the fact of the divine oneness, and of these three distinctions, has sprung the statement of the doctrine of the "Trinity." In pursuing the discussion, we may illustrate the three distinctions in the Godhead by terms familiar to science — Law, Manifestation, and Force.

The Existence of the Father. — What the Father is to the Christian world, Law is to the world of science. Not that law is the Father, but it is that through which the special manifestation of the Deity, called the Father, is made known to us. Law, natural and divine, is found everywhere. By it the animal, vegetable, and mineral kingdoms are bound together, controlled, and overruled. The elephant does not have the claw of a lion, nor the lion the tusk of an elephant. The maple does not bear the fruit of the pear, nor the pear the foliage of the pine. Salt does not have the crystals of sugar, nor sugar those of mica, or quartz, but each its own universal and eternal law of development, formation, and crystallization. What are these laws? We cannot see them, we cannot approach them; we do not know, on natural principles, what their cause, nor whence their ground of existence. They are hidden in the profoundest mystery. But they exist on every hand and in every kingdom above us, beneath us, before us, and behind us. In them we live, and move, and have our being. They are as universal as the universe, as eternal as eternity, as divine as the Deity.

Fichte, the most wonderful, and in some respects the greatest speculative philosopher Germany ever produced, taught that this "law of the universe" is God. But law is not God, nor a complete representation of God. The laws of the universe of every kind do not constitute all that is found in the universe, or all that is involved in the term "God." Aside from law there is manifestation, aside from law and manifestation there is force still unaccounted for.

This law-source is no more a complete Godhead than a man's intellect is a complete man without the will power which gives him motion, and without the visible organism which enables us to see him. To represent God thus would be to annihilate force and reduce visible creation to a mere idea. This was what Fichte boldly did, to give consistency to his system

Is not Christian theology more philosophical than Fichte in its representation that this "*universal law*" springs from a Being, a personal existence, designated by the term "Father?" The laws are not this Being; but may they not emanate from him? and through their presence may not his existence be made known to us? May not the Father in Christianity and the God of other schools be this great universal personality lying back of all existence, rising up in a kind of sublime, sombre, and silent majesty, a law-embodied Deity who sits above all, back of all, over all, immovable, immutable, immeasurable, and unapproachable, a smile for the innocent, a consuming fire for the guilty? The pantheistic world says, "This is my God." The Christian world says, "This is one, but only one form of the divine existence — the Invisible Father."

The Ministration of the Father. — As there is little controversy on the question of the administration of God the Father among the various schools of belief, we shall not dwell upon this division. It is sufficient to say that in him is bound together the universe as a unit, in him are harmonized and administered its laws. He numbers the hairs of our heads, and notes the fall of a sparrow. He rewards the good, and will punish the guilty.

The Logos, or the Christ of God. — What this Christ is to the Christian world, created and manifested nature is to the world of science. Not that nature is Christ, but, as in the case of the Father, may it not be that, through which the specific manifestation of the Deity called the "Son," or "*word*," is made known to us? All sensible men at present believe there is a created universe. They believe that a star is a star, and not an idea; that a rock is a rock, and not a mere belief. So far as we can judge, not a spot in the universe is without this actual or *possible* manifestation. The wings of the morning would find it in the uttermost parts of the earth. A flight to the heaven of heavens would find it there, and a descent into the bottom of the sea would find it there. This, then, which we see in the carpeted earth, in the rose-bud held in the hand of a delighted child, in the grass that nods to the breeze, or is crushed under our foot-fall — this which is seen on the mountain, in the valley, in the crystal rock, in the man walking the street, or hanging upon a cross, — in the sparkling stars over our heads, and in the black cloud that rolls up in the west, veiling the sun, and bearing in its bosom the hidings of his power, — is the Logos manifesting itself, a part of which manifestation is ourselves as a product, and in which manifestation we live, and move, and have our being.

The same may be predicated of this principle as of law. It is as universal as the universe, eternal in its actuality or possibility as eternity, and as divine as the Deity. Millions of our fellow-beings have called it God, have worshipped it as God. "Nature is God" and "God is nature" must be the theory of all who ignore the supernatural. But this manifestation does not constitute all that is involved in the term "God," aside from this, are universal law and force. May not this manifestation be represented in Christian theology by the terms "Divine Logos," "The Word,"

"God manifest," "The Christ of the Universe"? But bear in mind that this divine manifestation in nature is not, in essence, the personal Logos; it is only a direct emanation from him. It indicates the actual existence of him without whom "was not anything made that was made." Nor is he the Father or the Holy Ghost, any more than the works of nature are the laws, or force, of the universe. He is not the Godhead any more than the physical body of man is the whole man devoid of intellect and will; but may he not be, or rather become through Christ Jesus, the personal manifestation of the Godhead?

The Ministration and Especial Manifestation of the Logos. Anti-Trinitarians represent that the evangelical church believes in three Gods. This is not a true representation. On the contrary, may not its belief be fairly set forth in the following statement: There is nowhere but one manifestation of the personality or individuality of the supreme Godhead; and that one is the Second Person in the Trinity, the "*Christos*," the "*Anointed*" representative of the *three* divine personalities? If so, this would not be true during his walk on earth merely, but true since the morning of eternity. Did he not stand in the midst of that first creation of the sons of God, as he afterwards stood in the temple of the Jews, the one altogether lovely, enthroned amid all the attractive graces of the Deity, spotless and without blemish? With this thought before us, how natural and simple is the interpretation of those passages in the opening book of the Bible — passages which so forcibly exalt the human race. "And God said, Let us make man in our image, after our likeness. So God created man in his own image; in the image of God created he him, male and female created he them." Could God have created man in his own image if that image had not previously existed? The terms "image" and "likeness," here employed, are definite, not vague and imaginary. If it is not a likeness in matter that is meant, it must, inevitably, be one in form. If not in essence, it must, of necessity, be in semblance. Violence is done the Scriptures to make other interpretations. "Image" is a word taken from sensible things, and denotes likeness in outward form, while the materials of which the things are composed are different. "Likeness" is a term of more general application, and may indicate resemblance of qualities, both external and internal.

Reference to the original text will not change the translation of these words. So that, following the strict meaning of the text, God could not have created man in his own image, if that image had not previously existed. More than this, is it not reasonable to suppose that this manifestation was the one in which the Christ of God appeared, at first, the one in which he always has appeared and always will appear — the sublime ideal of the race, the type of perfected strength, beauty, and majesty, the only personal manifestation of the Father, and the Logos, and the Spirit? Is it the form of a bear, or an elephant, that satisfies our ideas of the divine manifestation? What form could walk the earth as its king, or fill the throne of heaven as its judge, with greater fitness than a perfect and glorified human manifestation, in the form and person of the eternal and exalted Christ? When we speak of Christ, then, something more is meant than the man human who walked the earth weary, hungry, and athirst, who sinned not, and died for us eighteen centuries ago. There is meant, in addition to this, the divine nature within him, which was eternal and infinite; the only definitely manifested form of divine existence ever seen by men or angels. He was the manifestation of Deity throughout the Old Testament dispensation, and throughout all dispensations; throughout the Christian era, and throughout all eras; from everlasting to everlasting. Such is the evangelical view based upon the teaching of the Sacred Scriptures. Through all the journeyings of the children of men, as of the children of Israel, this personality is ever present in one form or another — the cloud by day, the pillar of fire by night, or the rock from which gushes, at every turn of our journey, the waters of life. Says the apostle Paul, "Moreover, brethren, I would not that ye should be ignorant, how that all our fathers were under the cloud, and all passed through the sea, and did all eat the same spiritual meat, and did all drink the same spiritual drink, for they drank of that spiritual rock that followed them, and that rock was Christ." (1 Cor. x. 1, 3, 4.) "Abraham rejoiced to see my day," said Christ, "and he saw it and was glad." Abraham saw his day by seeing a specimen of it. He saw the God-man on earth. He saw him eat and drink just as the disciples did. He talked with him as they talked with him.

One day, shortly before the taking of Jericho, as

Joshua was reconnoitring, he saw a man with a drawn sword in his hand. So thoroughly real was he, that Joshua challenged him, and asked to which side he belonged. The man replied, "Nay, but as Captain of the Lord's host am I now come." Immediately Joshua fell prostrate. And the Captain of the Lord's host told him to loose his shoes off his feet, for the place was holy; then follows the statement, "And *Jehovah* said unto Joshua." That strange visitor was called, in the same sentence, "man," "Jehovah," and the "Captain of Jehovah's host."

"I saw," said Isaiah, "Jehovah sitting upon a throne high and lifted up, and his train filled the temple." Yet John declared that "these things spake Isaiah of Christ, when he saw his glory, and wrote of him." Ezekiel also saw, on the glorious throne, the form of a man of intense effulgence, and immediately after added, "This was the appearance of the glory of Jehovah."

Ascend the mount of transfiguration. Here we behold one moment the son of Mary. He was a man of sorrows. He was clothed in the ordinary garb of flesh and blood. The next moment the fashion of his countenance is altered; his face shines like the sun; his raiment is white and glistening like the snow. The disguise for a moment is laid aside, and "the inner glory rushed out in a flood of splendor." He is the same glorious person before whom the prophets fel as dead men, and from whom Moses hid his face; the same who had been present all the while with the disciples, but under a guise. Whatever we may think of the theory, the Scriptures represent that this is the supernatural man, the man from heaven, the God-man. This was the very same who descended and ascended, and who will come again at the last day to judge the world.

Is it unreasonable to say that the personage who has always occupied the throne of heaven, against whom Satan conspired; the voice that spoke to Moses; the flame, the bush not burnt; the mysterious visitor whom Abraham entertained, and to whom he prayed; the angel with whom Jacob wrestled and prevailed, gaining the title "Prince;" the form of the fourth that stood in the blazing furnace with the three trusty followers of God, and whose face, the king declared, was bright like that of the Son of God; the angel of the covenant, the babe born in a manger, the man that spake as never man spake, and died upon a cross, is the same existence, in every instance, — the same Christ of God?

Jesus of Nazareth. — We cannot pass this general division without speaking of Jesus, that special manifestation of the Logos, which is of so much interest to the race of men. The question which has been raised respecting him is, whether he were only a legitimate descendant of David, or something else and something greater. Was he, as we have suggested, a Supernatural Man? One need scarcely be told that the various schools of philosophy which have risen for eighteen hundred years, in opposition to the exalted claims of Jesus, are to-day of little account. Their representative men have thought that they were to shake this foundation of evangelical Christianity. Some had the hardihood to say so. But their theories have died into thin air, while this poor man's philosophy still lives. The views advocated by Voltaire and Thomas Paine are now rejected by all leading sceptics. The theory of Strauss, that Jesus was a mythical personage, once so eagerly accepted, is now discarded altogether. The Tübingen school, which arose from the dying embers of Hegelanism, once so popular, has vanished like a wreath of smoke, while the short stay of Jesus has filled the world with the deepest commotion, far and near. It is no more the world it was before he entered it. He charged its very atmosphere with the divine odors of grace and beauty. Modern non-belief makes the honest confession that the words of Jesus, in spite of all opposition, have passed through the world like a moral earthquake, — are still passing through it, leaving nothing standing but God's truth as he declared it.

Think of that character, held up, and held out to the world, and then, after a brief space of thirty and three years, by the will of God, dashed in pieces like a potter's vessel. Think of the broken fragments of that earthly existence, gathered up into a brief history, but containing power sufficient to change and purify the life of the whole world, whose broken body and bleeding wounds are sacredly commemorated by all the civilized nations of earth. Few are so radical as not to kneel at his table. Was he only a more exalted Plato, a more virtuous Socrates, a wiser Confucius, a mere philosopher among philosophers, the most disinterested and enlightened of teachers, the most patient of sufferers, and the most pure of moralists — or something more? Has God begotten another, a second son like him? Whence the force that kindled the marvellous power of his earthly life? What shall be said of the divine life risen from the dead, and still extant? There is a manifest growth. The seed is ripening. The fragments of the temple, broken in pieces and fallen to the ground, are in process of rebuilding. The life of Jesus has within a few years penetrated the heart of society and public history as never before. The press is teeming with his praises. Treatises bearing his name upon their title-page, are, and are to be, the vital books of the age. It is as if some higher and better thought had visited the race; as if some new power had broken, or was breaking, in upon us, through the life and cross of the Nazarene. The world is advancing towards him, slowly, but surely and grandly. It is spreading palms in the way of this "King of men." The air already rings with hosannas! What! the being who has wrought these changes only a "benevolent Jewish gentleman"? Nonsense! If he were what Carlyle, Renan, and others of like belief say he was, he was more than they *dare* tell us. The public now demands of these ethical and sceptical teachers to set forth explicitly what they mean. They are not definite. Do they fear to be? Why pass the question of Christ's nature in painful silence? Why not honestly confess that Jesus was Christ? Or is it their creed which hampers them? Are these great philosophers held within the narrow limits of the natural? If so, is not theirs a puerile philosophy, which will not allow her devotees to grapple with a great public question like the one under consideration?

The world thirsts for a divine Saviour more than for a perfect man. A ray of star-light, only indicating a better world, cannot satisfy the soul. A mortal rill is not large enough to quench immortal thirst. The race wants what those great souls, Socrates and Plato, panted after — a God-man, one who in eternal truthfulness is the highest man, *and* the present Deity. No system of philosophy can stand which does not provide or recognize such a one. If we reject Him who has come, we cannot expect another.

And has not Jesus done enough to justify the confession that the Spirit of God, which brooded over the waters and infant earth, inspiring the life and beauty which now gladden the eye with leaf, and rose, and tree, — that the Spirit, which inspires every divine thought in the human heart, begetting the divine life in the soul of every believer, — quickened also the life of Christ as no other has been quickened? Without such admission, must we not meditate in silence over the name, as does Carlyle? Do not the life and character of Christ remain an inexplicable mystery until the doctrine of a divine incarnation is admitted?

How charming, how thrilling in truth and beauty, is the doctrine of God in Jesus, the Christ! How harmonious the Scripture, "I am the first and the last: I am he that liveth and was dead; and behold I am alive forevermore, and have the keys of hell and of death." (Rev. i. 17, 18.) "The four and twenty elders fall down before him that sat on the throne, and worship him that liveth forever and ever, and cast their crowns before the throne, saying, Thou art worthy, O Lord, to receive glory, and honor, and power, for thou hast created all things. And they rest not day nor night, saying, Holy, holy, holy Lord God Almighty, which was, and is, and is to come." (Rev. iv. 10, 11.) These ascriptions of praise are paid, not to the Father, nor to the Spirit, but to the Christ of God. "And they sing the song of Moses, the servant of God, and the song of the Lamb, saying, Great and marvellous are thy works, Lord God Almighty; just and true are thy ways, thou King of saints." "And the Lamb shall overcome, . . . for he is Lord of lords and King of kings." (Rev. xv. 3.) Do not the above scriptures teach that Jesus, the Christ, is the eternal and only personal manifestation of Deity, and therefore the proper object of worship? "I say unto you, that in heaven their angels do always behold the face of my Father, which is in heaven. Philip saith unto him, Lord, show us the Father, and it sufficeth us. Jesus saith unto him, Have I been so long time with you, and hast thou not known me, Philip? *He that hath seen me hath seen the Father*."

There is no conflict. The Lord Jesus, laying aside his priestly robes, embodies all the glory of the otherwise invisible Deity. The rationalistic school desires to deify humanity. Why not accept the divine manifestation in the God-man? Are Christians to be called idolaters for worshipping the divine one clothed in the form of Jesus, by those who claim to see a God in every man? Consistency!

On the other hand, how perfectly the evangelical view harmonizes with the wants of every soul! It is not the laws of, or the force in, the tree that stands on the hill-side, or shades the door-way, which is of chiefest interest to us. We may wonder at the laws, and feel the absolute necessity of the life force; but the tree spreading its leafy tenting over us, the rock casting its friendly shadow in a weary land, come nearest to us. We may adore the Father, and feel the absolute need of the Spirit, and should ever pray that neither may be absent from us; but it is the manifestation of the Godhead, as in the visible, protecting arm of a father, in the love of a mother beaming in the eye and falling from the lips, the personal manifestation of Deity in Jesus Christ, the Supernatural Man, which alone, in eternity, can make us feel at home. Without the Second Person in the Trinity, heaven would be no place for mortals.

The Existence of the Spirit.—What force is to science, the Holy Spirit is to the Christian world. As a principle of science, force or activity is in everything. It crystallizes the mineral; it is the life of the tree; it bears the cloud through the sky; it is above and below us; in it we live, and move, and have our being; like the principle of law, it is universal as the universe, eternal as eternity, divine as divinity. How silently and gently the full moon moves through the heavens! yet it has more than three times the speed of the swiftest locomotive driven by the hand of a reckless engineer. Its weight exceeds by many tons three millions of the largest locomotives ever yet constructed. Since the reading of this chapter was commenced, the earth has passed through a space something more than thirty thousand miles. It has been freighted with twelve hundred million inhabitants, with mountains, oceans, vast forests, and solid continents. The planet Jupiter is fourteen hundred times larger than this earth; yet it moves through space five hundred miles per minute — sixty times faster than the swiftest cannon-ball. How great! how vast! how swift!

But the moon, the earth, Jupiter, every planet of the planetary system, and every star of the stellar universe, are acted upon by a moving and controlling force, — a will power, — which, as the omnipresent, invisible spirit of force, resides in a personality. It is that personality which "binds the sweet influence of the Pleiades, and loosens the bands of Orion, which bringeth forth Mazzaroth in his season, and guides Arcturus with his sons."

"Force, force, everywhere force!" exclaimed Carlyle. "Illimitable whirlwind of force, which envelops us; everlasting whirlwind, high as immensity, old as eternity — what is it?" Mr. Carlyle stopped, smiled, and then doubtfully gave forth his answer: "It is Almighty God!" Is this the *only* personation of Almighty God? This is eternal, self-existent, universal, immeasurable, unapproachable. It is the force element of the universe; it is the sanctifier of human hearts; it is the energizer of all life; it is the causation which gives motion among the stars and among the sons of men; the tremulous gleaming to the lightnings when they play across the sky, and the gentle whisper to the soul of man that tells him of duty and of God; it is that power which brooded upon the face of the waters six thousand years ago; it is that personality which breathed upon the abyss whence came animal and vegetable life; the same which overshadowed the virgin mother and inspired the life of the only divine being that has ever walked the earth; it is the spirit-power which now strives with all men, that it may beget in their hearts the divine life; it is as invisible as the fitful summer breeze that bloweth where it listeth; it is one of the personalities of the Deity, the Third Person in the Christian Trinity — the Holy Ghost.

The especial Ministration of the Spirit. — We may have been surprised that so little prominence is given to the personality of the Spirit in the New Testament writings. But this accords exactly with the statement of Christ. "Howbeit," he says, "when he, the Spirit of truth, is come, he will guide you into all truth; for *he shall not speak of himself*."

In studying the history of the race, however, we cannot have failed to discover certain great and sudden movements of mind and men, forward and upward, of whose cause science could not give us the slightest clew. We have been compelled to look for an agency back of men, in the divine, pure, and direct. This is true of all moral and social, as well as of all religious reforms. Emerson wisely says, "The religions we call false were once true."

An important question for us to settle is, whether or not the moving cause, in all things good, exists independent of the divine? — not the divine in man, but above man, in the invisible and supernatural. Remove this divine influence altogether, and it would be to the moral world like extinguishing the sun from the natural heavens. Men henceforth would grope and die; freedom would become slavery, and charity selfishness: few, if any, who are religious, would remain such, none would henceforth become such. In fine, every right movement among men is entirely embosomed in this divine cause. The radical school admit this of the divine *in* man; but is it not true of the divine *above* man, working in and through man?

The present is a dispensation entirely of the Spirit. If men reach the divine, or if they are at all affected by it, it must be, therefore, exclusively through the Holy Ghost — the divinity of force. Science is at present reducing all existing phenomena to the action of force and the correlation of forces. It is unconsciously indorsing the theory of the Christian church.

Let us be more specific. Are there not some movements which cannot possibly be accounted for through the agency of the divine in man? Take, for illustration, the great religious reforms and revivals of the world. Luther and Zwingle seem to stand in the forefront of the German and Swiss Reformations as the moving cause; but do we not feel, and are we not willing to admit, — unless we have an opposite theory to defend, — that the *real* cause, the cause which moved those men, was an outward force, above the human, which had been acting upon the public mind, and, having produced its work in that mind, sent Luther and Zwingle to give the alarm notes to Germany, Switzerland, and the world? Or shall we insist upon it that a clam and a jelly-fish have a desire to preach the Gospel, and will work up to it in time?

Theodore Parker, in a sermon delivered in Music

Hall, Boston, entitled "The Revival of Religion which we need," — which was indorsed by the learned and influential society to which he preached, — after condemning the popular notion of a revival, said, "This revival that we need will not come all at once, — *not* as the lightning shineth forth from the east even to the west, — not thus, but as the morning comes — little by little." Mr. Parker was then studying natural and existing causes. His reasoning was without flaw. Natural causes *could* produce no other than the revival he desired, and felt we needed. The revival that follows natural causes must, of necessity, come step by step, little by little, — the gentle dawning of a summer's morning, the swelling of a bud, the opening of a flower; and so, through natural evolutions and agents, we must pass to the millennium, after a thousand or ten thousand years of development.

Such is the theory of this eminent scholar and brilliant writer, and of the entire school which follows him. But will their theory produce the revival that swept over the country just after the close of the rebellion? Did that come slowly, little by little, step by step? Did it come from long-continued peace, from the faithful adherence to industrial pursuits and virtuous living? Was it the swelling of the bud, the gradual unfolding of a flower, the painting of a rosy morning on the eastern sky? Nay, rather out of the darkness of five years of war and blood did that flower bloom. It came like the coming of the Son of man; it was like the gleaming of lightning under a darkened sky; it swept from east to west, from north to south, until the cry for salvation was heard in every city and town. Was the cause natural? Nay, supernatural; and there was witnessed on earth the truth before revealed — "The kingdom of God cometh not by observation." It came then as it always comes — through the agency of a potent and active personation of the divine; that personality which is the tie between the finite and the infinite, between God and man, between the soul and the right; the loss of whose hold upon the world would be the loss of everything lofty and good, and the loss of whose hold upon the soul of man would be its inevitable and eternal ruin.

Review the positions already taken: We have discovered certain principles of law in the universe, which are of themselves invisible, universal, and eternal. As Trinitarians, we analyze and recognize in them a specific source from which all law emanates, and denominate the cause the First Person in the Trinity, the Father, who finds his only personal and visible manifestation in the divine Christ. We also have discovered that there is, on every hand, a visible manifestation of unseen principles. Natural science is pleased, goes into ecstasies over every department, but calls it all the work of nature. As Trinitarians, we go deeper, and recognize the cause of the works of nature, and regard it as divine. It is universal and eternal in one form or another. It is the expression of the Second Person in the Trinity. Or, employing the term which is found in the confession of the apostle Peter, it is "the Christ of God" — the only visible personal manifestation of the Logos. As Trinitarians, we also claim that Jesus of Nazareth is the only instance in which the Christ of God, or the Logos, has ever manifested himself in an incarnation, in a birth, and in a growth from childhood to manhood. This divine product, we claim, is the Supernatural Man.

We have also discovered certain principles of force in the universe which are also invisible, universal, and eternal. Natural science simply says these are the forces of gravitation, of cohesion, of life, and the like. As Trinitarians, we recognize in them a specific, direct, and personal cause back of the phenomena. These emanations spring from the Third Person of the Trinity, called the Holy Spirit, which is the person who speaks not only in the loudest thunders of the sky, but to the soul of man in accents tender as those of a mother's love. Like the Father, and the Logos, he finds his only visible personal manifestation in the central figure — the Second Person, or the Christ of God.

When we enumerate these three principles, and unite them in one, have we not reached the end of the line in all philosophy, in all nature, in all things in heaven and earth? Are not the conditions of the universe such, that there can be no perfect Deity without a Trinity? There is law, there is force, there is manifestation. Are not these three harmoniously united? So also may not the three distinct personalities lying back of these phenomena of nature be united in one and in but one personal manifestation?

Consider any one of these principles alone, or any two separate from the third, and we shall easily discover how far short of the true idea of God would be such an existence, or combination. On the hypothesis we have assumed, if there were only the Father in the universe, there would be that personality from which law emanates: he would be self-existent, eternal, omnipotent, omnipresent; but there would be no life, no force, no manifestation of that essence. Law would exist, but it would be a universal statute-book, closed and sealed forever to the eyes of men and angels. If the Holy Ghost only existed, there would be illimitable force on every hand — energy, activity, tempest, blackness, confusion. The personality back of this force element would be, like the Father, eternal, self-existent, omnipotent, omnipresent, but would exist without order, because without law, and without form, because without the element of manifestation. Again: If the Logos only existed, there would be mere manifestation, — more properly, perhaps, the source of manifestation, — without life and without specific form or beauty. Still, as a source of manifestation, he would be self-existent, omnipotent, omnipresent. Unite any two of these elements, omitting the third, and there can be no perfect Deity. Unite the Father and Spirit, for instance, and there would be law and force, but not an object in the universe appearing to the eye — no star, no solid ground, no tree, no flesh and blood — a creation only of ideas, — the God and universe of Fichte. Or, uniting the Father and the Son, there would result law and manifestation, but no life or activity; a tree full of leaves and fruit, but without life and growth. Everything would be perfect in form, but lifeless; a beautiful corpse, a petrified universe of beauty and grandeur, silent mountains, and a cemetery filled with magnificent and enchanting statuary.

Uniting the Logos and the Spirit, there would be force and manifestation, but no law, no order. It would be infinite powers flashing and thundering through the skies, without design or purpose; blind force, blind fate, blind everything everywhere, — the God and creation of Thomas Carlyle. But let there be the union of these three: let the Father be present, and infuse order into the universe; let the Logos speak the light and the works of nature into being; let the Holy Ghost breathe upon the scene; let Christ Jesus occupy the throne, and afterwards appear on earth, and be from first to last the only personal manifestation of the three personalities, and there would spring into existence a world of beauty; there would be a perfect man, a garden of Eden, a divine voice, and Jesus of Nazareth healing the sick and preaching to the people.

We think we do not misrepresent the Trinitarian when we say that he believes that the Father, though divine, infinite, and properly called God, is not a complete Deity; that the Logos, though divine, infinite, and properly called God, is not a complete Deity; and that the Holy Ghost, or Spirit, though divine, and infinite, and properly called God, is not a complete Deity; but that these three united, and appearing in one divine personal manifestation, are a complete Deity, and constitute the Trinity.

The voice which comes back from heaven and earth, from sea and air, from the word of men and the word of God, declares that there is only one God; but there is also another voice which proclaims, with equal emphasis, that there are three distinctions, or personations, in all things. The trinity of these forces is the harmonious note of the universe. They are not one first, and three afterwards, but one and three from the start. The correlation of divine and infinite law, divine and infinite force, divine and infinite source of manifestation, can produce a material universe. It cannot be produced without such correlation.

When the first star sprang forth from the hand of God, there was then the evidence of a Trinity which had no beginning, — a Trinity as the source of law, the source of manifestation, and the source of force, — harmonized and centralized in one manifested personality.

The doctrine, or rather the fact, of the Trinity is not merely a dogma of the church. It existed long before it was stated in the creeds of the church, long before the church existed, long before the birth of Jesus in Bethlehem, and long before the creation of either the earth or the universe. Deity cannot change these relations without dethroning itself. It is not a matter of wonder that the great masters of philosophy, Kalidâsa, Socrates, Plato, and Hegel, Bacon, Locke, Newton, and Leibnitz, were Trinitarians. As men profound in science, they could not be otherwise.

We may understand the subject but imperfectly while in this world. We are in one of the lower regions. The metropolis and royal seat of learning and theology are above and beyond. But these suburbs will ever be dear to us as believers, because we have here received our preliminary education. They will ever be sacred to us, and to the heart of the universe, because they have been the birthplace and home of that development of the Tri-One which we call the Supernatural Man.

"Satan himself is transformed into an angel of light." 2 *Corinthians* xi. 14.

"Now there was a day when the sons of God came to present themselves before the Lord, and Satan came also among them. And the Lord said unto Satan, Whence comest thou? Then Satan answered the Lord, and said, From going to and fro in the earth, and from walking up and down in it." *Job* i. 6, 7.

"Be sober, be vigilant; because your adversary the devil, as a roaring lion, walketh about, seeking whom he may devour." 1 *Peter* v. 8.

"And he said unto them, I beheld Satan as lightning fall from heaven." *Luke* x. 18.

"Therefore rejoice, ye heavens, and ye that dwell in them. Woe to the inhabitants of the earth and of the sea; for the devil is come down unto you, having great wrath, because he knoweth that he hath but a short time." *Revelation* xii. 12.

"Thus free, the devil chose to disobey
The will of God, and was thrown out from heaven."

POLLOK.

"The Christian Religion puts the Christian Devil above the Creator." THOMAS PAINE.

"Yet half his strength he put not forth, but checked
His thunder in mid volley; for he meant
Not to destroy, but root them out of heaven."

MILTON.

III.

SATAN.

THE theory of an evil spiritual agency, outside and independent of humanity, has had a place among the doctrines of the church ever since its formation, and ought to have had a practical bearing upon all its theories of sin and virtue, of religious life, character, and development. It is a doctrine, however, which has received so little fair investigation, that the ideas of poets have been mistaken for the truths of revelation: the Paradise Lost has been substituted for the book of Job, the poems of Montgomery for the teachings of Christ, and the observations of Southey for the Epistles of Peter. Since the extreme views held by Luther and the Catholics of his time, the theme has been rarely mentioned, with any degree of seriousness, either by sceptics or believers. Men have played with the subject much as boys do with the football, the ball serving only for the sport and the game.

But if Satan's existence and influence are realities, if they are matters of revelation or experience, if we are really involved, and doomed for the present to contend with this enemy of the race, and to meet, in one form or another, his cunning assaults, we ought to know it, and the facts should be stated to the world, not carelessly or jocosely, but soberly and fairly.

We shall probably be met on the threshold of the discussion by those who will remind us that the subject is involved in such mystery that it had better be passed in silence. We admit that mystery envelops it. The realm and field of Satan's action are not the seen, but the unseen. The facts of his existence are not comprised in ordinary history, but touch a range which is unexplored and unknown. So many were the difficulties hanging about the subject, so great the liability of its perversion, and the probability of a misunderstanding or misconception of it, in the time of our Saviour, that he taught concerning the devil, never in public, but only in the presence of his disciples. Silence is no longer necessary.

The danger of the present age is not from superstition, but from scepticism. While every question of religious faith and practice is freely discussed at the fireside, in the smoking-car, and place of business, by all classes of people; while the public mind is so unsettled on many of the vital questions of ethics and religion; while infidelity turns itself from one doctrine to another, seeking, by argument and assertion, to overthrow revealed religion, — the Christian public cannot keep silent if it would. Reasons for a particular faith must be given which are both biblical and rational. Whatever may be the difficulties enshrouding the particular doctrine under discussion, or any other, they must be met. Men must and will know where they stand. The Christian church, in this age as never before, must distinguish between fable and fact. It must establish its faith, not upon tradition, but upon revelation. It must not conceal its doctrines in a nook or corner of the house, but place them as a candle upon a candlestick, that they may give light to all the household.

In developing the subject, this twofold inquiry claims our attention: What are the teachings of revelation respecting Satan? and, Are its teachings such as commend themselves to the rational convictions of mankind?

Satan's Personality. — There is a large class of men, both within and without the church, who often speak and reason about the devil, but who seem to think he is only a fanciful personification, or representation — a figure, a type, or something else, of *sinful principles.* They have reduced him to a mere abstraction. The evils of the world and misfortunes of life they attribute in no way to Satanic influence, — to no outside pressure or temptation whatever, — but solely to the depravity or the irregularities of human nature. Revelation, however, states the case otherwise. It varies not in a single instance from presenting Satan as a real person, having power on earth, and to be feared among men. The different names by which he has been designated in the Scriptures are suggestive of his nature and personality. The term "*Devil*," for instance, which in the Greek means "the traducer, the calumniator," and in English, the enemy of mankind, implies personality.

The same is true of the term "*Satan*," which means an adversary, or a personal foe of the race. Of similar import are the Greek term "Apollyon," and the Hebrew "Abaddon," by which he is sometimes designated, which means an evil angel, or the angel of the bottomless pit. The forms of expression, as well as the particular words employed, suggest the same idea. He is always referred to in the singular number. More than twoscore times is he called "Satan," a term which is never employed in the plural number. Upwards of fifty times he is called "The Devil," invariably in connections requiring the singular number. He is called "The Prince" and "The God of this world," "A roaring lion," one that "Sinneth from the beginning," "Beelzebub," "Accuser," "Belial," "Deceiver," "Dragon," "Liar," "Leviathan," "Lucifer," "Murderer," "Serpent," "Tormentor." These expressions imply, beyond question, actual and individual personality.

If the Bible referred to Satan only under one class of circumstances, if it employed but one term, and that an abstract one, we might then regard his existence as only imaginary. But the frequent allusions to him, direct and indirect, — the great variety of circumstances under which he has been mentioned by inspired poet, historian, and prophet, by the disciples, and the Lord Jesus himself, — compel us to adopt an opposite conclusion. Christ was entirely mistaken, or there is a supernatural spirit of evil. The wilderness of Judea and the Apocalypse are scenes of actual presence, and displays of actual power. The daring and warlike imagery of the Scriptures, which represents God and Satan as sovereigns of hostile empires, means something. "The power of Satan," "The power of darkness," "The Prince of the power of the air," these are no fictions of distempered brains. There is no mysticism here. These are conceptions of terrible meaning to minds which felt the antagonism of literal and living forces which comprehended the ideas of loyalty and disloyalty, of life and death. The doctrine of Satan's personality pervades revelation. The body of it stands or falls with its admission or rejection. The doctrine in this respect is vital. No evangelical Christian can by any means ignore it. It is one of the constructive ideas of the inspired word. We can get rid of it only by rejecting the system of revelation in which it appears, everywhere present, everywhere consistent with free agency and existing evil, and everywhere uttering its warnings to be sober and vigilant.

Satan's Power.— Sceptics have often asserted that the "Christian's Devil," as represented by the church, possesses more power and influence than God himself. It is true that great prominence has been given to the woe Satan has occasioned on earth. True also that the Scriptures represent him as a being of terrible energy. It is this that gives point to their warnings against him. In this respect revelation is rational and consistent with itself. It may be true that the potency of the Evil One was not greatly diminished by his fall. Evil men exert as powerful influence as good men. We all feel that the strength of human nature, will, and influence remains in terrible force, though men are wofully fallen and sadly depraved. On this principle, in power of will, in energy of character, Satan may be as unchecked and mighty to-day as when he bore the lights through heaven; though it is true that the tendency of his course, in the long run, is to chains and fire. Great intellectual power, great activity, and great energy must certainly be predicated of him if he is a fallen angel, and are certainly attributed to him throughout revelation. Our own feelings, at times, suggest the same spiritual activity and energy. Who has not felt it when chafed and detained by some pending or impending emergency? Who is so sluggish as never to have felt that if he could break away from this flesh and blood that cramps him, he could then reach the mighty aspirations of the earnest, panting soul within? The physical body diminishes power; it does not increase it in a single instance. "It is sown in weakness," because it is physical; "it is raised in power," because it is spiritual. Evil spirits, which are fallen angels, must from necessity possess great power and influence. Plato, and after him his followers, taught that the devil and his attendants were the governors and lords of men, as men are of cattle. Thucydides and Livy, hoping to avert evil and secure good, worshipped them. Judging, therefore, from the forcible language employed in the Scriptures, from the nature of spiritual power, and from the observations and teachings of philosophers, it is not surprising that the impression has gone forth that the control of the universe is about equally divided between God and the devil. But the Scriptures nowhere indulge such an idea. They everywhere assert, by word and type, that Satan's government, though powerful and aggressive, exists only by permission, both as to extent and duration, — that it is *entirely* under the control of the Almighty; so much so, that one word from his lips would banish Satan forever from the earth. He could not strike another blow, destroy another victim, or deceive another heart, were God to say, "Thou shalt not!" Revelation represents that he fell from his first estate, that he will be banished from the earth, and that his kingdom, which has had such control, will end anon in total ruin. Does not the cause of truth hope for, nay, sigh for, the time to come when the inspired and sublime prophecies respecting him shall be fulfilled, and when this leader and his followers shall be tormented with conscious defeat and biting remorse, day and night, forever and ever?

Satan's supposed Ubiquity. — It is sometimes charged upon evangelical Christians that they believe and teach that the devil possesses the divine attribute of omnipresence. There may be some occasion for this charge, but it can have arisen only from careless phraseology on the part of Christians, or from a negligent interpretation of Scripture. The Bible, it is true, represents Satan as a being whose baleful influence is everywhere felt, but it nowhere speaks of him as personally *ever* and *everywhere* present. On the contrary, it always speaks of him as a moving personality, *ever* on the move from place to place, which precludes the idea of omnipresence. He is represented as "going up and down the earth," as "going to and fro in the earth," as "coming to," and "going from," Christ and humanity. There is no deviation from this thought, as in case of the Deity. The Scriptures attribute omnipresence to but one, that is, God. Revelation does, however, directly and indirectly predicate the same characteristics respecting Satan's *activity* as respecting his *power*. They are such as adorn a spiritual existence. One of his names was "Lucifer," "the light-bringer" (or bearer) of the primeval universe. He is a fallen spirit, but he retains the activity of an angel. Did he move no faster than light, he could go four times round the earth and back again in one second. He could strike his blow, sow his seed, and leave it everywhere in his trail to germinate and ripen. Without doubt he can move with much greater rapidity than this even. Spirit can move like thought, and compass infinite distance, and accomplish a world of evil in the least duration of time.

In addition to this, revelation teaches that Satan's government and kingdom are representative. In this respect it is a model government. In league with him, in unity of purpose, one and inseparable, are all disloyal spirits in the world and universe. The devil can thus have his agents in all places at the same time. It is his great number of powerful and active accomplices which enables him to do a work that, apparently, requires his constant and personal presence everywhere. Though it is true that through his agents no one has escaped his notice and influence, still, in point of fact, personally, he may never have visited half the inhabitants of the globe. He is, however, in universal and constant communication. He is the central telegraph operator. He sends his despatches along the whole line. He himself is only present where the lines converge, where great interests are at stake, as at the headquarters of the army. He gives his orders, and the work goes on as well as if he were personally present. Without thus distinguishing Satan from his emissaries, it is perhaps not a matter of surprise that he has been represented as everywhere present. In this restricted and qualified sense he *is* omnipresent. He is the commander-in-chief in his camp, fighting a dozen battles the same hour. Napoleon, while in the palace of the Tuileries, was said to be at work in Portugal, Belgium, and France at the same moment. Over the tomb of Charles V. is engraved, "Dominator of Europe, Asia, and America," though he had personally seen only a part of Europe. It is by this representative scheme that Satan is enabled to rule his empire and carry on his kingdom.

This rebel angel chief moved and stood first because he was first. He still holds his position among his confederates, because he is above them all, and is the most powerful and active being God ever created.

Those who attend him are likewise active, powerful, sinning, suffering, miserable, yet persistent and obedient to their leader. Under his direction they are, doubtless, everywhere present.

Satan's Moral Character.—As Satan has been represented to us in the works of poets, he is a being to be admired and commiserated, rather than despised. Grandeur and sublimity have been thrown about him, in place of the stains of crime and sin. Mr. Macaulay, in criticising the poem of Montgomery entitled "Satan," says, "The poet, with the exception of locomotion, has failed to represent a single Satanic quality. We have yet to learn," he continues, "that Satan is a respectable and pious gentleman, and we would candidly advise Mr. Montgomery to omit or alter about one hundred lines, and republish his volume under the name of Gabriel." "Satan," says Carlyle, "was Byron's grand exemplar, the hero of his poetry, and the model, apparently, of his conduct." Lamb, in one of his letters, passes the following very just criticism upon Southey: "You have all your life been making a jest of the devil: you have flattered him in prose; you have chanted him in goodly odes. You have been his jester, volunteer laureat, and self-elected court poet to Beelzebub." Milton is chargeable, to some extent, with the same mistake. Every critical student of the Bible must have felt that the representation is entirely wrong which presents to the world such a grand and majestic Satan. A criminal, however great and daring, powerful and active, is not a majestic man, is not a grand or great hero; on the contrary, he is no man or hero at all. Satan is a criminal, and any other representation is incorrect. No other can in any way be derived from the Scriptures. They leave but one impression, and that is this: Satan is a being of supreme meanness, vile as the vilest, basest of the base, and heartless as a stone. His breath is poison. His touch is death.

Such are the teachings of revelation respecting the personality, power, ubiquity, or activity, confederation and moral character of Satan. Let us now inquire if these representations commend themselves to the rational convictions and experience of humanity.

Few observers of men and society will deny that there are certain phenomena in the world for which it is exceedingly difficult to account, except on the supposition of an unseen and evil cause, or agency, producing them. It was no other than a rational observation of facts which led the ancient philosophers to teach that every man has two spirits attending him, one good, the other bad. An evil personal existence, in the judgment of Plato and his followers, could alone explain the evil phenomena of the world. Those rugged philosophers who grappled so resolutely with existing facts felt there were beings whose forms were hidden from mortal eyes, but whose impressions were plainly visible as they laid their shadowy hands upon those of their fellow-men who had gone farthest into rebellion. They felt that the horrid suggestions of crime, which often suddenly, and without any apparent cause, hurl men into perdition, could not be causeless, but were the instigations of this corrupt enemy of the race. They did not believe that the spirit of deception which had destroyed whole nations, the spirit of malignity which sometimes possesses mankind to an alarming extent, the spirit of selfishness, of superstition, of crime, of out-breaking sin, of blasphemy, of cruelty, existed independent of an intelligent cause of some kind, somewhere. They assigned one, in substance the same as that of the Scriptures. Can we do better?

A baleful shadow overhangs the earth. It appalls us. On every hand we see it, and in a multitude of forms. What is our theory of its origin? There is a great rebellion in the universe; a rebellion which has the appearance of having been originated, not by chance, but by genius; not by the genius of evil floating about in the air unimpersonated, but by the genius of a powerful and active evil spirit, in confederation with a legion like himself. This we say is the appearance of the present rebellion. Let the rationalistic philosophers of the nineteenth century account for it.

It is a curious fact that those people who reject the doctrine of a personal devil with the greatest vehemence, are also the people who are ever insisting that men are inherently good, and not bad. "There is no Satan except what is in man," they say, "and there is none in man." But there is sin, there is guilt. Men hate God, and say harder things against him than they do against the devil. Two kingdoms surround us. It is of no use to mince the subject of evil in the world. It exists, a vast amount of it. It is in every walk and work of life, in every profession and in every business. The man who has not seen it is a blind man. The question is this: Did all the evil of the world, all this gigantic rebellion, originate in nothing? Is it a causeless product of the atmosphere, or the soil? Revelation gives an adequate cause for it: can we do better? What if, by argument, sophistry, or assertion, we could succeed in banishing from our theories and from the world the Satan of the Bible? Should we not still have a world full of mysterious and evil phenomena which require explanation, and which can receive it only upon the ground of a personal, powerful, and active spiritual agency? Bad men exist: why not bad spirits? why not devils?

Is one more unaccountable than the other? Is it not, in the light of a rational observation of existing facts, far more unreasonable to deny the existence of Satan than it is to acknowledge it? Does not the doctrine remove, by far, more difficulties than it imposes? Looking at men as they are, and the world as it is, are not silence, or the devil, our only alternatives?

Phenomena of Evil in Individual Experience.—We find, upon self-inspection, that our temptations, though manifold and enigmatical, evidently arise from three distinct sources, and are of three distinct kinds. There are temptations from the world: all know what they are, and have experienced them. There are also temptations from the flesh. Between the two classes we can easily distinguish. There is also a third class, which, upon strict analysis, appears to differ entirely from those of the world and the flesh. Who has not been startled at times with those evil suggestions which flash into the soul without apparent cause or connection, let fly against us like burning arrows from an unseen hand. They are "fiery darts," as the apostle forcibly calls them. Good men have confessed that without the slightest reason, and from no recognized agency, they have felt of a sudden an impulse to commit the most horrid crimes ever perpetrated. They would tempt and ruin some victim, strike some fatal blow, or leap from some precipice upon the rocks, or into the sea. How mortifying, how humiliating, for a pure heart to encounter such experiences! It is some relief to feel that we are not the sole cause of their existence; that we are not so bad as the instigations would lead us to think we are; and that, when we drown or quench these darts of fire, no harm will befall us. The question recurs, Whence this peculiar form or style of temptation — these depressions that come upon us when we have done the best and have the least occasion for them? The hardness of heart, the restlessness of aim and purpose, these and other evil suggestions, have they no cause? Are these the forms of temptation which ordinarily come to us from the world and the flesh? Every thinking man, in accounting for such personal experiences, feels that it is folly to have recourse to abstractions. It is a pygmy philosophy which does not recognize in them a producing evil force, or which attempts to ignore their existence altogether. The tempest that springs suddenly out of a dead calm, tearing the sea from its foundations, and flinging it against the skies, must have a powerful cause somewhere; seen or unseen, a cause there must be. The frightful heaving of a burning volcano must be produced by an existing force. So also must this spiritual earthquake, this frightful sea of evil passions, which surges about and sometimes threatens to ingulf us, be produced by a power not figurative, but literal. Actual force in a living spirit, as the psychological root, becomes an absolute necessity.

Rebellious and Sinful Conduct of Satan. — It is claimed by objectors that it is unreasonable to believe that an intelligent being, who stood next to the Divine Manifestation in God's glorious and harmonious empire, should have departed so far from rectitude and virtue as to attempt to dethrone the Christ of the universe. We are free to confess that it was a strange stroke of policy and ambition. Not only strange, but sinful beyond measure, destitute of all defence; it was lawless, anomalous, mysterious, and inexcusable. "Sin," says Charles Beecher, "has no excuse." The most, perhaps, we shall ever know of that transaction is the inevitable conclusion to which revelation leads, and where it leaves us. Satan, at the time of his fall, made a voluntary choice to be influenced by pride and treason. While we would not attempt to account for this inexplicable and continued choice, we are led to ask whether any other explanation of the existence of evil in the world is more rational than that given in revelation, which associates with it the fall and present influence of the devil?

Have not those states of a country which have been the least oppressed, which have been the most highly favored, possessed of peculiar rights and privileges, where the frosts of winter scarcely touched, and where the orange blossomed and ripened, — have not such states been known, without reasonable provocation, to organize treasonable movements against a government that has always blessed and favored its people? Does history represent that such movements are planned and executed among the dregs of society? Will the leader usually be found to be a man who has been oppressed by the government, and driven to madness by personal abuse? Is not the chief secessionist and rebel usually a leader of acknowledged power, of superior mind, and of marked intellectual sagacity? May we not safely say that all movements which result from pride and treason spring from above, and not from beneath, the masses? Is not sin "of patrician rank, not plebeian; of celestial growth, not terrestrial?" *

* Charles Beecher.

Do not the Scriptures, therefore, state what is most natural, judging from what is seen, when they inform us that sin entered the world by one, the universe also by one — one standing not at the foot, but at the head of his order? Could any but an angel of the highest rank have originated such a baleful shadow of evil as now darkens the hearts of men and stains the purity of the universe?

Once having entered upon this path of ruin, nothing is more natural than for Satan to continue as he is, and do as he does. The higher the being, the brighter the genius, the more certainly will suffering be preferred to the voluntary humiliation of pride. It is unnatural for any fallen intelligence to repent. Any other created being in the universe will sooner, more easily, and more naturally repent than the devil. Who made it unnatural — God? He made it possible, because he has made his creatures free; they have made it natural, because sin, followed, becomes natural, and because, the step once taken, the tendencies once set in a given direction, it is *un*-natural to move in the opposite direction. The old soldier loves the booming of the cannon, though he can no longer command the battalion. The age-stricken savage loves the wild war-whoop and bloody scalping-knife, though he can no longer sound the one or wield the other. He loves them because it has become natural. So Satan and his confederates love the course they have pursued, though it can be tracked from the beginning to the end with ruin and blood.

As young, comparatively, as the earth-born race is in crime, did not God hold it in check by Providence, conscience, and his spirit, its natural tendencies would lead it to follow but one course; there would be but one profession, and no loyal heart would beat. When any being, as in the case of Satan, passes beyond the restraints of God's spirit, his character has become fixed and eternal. There is not power enough in the universe to change it. Satan has gone so far that he cannot change if he would, and would not if he could. The devil penitent! A penitent devil would be no devil He is no more penitent than when he attempted to snatch the sceptre from the Son; no more penitent than are those hardened traitors who would rule a nation they could not conquer, and who would reënact the murders and starvations of prison-pens!

Satan would this moment strike Christ, the Infinite One, from his throne, if he were able, and usurp his place. Nothing would suit him better. He is the embodiment of the old infidel cry of France — "I wish I could dethrone the Almighty! Away with him!" He is the malice of Iago let loose upon the race. Still persisting in his work, he rests neither day nor night, but plunges through the world on his mission of evil, seeking whom he may destroy. He is not destitute of motives in pursuing this course. He is stimulated at every turn by the expectation of gaining something, the delay of final punishment, perhaps, or victims, subjects, company, at least.

He knows that every victim he gains, and every conquest he makes, will lengthen his earthly probation. Like the demoniacs in the country of the Gadarenes, he agonizes to escape from the abyss and remain on earth. He knows, also, that man is rising to a point far above himself, though lower by creation; that the "seed of the woman," with Christ at its head, is to fall with crushing weight upon him as soon as it is sanctified, and that thereafter no new conquests to his dominions can be made. Satan is following both a natural and an unnatural course; one that is unreasonable as it can be, but no more unreasonable than are the workings and phenomena of pride, selfishness, and treason, which everywhere meet the eye and tempt the heart. While, therefore, "misery loves company," — while there are a temporary but fiendish relish, satisfaction, and delight in seeing others sin if we sin ourselves, — and while Satan is permitted to walk among men, it need not be a matter of surprise that truth struggles for its existence, and that a well-organized spiritual carnival has polluted the earth for six thousand years, and will continue to pollute it until this common foe is exiled. We may rest assured that all the jealousy and malice of his diabolic nature will be roused against mankind, and that whenever he can ruin a member of the victorious race on the outposts or in his own territories, he most certainly and most naturally will do it.

The Permission given to Satan to tempt and destroy the Human Race. — It is claimed by rationalists, that, even if Satan should choose a course so fatal to his best interests, God would not allow him to tempt and destroy humanity. But God allows the world and the flesh to do this; why is it more unreasonable that the devil should receive the same permission? Who is sure that the world and the flesh do not destroy the greater number?

In the university of humanity thousands fall during the period of discipline. Shall we demand of God to bolt its doors, that none may enter it? Could he justly and wisely do this, if all *can* be safely and thoroughly disciplined? if all *can* take honorable diplomas and receive creditable dismissals? Is not he who conquers the world and the flesh worth more by that discipline than the thousand who needlessly fall? Is not trial better than freedom from it? Cannot the race afford to run frightful risks to gain what is in store? Is not risk everywhere the price of great victories and glorious achievements? Does not the man who resists most perfectly the most powerful and subtle temptations become thereby the strongest man — the hero-man? God permits the evil one to do his work, then, not for our injury, but for our highest good.

The spirit that struggles up through the scum of society becomes its brightest ornament. The most brilliant cut diamond was once rough as the pebble in the street. Its cutting has disclosed its value. One ripe piece of fruit is worth the ground covered with blights. We bow before Him who comes with red garments from Bozrah. Have we not learned that Omnipotence itself cannot create human character? that it is a thing we make ourselves? and that to make it well, we must be left to *contend?* If God made it impossible to sin, we should not be men, but machines. If we were left without temptation, we should no longer possess virtue or heroism. We *need* the sudden and peculiar assaults of Satan, in order to secure the perfection of a Christian — a Christ-man.

This was His trial. While God shows his mercy to Satan, both in allowing him, for a season after his fall, to remain in his presence, and in giving him a respite on earth before his final banishment, still the wrath of Satan shall be turned to God's praise, and shall work nothing but good to the heir of heaven.

Hear the apostle: "Be sober, be vigilant; because your adversary, the devil, as a roaring lion, walketh about, seeking whom he may devour; whom resist steadfast in the faith. The God of all grace, who hath called us unto his eternal glory by Christ Jesus, after that ye have suffered a while, make you perfect, establish, strengthen, settle you. To him be glory and dominion forever and ever. Amen." Satan's power, according to the Scriptures, is permitted, not out of respect to him or his kingdom, but that men through resistance may be made perfect, established, strengthened, settled. In every temptation that befalls us God has regard to our eternal interests and to our highest development. His object is to make kings and priests of mortals. His plan is to qualify them to administer the laws of those kingdoms and worlds from whose thrones Satan and his followers have fallen. The Creator is to vindicate to the universe his long-suffering and tender mercy, and to demonstrate that the principles of his government are right, and will endure forever; that they can stand safely amid all the fearful and deadly assaults made against them.

It may be observed, also, that the sceptical objection in question overlooks a fact which should ever be borne in mind,—this, that during our probation God has strictly limited Satan's influence over us. He has created us with endowments, and thrown about us counter-influences. sufficient to enable us at every turn to cope successfully with Satan and all his accomplices. Men are daily and hourly conquering him; not all, but some. All do not; all *can*. Though Satan can and does afflict us sorely in the trial; though the ancient and sorrowing patriarch on the plains of Uz is humanity in miniature; though Sabeans, Chaldeans, lightnings, diseases and deaths are hurled with amazing accuracy and rapidity, one after another, upon us by this unseen hand; though when he meets us it is personality against personality, agency against agency, spirit against spirit, just as real as in the time and temptation of Christ; though he does allow us no peace, and does bruise us in the conflict; though his daring, skill, and malignity are unequalled; though he is constantly seeking to weave us into his subtle and ever entangling web, which ends in fire of wrath insufferable; though he lays hold upon those, by permission, whom God forsakes, springing upon them like an assassin in the night, as a strong man armed upon the defenceless, — still the human soul can be, and ought to be, and *must* be, his master; otherwise its destruction is inevitable Satan can tempt only; *compel* he cannot. Resistance in a child will put him to flight. If men are ever bound to his chariot-wheels, — and unless they resist him they will be, — it is only because they have allowed him to bind them there. If they are his servants, led captive at his will, it is only because they have yielded themselves servants to obey him. He tramples upon men only when they bow before him. He takes the sword from them only when they tender it to him. He can never enter and hold possession of the soul, unless we deliver to him the key. We are made prisoners never by force, always by surrender; but when a final surrender has been made, the slaughter is terrible. The pleasant baits are then thrown aside; smiles give place to frowns; and absolute malignity takes possession; we become helpless victims in the hands of an experienced wretch. It is Indian warfare—indiscriminate slaughter; no quarter shown, no regard to the rules of war, to the pledges and promises given. The devil pity his victim? No, never! He who makes men presume to commit sin, and then despair of being forgiven; he who speaks gently when he would lead them aside, but afterwards thunders into their consciences the accents of damnation; he who cruelly insults his victim, lashing him into madness, playing the oppressor, tyrant, and usurper over him,—*he* knows no pity. An emotion of pity felt by him would leave the universe without a devil. O, fortunate it is that we can resist such a being if we will!

Warnings of the Scriptures against Satan.—The inspired writers speak as though they felt that the human race was exposed to constant and fearful peril. And when we pause to think, do not startling facts, as well as the Word of God, crowd us on to strange conclusions? Is not human life fearful? Who are we, that we should face these deadly foes that throng our pathway, with such odds against us? Can we be safe by remaining careless and inactive? Can we look upon the world about us, can we explore our own souls, and be indifferent to the fact that this "Leviathan" is actually passing up and down the earth, seeking whom he may deceive and devour? The entire spirit of revelation leads to the conclusion, that every man is known by Satan through his own visitation, or through some obedient agent, and that, if we can be ruined, he knows the particular method which will be most effectual, and the time when we shall be least on guard. We have strong appetites, passions, or impulses. He knows it; knows it too well. He turns his hand skilfully, ever varying his assaults. If we are merry, he allures us to carelessness and thoughtlessness; if sad and pensive, he tempts to some desperate deed. He does his work by fair means, or foul; by telling the truth, or a lie; by swimming with the current, or stemming it; by remaining silent, or becoming noisy and garrulous; by frowning like a demon of darkness, or glistening as an angel of light. He becomes a deceiver, a serpent, professed friend, avowed enemy; anything and everything to suit his purpose and gain his end. Eve is walking in the garden of Eden: her eye rests upon delicious fruit. Satan knows, at a glance, his victim. Choosing for his agent the most sagacious animal of the field, he speaks to her: "Thou shalt not surely die in the day thou eatest thereof." "Eat! eat!" was his coaxing invitation. The woman ate; and spiritual death has followed the race from that day to this. The same voice is now heard on earth though Eden is lost: "Eat! drink! You shall not die in the day thereof;" and his new victims tremble, yield, and are plunged into the first and second deaths. What is true of animal appetites is equally true of mental tastes and human passions. It is true of every passion and impulse man is heir to. If we yield to Satan at a single point, he will most certainly control events to suit his purpose. His purpose is to accomplish our spiritual overthrow. He sees that one man can only be led to curse God and die through adversity: he sends adversity, and often ruins his victim. He sees that another, by uninterrupted prosperity, or favor of circumstance, will be most likely to remain unmindful of the claims of God: he allows that man to prosper. He plants in his yard the olive, while he sows the seed of the myrtle in that of his neighbor. He allows some men more peace while sinners than they would enjoy if righteous. He sees that silver and gold will block the door of heaven against some men. He suggests to them, by various means (he is seldom at his wit's end, except before Christ and his image), what are the best investments. He thus causes money to be taken from the treasury of one, and piled up in that of another. Some are rich because the devil is permitted to help them; others are stripped of their property by his agency, as in the case of Job. He would be glad to help any person to great wealth; he would be glad to point his wit, illustrate his arguments, polish his sentences, and do for him a thousand things, if he could only thereby induce him to fall down and worship. He would do all this, however, not because it will be of any real advantage to the man; not that he cares a whit for his prosperity; not that he cares for men to acknowledge him as the cause of their success. Like the skilful hunter, he tries at every point to conceal his person while pursuing his game: he would not have men tormented by thoughts of him before their time; but he would do all this, that, through wealth or ease of circumstance, by some temporal promotion or literary success, he might, at length, in a critical and unsuspected moment, plunge humanity into ruin and endless sorrow. He is an old and experienced wretch and craftsman: on his territories one cannot outwit him: take a pound from him, and he will take hundreds from you. He stakes nothing, comparatively, in his throw, while man stakes everything. It is an apple against Paradise, a handful of gold against heaven.

The warnings of revelation to the world are therefore timely. It would not be a sufficiently full revelation without them.

An additional thought meets us at this point. Does not the permission God gives Satan to punish wicked men in this life make it rational to believe that the same permission will be extended to him after death? Men cannot escape the conviction that it is the most fearful thing on earth to fall into Satan's power, and experience the remorse which he develops in the soul of the sinner. He writes thousands where the law writes but fifty. He stains an ordinary sin with the blackness of perdition. A record of the madness, insanity, and suicide to which he has driven his victims would constitute the saddest volume ever written. Impenitent men, sinking under the hand of death, and into the power of Satan, have cried out, with an agony so terrible, upon nearing his visible presence, that even the sceptic and infidel have been appalled. He flashes the vision of his presence upon the soul of the inebriate; he sends to the couch of the murderer "the ghost of him he slew;" he wrings confessions from the lips of criminals of every grade, and then blackens them with disgrace and crushes them with despair.

If he can lash the sinner so fearfully in this world, if he can insult and abuse the human soul to such an extent in its present condition and freedom, what torture will not this powerful, active, and heartless being inflict when all his skill, wit, industry, energy, and malice have full play! Can he do otherwise than terrify into complete madness, until repose would be more peaceful on a bed of living coals than in his presence? The sting of death is sin — sin pointed, barbed, and poisoned by Satan.

Is any theory of the church more rational than the one which aims to save men from being victimized by such a mysterious and tyrannical enemy? Is it not a sublime warfare that it wages against him? Is it not a righteous indignation that speaks from its pulpits, and burns upon its altars, against such a deadly foe of virtue and of truth?

With deference and kindness to all, we believe that that theory is alone consistent and rational which admits that there is a supernatural spirit and world of evil, and which exhorts mankind to be armed with the supernatural helmet, breastplate, and sword before which Satan falls, and which extorts from him his old cry of terror, "I know thee, who thou art," as he meets the image of Christ in the human heart.

But the Scriptures speak to the church in no less important terms than to the world outside the church. They represent that the very elect are not overlooked by Satan. He stood at Joshua's right hand, to accuse him; he moved David to number Israel, and disobey God; he sifted the apostle Peter; he continually buffeted Paul, and hindered him once and again from going to the Thessalonians.

He is the great deceiver, as well as the troubler, of Israel; he enacts, under mask, a most dangerous part in the house of believers; he takes the place of the Holy Ghost; he sometimes gives us the seeming "witness of the Spirit," when we are not entitled to it; he assumes the office of comforter, counsellor, sympathizer, and helper. There is not a solitary work of the Divine One which he does not skilfully imitate. He is an angel, a Saviour, or a devout worshipper; he is a wonderful counterfeiter; skilful and variable are his tactics; he assures some men that they are sufficiently good — good as they can be; he tells others that they are not sufficiently good, but that it is useless to attempt to become better; to some he says, "You are wise," to others, "You are foolish;" to some that they have sinned away the day of grace, to others that there is no day of grace; to some he proclaims the doctrine of unconditional election, to others the doctrine of universal free grace; to this one, this thing, to another, that thing, without regard to truth, but with sole regard to his own success and their ruin.

There are those who are represented as being surprised on the day of judgment that they are condemned. The truth will then appear, for the first time, that they have been deceived. Satan had been repeatedly telling them that they were doing their whole duty, when they were neither living in love and charity with their neighbors, feeding the hungry, nor giving a cup of cold water to the thirsty traveller by the way-side. How, then, it may be asked, are men to know what they are — whether servants of God, or the devil; heirs of heaven, or of perdition? Revelation informs us of but one absolute ground of security, and of but one absolute condition of safety. The ground of security is the atonement of Christ, and the condition of safety consists in devoting ourselves, soberly and earnestly, to the service of God, in vanquishing Satan by nearing and accepting Christ, and by following the example of Christ, not once a week, but daily and hourly. Safety depends in looking upon this life as a hard fight, — a hand-to-hand fight, — in which the Cross of Christ and a devoted life are our only protection. In possession of these, if Satan tells us we are numbered among the elect, we can reply, We know it. If he tells us we have sinned away the day of grace, we can tell him he lies. We can face the adversity which he is permitted to send upon us, and trust our integrity, as did the afflicted patriarch. But without this devotion, nothing is secure. Fancied security, under such circumstances, is but a dream, excited by the gentle, soothing, but fatal whispers of this evil one, saying, "It is well, it is well," when it is not well; saying, "You are safe, you are safe," when you are not safe. "Who shall ascend into the hill of the Lord, and who shall stand in his holy place?" Let the reply be engraved upon the walls of church and home alike: "He that hath clean hands and a pure heart; who hath not lifted up his soul unto vanity, nor sworn deceitfully."

These, these of outward and inward purity, are the loyal and impregnable hearts of God's universe. God will trust more to these than to all the swords that have dripped with blood. Many a pugnacious man would volunteer to fight the devil with fist and club. The ink-bottle encounter by Luther is not the most heroic. Virtue and resistance are alone valiant in this contest. It is the blow struck for Christ which is a blow directly upon the head of Satan. It is the blow dealt in support of error that adds to his malignant power, lengthens his earthly probation, and strengthens his dark confederacy.

"It is not expedient for me, doubtless, to glory. I will come to visions and revelations of the Lord.

"I knew a man in Christ above fourteen years ago (whether in the body I cannot tell, or whether out of the body I cannot tell: God knoweth): such a one caught up to the third heaven.

"And I knew such a man (whether in the body, or out of the body, I cannot tell: God knoweth): how that he was caught up into Paradise, and heard unspeakable words, which it is not lawful for a man to utter." 2 *Corinthians* xii. 1–5.

"Wherefore, seeing we also are compassed about with so great a cloud of witnesses, let us lay aside every weight, and the sin which doth so easily beset us, and let us run with patience the race that is set before us." *Hebrews* xii. 1.

"Now the Spirit speaketh expressly, that in the latter times some shall depart from the faith, giving heed to seducing spirits, and doctrines of devils;

"Speaking lies in hypocrisy; having their conscience seared with a hot iron." 1 *Timothy* iv. 1, 2.

"This know also, that in the last days perilous times shall come.

"For men shall be lovers of their own selves, covetous, boasters, proud, blasphemers, disobedient to parents, unthankful, unholy, without natural affection, truce-breakers, false accusers, incontinent, fierce, despisers of those that are good.

"Traitors, heady, high-minded, lovers of pleasures more than lovers of God;

"Having a form of godliness, but denying the power thereof: from such turn away.

"For of this sort are they which creep into houses, and lead captive silly women laden with sins, led away with divers lusts;

"Ever learning, and never able to come to the knowledge of the truth.

"But they shall proceed no further; for their folly shall be manifest unto all men." 2 *Timothy*, iii. 1–9.

IV

PERMITTED AND PROHIBITED SPIRITUALISM.

CHRISTIAN people have often attempted to support truth with artificial props and expedients, instead of trusting it to the virtue of its own vital power. When the Puritans came to this country, they thought the interests of religious faith required them to abolish all the forms and polity employed by the Established Church of England. Plainness of dress, unadorned churches, the absence of all instrumental music, and standing, instead of kneeling, while in the act of prayer, were things religiously enjoined. A few years ago, during and just after the Miller excitement, certain important and glorious doctrines of the church were passed in silence. The doctrines of the millennium, of the second coming of Christ, the prophecies of Daniel, the disclosure of the future by our Saviour, the Apocalypse of John in Patmos, were rarely alluded to in the church or at home. To some extent, we find at present another illustration of this same tendency and timidity concerning the developments and claims of modern spiritualism. The church has been betrayed thereby into an unfortunate and painful silence respecting the condition of our friends after death. Whether they are consciously active or inactive, whether they make us frequent, occasional, or no visits, are questions rarely asked except by professed spiritualists. The mourner has been denied every shadow of comfort from this source, and from the child has been taken away all impressions of the presence of a mother or a friend in his journey and struggle through life. The effort of the church has been to banish the dead to the greatest possible distance from the earth, and into perpetual inaction. Truths which were once preached with an inspiring force and confidence, awaking in the heart a desire for a new and better life, have been denied all discussion except in secret, and all support except in our convictions. This condition of things, however, is not a subject of congratulation to the church, but rather one of regret. The church has gained no power thereby; it has betrayed a certain weakness. It has gained no hearers, but has left comfortless many hearts which might have been cheered. Whatever temporary advantage may be gained by modern spiritualists, the church ought fearlessly to speak its convictions. Through timidity it should not withhold the publication of any scriptural doctrine. The deepest and highest truths ever lie nearest to the deadliest heresies. The most dangerous counterfeit is most like the genuine coin. The greatest lights have continually beside them the darkest shadows, and the snow is always whitest and purest at the mouth of a grave.

Permitted Spiritualism will first claim our attention.

Few will deny the statement that mankind may receive certain impressions from a deep and pure spiritual life, which cannot be received without it. May there not be such purity of heart and life as to allow one to talk with, or even walk with, God, as Enoch did? This kind of communication is granted, however, not through the mediation of others, but directly and by means of impressions. It consists in permitted visits to hearts, rather than to eyes, or ears. They are invisible angels of mercy, which come to the good, often unsought, but never unwelcome.

The apostle Paul, in one of his most forcible and beautiful exhortations, represents mankind as running on a race-course, upon either side of which he supposes that illustrious witnesses are standing in great numbers. The connection in which the passage occurs conveys the impression that the dead of this world are among those witnesses, in a thick cloud to us, but in a cloud so thin to them that they are able to hear distinctly our songs of praise, our voices of sorrow, and our footfall echoes upon the pavements of the highway to immortality. Revelation elsewhere invites the belief that by means of impressions these friendly witnesses, unrecognized, communicate with us, inspiring our hearts and cheering our lives.

In addition to this impressional communication from the immortal world, the Scriptures tell us of something more, and different, involving audible and visible manifestations which have sometimes spoken to the ear and flashed before the eyes of men. This is not unreasonable, nor impossible. What evangelical Christian will not admit that Christ is always with his followers? Who will deny that he could, as an ever-present being, reveal himself instantly in the same or in different forms, in the same or different places, as a friend or companion? Was it impossible for him, after his resurrection, to appear as a Jewish traveller and stranger on the road to Emmaus; as a gardener to the women at the tomb; to Cephas in one place, and to all, if circumstances had required it, at the same instant? Cannot the Holy Spirit manifest his power, on the same evening and at the same hour, to the multitudes of worshipping Christians everywhere? Cannot God manifest his power in the sun shining in the heavens, in the leaf trembling in the breeze, or in a rose-bud crushed in the hand of a child? May not that vision be a reality which has left

> "A smile so fixed, so holy, on the brow,
> Death gazed, and left it there;
> He dared not steal that signet-ring of heaven"?

May not "thy rod and thy staff" have a vital meaning to every dying Christian? May not the promise of Christ, "Not as the world giveth give I unto you," be so verified that no Christian shall be left to go through the dark valley without the visible manifestation of his Saviour to precede him? Do not the voice that spoke to Moses in the burning bush, — the mysterious visitor whom Abraham entertained, and to whom he prayed, — the personality with whom Jacob wrestled, — the form of the fourth in the blazing furnace, — the vision of the host of God granted to Elisha and his servant, — the visions of Cornelius at Cesarea; of Paul, who knew not whether he were in or out of the body; of John in the Isle of Patmos,— furnish ample ground for the foundation of a rational belief in the existence of a spirit-world near us, and that communication with it, through agencies not human, is not impossible or unreasonable? If, then, the Bible teaches the startling and sublime doctrine that the dead are ministering, or tempting, spirits, as they are good or bad, let the church hesitate no longer, but accept it, trusting that its excrescences will in time be removed. If it is perverted, it will only have suffered the fate of all other doctrines. Certainly men will linger less in the graveyard, if convinced that the dead are elsewhere. When men are wont to cherish the healthy convictions of an unseen, but of an actual, active, and immediate future, they will have a pulse of less flurried beat, nay, one that shall beat quick and deep for Christ and heaven.

We are now prepared to consider the subject of

Prohibited or Medium Spiritualism. — There are many things which have been passed to the credit of medium spiritualism which have nothing whatever to do with it. The phenomena of clairvoyance, mesmerism, and animal magnetism are brought forward as the fruits of spiritualism, and as direct evidence that the dead communicate with friends through the agency of mediums.

Let us look at these manifestations for a moment. It is claimed that there are certain persons who are able to see objects concealed from eyesight, and remote; that they can tell us accurately how our friends, hundreds of miles distant, at a given moment are engaged; what is at present, and what is in the future to be, the condition of our business, and why we are pleased or depressed. These persons are said to be able, under certain physical or mental conditions, to speak a language of which they are ignorant, play upon musical instruments with which they are unacquainted, converse fluently and intelligently upon subjects with which they are not familiar, explore our memories, and catch the impressions there recorded before we note them ourselves, and thus to surprise us by speaking of that which we had forgotten.

Besides these transactions, which, for the sake of the argument, we are willing to admit, there are certain other things pointing in the same direction, with which we are all familiar, and which we are compelled to admit. We often receive a mental despatch, and make preparations to receive our friends before they announce themselves at the door. In company, we are often surprised to hear some one remark upon the very topic which was silently working in our own thoughts. We have spoken of the same thing at the same time with some other person near us. Often we have been thinking, during a previous week, upon the very subject which the preacher announced on the Sabbath for the theme of his discourse. All these phenomena show a deep and unexplained communication of soul with soul, of spirit with spirit; but not with the spirits of *dead men*. They have nothing whatever to do with anything but the living. The time is coming when this department of psychology will be reduced to a definite science. It will become of great practical utility to the race, and will work itself clear of all connection with modern spiritualism. It may supersede the magnetic telegraph as a means of communication, and the detective police as a means of ferreting out public criminals. A hundred years will develop marvellous changes in human affairs, and make steam and lightning slow and clumsy. It is only because of the present undeveloped condition of the psychological sciences that spiritualists have seized upon them, and through their agency have been enabled to win many converts and delude many hearts.

But, aside from these things, modern spiritualists have not scrupled to employ direct and intentional deceit in their transactions. A kind of skilful dexterity — a sleight of hand — has often done a work which has been attributed to spirits. The Japanese jugglers could pass for splendid mediums. Of all this legerdemain, however, under the name of spiritualism, there is but one thing to be said, and that is in its condemnation. The person who will thus voluntarily deceive another; who will affirm that certain phenomena are produced by the dead, when he knows they are produced by trickery; who pretends to call back the departed spirit of a friend to console the living, and who knows there is no truth in it, — does he not deserve to be branded as a villain? and ought he not to be forever exiled from respectable society? Is he not a liar, a thief, and a robber?

Classification of the leading Medium Spiritualists. — It may be difficult, if not impossible, to make a complete classification of all those who are more or less pledged to the support of spiritualism.

Many good people, no doubt, have entered the ranks

of spiritualism. They are there in consequence of having lost friends, and from being filled with absorbing desires to communicate with them. Such persons deserve not words of condemnation, but need words of warning. When brought into the presence of real or pretended mediums, they listen, yield to their clairvoyance, jugglery, or necromancy, and, at length, under the weakness of a broken heart, or excited imagination, obey every command that is given. It is among these dilapidated and sorrowing tabernacles, these ruins of former happiness and prosperity, that the medium revels without hinderance, as ghosts are said to haunt gloomy and deserted houses.

There are also restless and inquisitive men who are spiritualists. They are eager, in any and every way, to obtain possession of the secrets of the unknown world. They are ready to listen to any voice, and obey any command, but that of revelation. They would gain heaven, but in a forbidden path. Dissatisfied with the crucifix, they weave a garland of imaginary flowers, which they call Christianity. Dissatisfied with the life they have led, they resort to spiritualism ; call it religion, and themselves religious. Among this class are found the more daring and persistent of the order.

In addition to these, there are those among spiritualists who possess cool heads and steady hands. They claim to be investigators. They assume nothing, they profess nothing, and pretend to deny nothing. They are spiritualistic philosophers. From this class have arisen the most pitiable dupes of this delusion. Others will be found, who hope, by associating with mediums, to reap some pecuniary advantage in their business transactions, or gain some practical knowledge hidden from others.

Lastly, there will be found those who are sensual and devilish men. They are spiritualists simply because spiritualism affords them the best of opportunities to indulge their corrupt passions and perpetrate their fiendish schemes upon willing or ignorant victims.

Fruits of Medium Spiritualism. — All our readers may not be apprised of the fact that spiritualism has assumed a somewhat remarkable political attitude, and that many leading public men in America and Europe indorse its positions, and are ranked among its believers. The following statement, published in "The Spiritual Age," certainly has the merit of being unambiguous: "Let us assume," says the article, "a political attitude, and make the world feel that we are no longer to be trampled on with impunity." In answering the question of their political designs, they reply, "The design is to crush, destroy, and break in pieces all existing forms of government, and build a form which shall be a Theocratic Democracy. Every man will be his own ruler, and his natural demands his highest law."

An article published in "The Telegraph," under the title "Practical Spiritualism, Purposes, and Plans," contains the following: "It is hardly to be supposed that an enterprise so startling to the world as the spiritual movement, would have for its grand end anything like the presentation of mere phenomenal exhibitions. The great purpose is of a much broader nature, and of a more thoroughly practical spirit."

"Spiritualism," continues the article, "is the mother of all institutions for external uses, therefore the mother of the states, and in the combination takes the place of the union of church and state. It is the purpose of spiritualism to so educate a class of persons in certain practical functions, that they shall become pivots of groups in the coming new social order."

The following statement may be found in a "Soldiers' Tract," published by the spiritualists, July 4, 1861: "The next government which shall arise over this people, and which is even now drawing nigh from out the angel-world, will be a Theocratic Democracy, — God ruling through mediumistic man. . . . And then, as Spiritualism and Celestialism march over the land, the master-souls, once denizens of time, will influence men's acts; the spiritual congress above will guide in all wisdom and truth the councils assembled here below."

At a meeting of spiritualists held in Abington, Mass., a noted spiritualist made the following remarks: "The time is speedily coming when every one who has opposed, scorned, reviled, and persecuted spiritual communion will be brought to the altar of sacrifice; will suffer sorrow, regret, affliction. . . . It will be a bitter cup, but a necessary remedy for the present sickly morals and religions of men. It is in the power of the spiritual world to make any poor man rich in one day, — to make any rich man poor in one day; to make a well man sick in a moment of time, or to make a sick man well; to take life, or to continue it; to make woe in the human heart, or joy and gladness there. . . . Imminent and immediate dangers to earthly prosperity hang over all opposition to spiritual communion."

This is the temper they show, and such the politics they publish. But more than this: leading spiritualists feel at liberty to perjure themselves in courts of justice, defy the judge on the bench, laugh at the jury in the box, and violate the most solemn compacts and agreements, at the direction of a medium. They affirm that the claims of the state are superseded by spiritualism; that human society is nothing, that human law is nothing, and that spiritual communication is everything. In view of such published statements, can we not justly pronounce the leading spiritualists of America traitors? Do they not declare themselves in waiting to inaugurate a form of treason more deadly than that of the Southern Cotton Oligarchy? Had they the power and courage, would they not do as bad a thing for the nation to-day as the devil could do, were he present as their leader?

But again: Leading and influential spiritualists seek the subversion of all true religion, as well as government. They reject the Bible. Sin, in their creed, is only the casting off of the gross part of human nature, and is strictly in accordance with the will and pleasure of God. The doctrine of a personal devil is entirely ignored. "Man," they say, "must be devoid of good sense to believe anything of the kind." Christ, as a personal Saviour, is thus disposed of: "No man should rely upon any Saviour outside himself. Each and every man is a Saviour, a God

Christ is no more the Son of God than was John Howard or George Washington."

"'The Age of Freedom," published at Berlin Heights, Ohio, contains the following: "What a horrible phantom, what a soul-crushing superstition, is this idea of an overruling, omnipresent, all-powerful God! . . . Belief in a God is degrading, whatever the character ascribed to him. Where is your God? I can stand up, and look him in the face, and affirm that I have a right to 'life, liberty, and happiness,' whether it is his pleasure that I shall enjoy them or not."

Blasphemy is justified; and in public assemblies God is set aside in mockery, and prayers are offered directly to an imaginary Satan. The leaders of this society are sceptics, infidels, and atheists.

In addition to this, are we not justified in the assertion that no order, in any civilized land on earth, ever taught a more corrupt morality than that which the leading spiritual publications of the day advocate? We cover a broad field when we say that spiritualism allows and justifies any act which is prompted by the lusts of a depraved heart. At a national convention of spiritualists, held at Chicago, it was provided, that "no charge should ever be entertained against any member, and that any person, without regard to moral character, might become a member."

At the Rutland Reform Convention, a female spiritualist, as reported in the "Banner of Light," made the following remarks in support of the rights of women: "She must demand her freedom; her right to receive the equal wages of man in payment for her labor; her right to have children when she will, and by whom she will." "This," says a certain writer,* who has thoroughly canvassed the subject, and to whom we are indebted for the compilation of these quotations, "means nothing, and can mean nothing, but indiscriminate and debasing lust."

The author of the "Educator" became the father of an illegitimate child by direction of the spirits; and the course of the guilty parties was thus justified in the editorial page of the "Spiritual Telegraph," published in New York: "It is reserved for this our day, under the inspiration of the spirit-world, for a quiet, equable, retiring woman, to rise up in the dignity of her womanhood, and declare, in the face of her oppressors and a scowling world, '*I will be free*.'... And no man or set of men, no church, no state, shall withhold from me the realization of that purest of all aspirations inherent in every true woman — the right to re-beget myself, *when, and by whom, and under such circumstances*, as to me seems fit and best."

The wife of the founder of the free-love institution at Berlin Heights, Ohio, sent a letter to the "Detroit Free Press," of which the following is an extract: "My husband was the founder of the Berlin Free-love Institution. He has been a believer in that free-love doctrine for about three years. A year ago or more he left home, ostensibly upon business; but he only roamed around in search of free-love companions; having found a small number of which, he took them to Berlin, and founded the infamous den of lust which now exists there. He left me with three little chil-

* Miles Grant.

dren to provide for, and nothing to do it with but my hands. I have stood for four days in the week over the wash-tub, laboring until my strength has many a time given way entirely, for the sake of a little money with which to feed my children." Had the devil a wife, could he be more faithless and heartless than that man!

When we recall the evil that spiritualism has done to society, — when we think of what it proposes to do, — notwithstanding all its insinuating threats, ought it not to be denounced? In the name of the state ought it not to be denounced? It reeks with treason. In the name of God and religion ought it not to be denounced? It seeks to rob the world of all faith in Christ, and offers no substitute. In the name of all things pure and good ought it not to be denounced? It would send sensualism into every household unrebuked, and rob us of everything we cherish most sacredly. Nothing in society should receive a more bitter and scathing condemnation than medium spiritualism.

Dr. B. F. Hatch, husband of the noted Mrs. Cora V. Hatch, afterwards Mrs. Daniels (what by this time we do not know), makes the following published statement: "I have known many whose integrity of character and uprightness of purpose rendered them worthy examples to all around, but who, on becoming mediums, and giving up their individuality, also gave up every sense of honor and decency. . . . Iniquities which have justly received the condemnation of centuries are openly upheld; vices which would destroy every wholesome regulation of society are crowned as virtues; prostitution is believed to be fidelity to self; marriage an outrage on freedom; love evanescent, and, like the bee, should sip the sweets wherever found; and bastards are claimed to be spiritually begotten. . . . I most solemnly affirm," he continues, "that I do not believe that there has, during the past five hundred years, arisen any class of people who were guilty of so great a variety of crimes and indecencies as the spiritualists of America."

Taking for granted only what is claimed by spiritualistic leaders, what is published in their journals and practised in their daily walk, should not all moral and patriotic citizens, in order that "the community may live in peace, that the citizen may feel himself safe in the bosom of his family, that our streets may be safe to walk in, that our land may be a country fit to live in," — rebuke and loathe spiritualism, with all its legion of nameless crimes? And then, if persisted in, should it not be punished by the enactment and enforcement of rigorous and wholesome laws?

When spiritualists have the effrontery to teach such base immorality and corrupt sensualism; when they publicly announce that all matrimony should be condemned, except that which is voluntary, temporary, and terminable at pleasure; when in public they advocate, and in private practise, the principles of free love, which destroys whole communities, degrades the individual, and obscures the brightest sun-light of homes and hearts; when they trail in the dust all that exalts woman above the condition of a slave, or a brute; when they constantly seek to sap the heart of all virtue, and generate in it the elements of atheism, falsehood, and shamelessness; when they crush the voice of conscience, make of purity a name, and of correct tastes false pretence, — when they advocate these things, practised in all ages only by the vilest and meanest of human beings, it is not only high time that public sentiment had broken the silence, and pronounced its awful verdict of condemnation, but high time also that we had paused to inquire respecting the producing cause of this corrupt brood of iniquities and crimes.

Is it a question of small importance which at this point confronts us? Is there not evidence that a well-organized and treasonable plot has been instituted against society, morality, and religion? Have so many human beings by accident fallen into line with such military precision? Setting aside the phenomenal exhibitions of clairvoyance, animal magnetism, and deception, does it not seem that there is a skilful leader in the unseen background? Is not that spirit of deception unaccountable on natural grounds which leads husbands who love their wives, and wives who love their husbands, to turn their faces from one another, and set them as flint downward? which excites in their hearts the dream that they cannot find in their own homes, and at their own firesides, the purest and deepest earthly felicity granted to mortals? Must not there be some controlling influence at work when men are led to curse church organizations with which they have been in communion, and which have never injured them? Is there any known natural cause which can account for the blasphemy that falls from the many lips whence but lately were uttered fervent prayers to Jehovah? Are such sudden changes sprung upon the race by accident? Can those who deny that the cause of this evil exists in the human heart, also claim that no cause of any kind exists? If not internal, must it not be external? Must not those who claim to see in this conduct and in these declarations only the evidence of human depravity, admit that it is a depravity which has an individual intelligence, apart from the subject it affects? Perhaps history will throw some light upon these questions.

Though the Egyptians, the Canaanites, the Chaldeans, and the Greeks had their spirit-diviners; though St. Jerome, one hundred and fifty years after Christ, mentions invocations of spirits as a fact which no one thought of disputing or doubting; though Lactantius, in the third century, makes similar statements; and although there has been a belief in something of the kind in all ages, still, without much difficulty, can we not designate certain epochs of spiritual manifestations, which, in importance and extent, pass entirely beyond the ordinary range of such things? The terrible displays of demoniacal possession which are recounted in the New Testament occurred just before and during the time of Christ. The period of German witchcraft arose just before the age of Luther. One hundred thousand persons were then executed. Witchcraft, or spiritualism, in England, made its appearance just prior to the great revival in the fifteenth century. Thirty thousand persons were then executed. American witchcraft was at its height just before the great awakening under Edwards and other reformers. And the modern developments were started at Rochester,

New York, just before the greatest revival which this country has ever known. Do not all these point in the same direction, and await what has not yet been given — a satisfactory, scientific explanation?

Men who deny all supernatural phenomena may assert that these people were deceived, — that Christ and his disciples, as well as St. Jerome, Martin Luther, John Wesley, and Cotton Mather, were deluded. But is such a flat denial, for the purpose of avoiding an inevitable conclusion, the part of a true philosopher? Looking at these facts as they are, do they not indicate something besides random shots? Does not the curtain seem to conceal a chief actor? Looking upon present developments, and judging from past transactions, is not the world on the eve of some glorious religious movement? May not a malevolent intelligence, now as before, flaunt his disapprobation in the face of society? The church of Christ is the last organization to take alarm at these things.

Turn to sacred history. The possibility of satanic agency in spiritualism we base upon the Bible. It speaks unqualifiedly of demoniacal possession, though it does not tell us what it is; of witchcraft, without describing it; of necromancy, without offering explanations; and of those having familiar spirits, without disclosing their origin — whether they are from earth or hell.

In the New Testament we are referred to Simon Magus, Elymas the sorcerer, and the young damsel from whom Paul cast out the spirit of divination. Had these persons lived in modern times, they would have passed for noted spiritual mediums. It is worthy of remark, also, that the Bible, in its reference to these practices, is distinguished from every other book of ancient date by its unvaried condemnation of them. It paints a doleful picture of demoniac possession, it condemns all forms of witchcraft, and pronounces a lasting curse upon every necromancer. Listen to its solemn injunctions and commands: "Regard not them that have familiar spirits, neither seek after wizards: I am the Lord your God." (Lev. xix. 31.) "And the soul that turneth after such as have familiar spirits, and after wizards, I will even set my face against that soul, and will cut him off from among his people." (Lev. xx. 6.) "And when they shall say unto you, Seek unto them that have familiar spirits, and unto wizards that peep and mutter, should not a people seek unto their God? for the living to the dead? To the law and to the testimony: if they speak not according to this word, it is because there is no light in them. . . . And they shall look unto the earth, and behold trouble and darkness, dimness of anguish; and they shall be driven to darkness." (Isaiah viii. 19, 20, 22.) "When thou art come into the land which the Lord thy God giveth thee, thou shalt not learn to do after the abominations of those nations. There shall not be found among you any one that useth divination, or an observer of times, or an enchanter, or a witch, or a charmer, or a consulter with familiar spirits, or a wizard, or a necromancer. For all that do these things are an abomination unto the Lord: and because of these abominations the Lord thy God doth drive them out from before thee.

Thou shalt be perfect with the Lord thy God. For these nations, which thou shalt possess, hearkened unto observers of times, and unto diviners: but as for thee, the Lord thy God hath not suffered thee so to do." (Deut. xviii. 9–14.)

Do not these facts of history, and these representations and commands of Scripture, leave the impression that communication with the invisible world is possible, not only by the means of a pure life, but also through the agency of certain persons who have "familiar spirits," are "possessed of demons," called "witches," "necromancers," and, in modern times, "spiritual mediums"? Can any candid student of the Bible deny the possible presence of demons on earth and among men? Did not Christ frequently encounter them? Did he not often forbid them to speak? Did he not frequently address them personally, and apart from the individual in whom they dwelt?

The word translated "hell," in 2 Peter ii. 4, is "*Tartarus*." It occurs nowhere else in the Bible. A large number of the most learned and critical commentators, including such names as Drs. Ramsey, Cudworth, Parkhurst, and Whately, together with the learned Grotius, agree that the word, in a physical sense, according to ancient classical writers, means the atmosphere of our earth. The passage then would read, "God spared not the angels that sinned, but cast them down to the atmosphere of earth." Our atmosphere is a temporary home for demons. Satan himself is "the prince of the power of the air." Who that has lived in the world doubts it? Sad the lot of mortals, did not angels of mercy visit and comfort them.

While we can and ought to deny the supernatural agency of human spirits in the transactions of spiritualists, unless they have first become demonized, can we, with the Scriptures before us, also deny the agency, or presence, of everything supernatural? Had we not better suffer ourselves to be led by the plain language and evident impressions of fact and revelation? Have all these representations in the Scriptures no foundation? Have all the evils of Spiritualism in society no powerful cause acting in the background? Would it not seem that there must be an agency, — an active, intelligent, and malignant agency, — somewhere? Have you visited "the circle," and received a message purporting to come from a mother or child, from father, husband, or wife? Be not deceived. May it not be something besides a message from the dead — even the sly and seductive, crafty and deadly voice of Satan, though clothed in salutations gentle as those of a mother?

"For seven years," says Dr. P. B. Randolph, once a noted, but subsequently a reformed spiritualist, "I held daily intercourse with what purported to be my mother's spirit. I am now firmly persuaded that it was nothing but an evil spirit and infernal demon, who, in that guise, gained my soul's confidence, and led me to the very brink of ruin." "Five of my friends," he continues, "destroyed themselves, and I once attempted it, by direct spiritual influence. Every crime in the calendar has been committed by mortals moved by these viewless beings! Adultery, fornication, suicides, desertions, unjust divorces, prostitution, abortion, insanity — I charge all these upon them!" Do such fruits spring from a mother's counsel? Can sweet fountains send forth such bitter waters? Can good trees yield such corrupt fruits? Can any observer fail to see that there is in spiritualism a personal agency at work, under covert, to accomplish the subversion of all things good? If there be a personal devil, could he do more to alienate the world from Christ than is being done by this order of "free-thinkers"?

So far as there is anything supernatural in spiritualism, we can trace the system home to its fountain-head — the abode infernal. In the "darkened circle," man stands in another world; face to face with supernatural and malevolent beings — **demons.**

A SUPERNATURAL LIFE.

"When the wicked man turneth away from his wickedness that he hath committed, and doeth that which is lawful and right, he shall save his soul alive.

"I have no pleasure in the death of him that dieth, saith the Lord God; wherefore turn yourselves, and live ye." *Ezekiel* xviii. 27, 32.

"Without me ye can do nothing." *John* xv. 5.

"Work out your own salvation with fear and trembling. For it is God which worketh in you both to will and to do of his good pleasure." *Philippians* ii. 12, 13.

"Marvel not that I said unto thee, Ye must be born again." *John* iii. 7.

"I need a cleansing change within;
My life must once again begin:
New hope I need, and youth renewed,
And more than human fortitude;
New faith, new love, and strength to cast
Away the fetters of the past."

HARTLEY COLERIDGE.

I.

CONVERSION.

AFTER a day of toil passed amid the busy scenes of a public feast at Jerusalem, our Saviour retired in the evening for the purpose of prayer or repose. From the reading, we infer that it was near or past midnight, when he was waited upon by a Jewish senator of high standing, who desired an interview with him. This visitor had been convinced, from the miracles and public teachings of Christ, that he was no ordinary personage, — that he must be, at least, a prophet sent of God. He felt, with many other devout Jews, the utter inefficiency of the forms and life of the Jewish religion. He consequently came to this new teacher for the instruction he desired and felt he needed. A constitutional timidity, and the avowed scorn of most of the Jewish rulers towards Jesus, easily account for the secrecy of the midnight visit.

To what hour the interview was protracted we are not informed. Of the various subjects discussed we are ignorant. Here, as elsewhere in the Gospels, only the chief points, those which are vital in affecting the right development of character for the eternal future, are recorded. The great principle set forth, and the one around which the entire conversation was made to revolve, is the direct and positive announcement of Christ respecting the necessity of conversion. The declaration is full of mingled pathos and moral grandeur. It involves the *possibility* and *absolute necessity* of "conversion," "change of heart," or "new birth," as the commencement of the supernatural life has been variously termed.

There is a theological distinction between conversion and regeneration. Conversion is strictly a human act, in accordance with a divine requirement: it is a duty. Regeneration is strictly an experience begun and completed through divine agency: it is a gift from God. The old definition is a good one: "Regeneration is a change wrought in man by the Holy Spirit, by which the dominion of sin is broken, so that, with free choice of will, he serves God."

The strictest analysis would require a separate treatment of "conversion," "renewal," "regeneration," and "sanctification." We intentionally overlook these technical differences, and shall regard the "new life" in its completeness. The schoolmen and the ecclesiastical fathers did this. Christ and his disciples invariably pursued the same course.

A change of character, analogous to that of the new birth or life, is possible, and of frequent occurrence. This proposition hardly needs the support of an argument. Most men have experienced the change of feeling and of character which is produced by advancing years and the ever-changing outward condition of things. In process of time, a man's likes and dislikes may be constitutionally revolutionized. Our personal identity remains the same; that is, henceforth eternal; but the character, of necessity, changes. Character is that which decides what we are, and marks us out, individually, from all others.

We pass through a crowded thoroughfare. We meet multitudes going hither and thither. We look into their faces, and they into ours. We pass them, never to pass them again, and reach our journey's end. We are affected by all this. We are not the same in our feelings and character after the journey that we were when we commenced it: we are better or worse. There is no restoration to former conditions. Every evening, when the sun falls in the west, we are not only not in space and duration where we were when it rose in the east, but we have become a part of all we have met; changed by every impression, given and received. This is the reiterated story of every morning and every evening to every man and child. Without a renewal of our conditional or naturalization certificates, we cannot perform the parts assigned us.

Men must really, vitally, mentally, morally, and, in a limited sense, spiritually, be *born again daily*. The thing is possible; it takes place; it is not Christian regeneration, but approaches and partially illustrates the meaning of the command of Christ to Nicodemus, "Ye must be born again;" or, by a more correct translation, "Ye must be born from above." This ordinary change of character, like evangelical conversion, may be gradual and partial, or immediate, entire, and absolute. We enter a home to-day gladdened with the prattle of childhood, where every member of the household is wearing the smile of life, health, and joy. We may be called a week hence to enter the same home, and to enter it because the song and music of a week before have been hushed. We shall feel the hand of the strong man tremble in our grasp, and fail to see the veiled face of one who would hide a mother's love and grief from the world. Then and there will be brought to pass the saying written, "While the sun, or the light, . . . or the stars be not darkened, nor the clouds return after the rain: In the day when the keepers of the house shall tremble, and the strong men shall bow themselves, and the grinders cease, and they that look out of the windows be darkened, and the doors shall be shut in the streets: . . . because man goeth to his long home, and the mourners go about the streets." That is not the same household of the former week, but another. The name on the door is not changed; the local relations are the same; the surrounding ornamental trees cast the same refreshing shade, and the fragrance of the rose finds its way into the same halls: but that bit of crape hanging at the window, or pendent at the door, is the symbol of another home. The looks, the speech, the thoughts, the future plans and life-motives are changed; in certain respects they are entirely revolutionized. A moment has done the work.

In some cases the mourners know not where to direct their weary pathway. They have been, or are, born again into new scenes, and days of grief and sorrow. During the pangs of the change, God sometimes sets apart the household from the world for a season. It is an awful blow — a shock whose effect remains for life; in some cases even deepening — the pebble dropped, and the wave continuing.

> " Our house is emptied of delight;
> It is no more the house of joy
> That once shone with his presence bright,
> That echoed to his laughter light,
> His bounding step upon the stair,
> His joyous accents everywhere:
> It is no more our home without our boy."

What is true here, and to the extent discussed, is true still farther, and to such an extent, under these and other circumstances, that an entire change may take place, so radical, that a man will hate what he once loved, and love what he once hated. Human character is capable of this change. It is not an uncommon, we were about to say not a difficult, step from one extreme of like or dislike to another. Who has not found himself loving the company, services, and surrounding circumstances which he once loathed? Who has not followed back, with equal zest and pleasure, the path he walked in the outward journey of life? A young man, who had wasted a large patrimony in a profligate life, while hanging over the brow of a precipice from which he had determined to throw himself, and for which purpose he had gone thither, formed a counter-purpose — that he would return to his home, and regain what he had lost. It was all the work of a minute. The purpose he had then formed he kept. He began his new life by shovelling a load of coal into a cellar; he proceeded, step by step, until he had more than regained what he had lost, and died a millionnaire. In a worldly sense, he was converted. This is not a solitary, but a representative, case. There are thousands like him in their resolves and efforts, if not in their success.

These facts demonstrate the possibility of a radical and sudden change of life and character. This, then, is our reply to the objection urged by so many respecting the unreasonableness and impossibility of such a change, that nothing is more common, or more necessary, in life, than a change, — than a conversion from one class of feelings to another, — from one state of character to another, — from one condition of life to another, — from being influenced by one class of motives to being influenced by an entirely different class, — from being born once to being born again. When this conversion is commenced through religious motives, and is carried on by divine agency, then it becomes religious, instead of social conversion. This constitutes the vital difference between the two.

A change of character not only analogous to, but one involving all the conditions of the new birth, as enjoined by our Saviour upon this Jewish ruler, and as taught by evangelical Christianity, is both possible and of frequent occurrence. In discussing this statement, our first endeavor should be to ascertain, if possible, the exact meaning of the terms employed. The language of Christ to the ruler is, of course, figu rative, but is no less forcible, explicit, and beautiful It was a law among the Israelites, that a foreigner, before he could become a Jewish citizen, must pass through certain ceremonies, and take upon himself certain obligations. This being done, he was ever afterwards admitted to the rights and privileges of Jewish citizenship. His first birth was thus overlooked. He was regarded as born again in Judea. Our term *naturalization* * has been employed to express, with peculiar force and clearness, the same idea, the transaction being that process by which a citizen of another country becomes as if born in this. For all real and practical purposes he is native born. With this interpretation, we see the force and point of the Saviour's question, "Art thou a *master* in Israel, and knowest not these things?" The additional phrase, "born of water and the Spirit," need not involve us in any fresh difficulty. It presents merely the agency producing the change, — the Spirit of God, — and the water, which is only employed as the symbol of the change; useless in itself; useful only as a public testimonial, and necessary only in the fulfilment of a positive command. Collecting all these thoughts, we may present this as the literal meaning of our Saviour's address to Nicodemus. The new birth, or the birth from above, is the conformation of the life and practices of the individual, through the agency of the Holy Ghost, to the laws of Christ's kingdom. It is changing the allegiance from one ruler to another. It is the man who has been serving the kingdom of this world becoming naturalized and serving the kingdom of God. Or, holding ourselves more closely to the

* Bushnell.

figure of a birth from above, the principle taught by our Saviour may be presented thus: The Holy Ghost, if admitted into the soul, and if cherished there, begets a new and divine life, which is subsequently developed. and which manifests itself through the sensibilities, intellect, and will. The different conditions expressed by the terms "conversion," "justification," and "sanctification," begin at the same instant. But not until the old man gives way entirely to this new one, not until the subject is really and vitally a new creation throughout does the work reach its completion. It is then called *entire sanctification.* Why need writers mystify so simple a subject?

Let us pause for a moment to answer one or two questions which naturally arise when this theme is presented. Is the change *instantaneous?* If pressed for the answer, we should say, yes, theoretically. The change from a wrong principle and motive in life to a right one, from partial to entire purity, must be instantaneous. But practically there may be, or there may not be, a *consciousness* of any such sudden transition. Conversion is never a *development*, but is a *crisis* in every instance, perceived or unperceived. Sometimes it is so startling, the conviction of sin so deep, the relief so overwhelming, that the subject with unmistakable accuracy can designate the very day and the hour when this change took place. He can answer the question, "Where were you converted?" as readily as "Where did you go to college?" "Where were you born?" said an English bishop to Summerfield. "In Dublin and Liverpool," he answered. "Were you born in *two* places?" said the bishop. "Art thou a master in Israel, and knowest not these things?" replied Summerfield. The conversion of such a person is like the phenomenon which would occur should the sun rise suddenly at midnight, appearing at once on the meridian, standing there, or moving ever onward, without eclipse and without cloud.

On the other hand, the change sometimes takes place in such a manner that the subject only knows by the review of months, and possibly years, that he is not the man he was. It is, perhaps, more frequently the case that the light struggles for a season with the darkness; doubt is mingled with hope; clouds hang about the horizon, or even shut in the heavens, with only an occasional glimmer of light. With the majority of people in a Christian land, conversion is like the dawning of the morning in the east, in which the change from deep night to commencing day can scarcely be marked. It is so gradual that you can select no points, or sudden advances, until the sun appears. The beholder knows it was once dark: he knows equally well that it is now light. "One thing I know," exclaimed the blind man to the hard questions of the Pharisees — "that whereas I was blind, now I see." The child, learning the alphabet, may not know when it is mastered. The thing of importance is, can he read?

So far as the soundness or the crisis of conversion is concerned, it makes no difference whether it is like the "torrent frozen in mid air," the "lightnings pinioned while playing across the clouds," or like the slow and gradual development of childhood into manhood. The only question that need concern us is, whether or not the heart is now devoted to God and to his service? Has there been a change of character or of citizenship? Are the chief interests transferred from this to the world to come? Have the sins with which he was laden disappeared? Does the man know that a change — a spiritual change — has actually taken place? Is the soul roused to its true dignity? If so, that is enough. The man has been converted. With no time specified, "without a form to signalize it, without a whisper to proclaim it to the world, there will be joy in heaven." *

But must not this change, if radical, be attended with great distress of mind, or tumult of heart and conscience, before, and with a thrilling joy, which re-creates the world, during and immediately after conversion? These experiences may occur, and they may not. They may, and they may not, be any part of conversion. They are dependent upon the constitutional tendencies of the man, and upon his previous life. The highwayman, arrested by God's spirit while in the act of murder, will, most likely, have a tumultuous experience. It will differ entirely from that of the innocent child starving by the road-side. There will be discovered precisely the same differences in experiencing this change that occur in the events of practical life. No two persons will, or can, appear precisely the same under the same circumstances, whatever these circumstances may be.

Take the common illustration: Two sisters lose a much-loved brother. In the bosom of each there will

* Phelps.

be a deep sense of loss, and loneliness, but the amount and kind of emotion at the grave may be very different. In the one will be seen the gush of tears, while not a tear moistens the cheek of the other. The one will turn away from the silent grave with outbursting sorrow, the other in silence, but with a cold, dark mountain upon her heart. One mother may never weep, whose sorrow is as intense as that of her who is bathed in tears at the slightest sickness of her child. These manifestations are the result of constitutional tendencies. They argue nothing, one way or another, as to the soundness of conversion. Conversion is not a question of smiles or tears, of sunshine or clouds. It is not a question of this or that emotion or feeling, any more than it is one of time and place. It is a simple question of a change of character through a divine agency, induced by religious motives, without regard to the time or the manner of its accomplishment. It is, therefore, the sheerest folly to attempt to force every religious experience into the same mould. It cannot be stereotyped. To give directions in each individual case respecting how a man must or must not *feel*, is the last business of the preacher. If any person waits to have a religious experience exactly like that of some one else, he will wait forever without receiving it. There are no exact repetitions. If you find them, one is a counterfeit. Seize the hand of Christ in your own way; step forth; all will be well.

But, again, it is asked, Is this birth from above such that we can always decide correctly whether the individual who makes the profession has, in reality, experienced the change? Will the conduct, at all times, unmistakably foreshadow it? Is the mark always in the forehead? Go to the dress parade of a regiment. There are the soldiers, — under the same uniform, obeying the same commands, equally prompt and equally perfect in their execution. That is what appears to the eye. But the principle involved in the new birth looks at nothing of this. It strikes off, or rather through, the uniform, munitions, and arms, and with the eye of God stares at the heart. It sees more than passes under the human eye. There is the same apparent obedience among the men; but one is a traitor, who will betray the command for thirty pieces of silver; another is a deserter, who leaves his companion alone in the long march and deadly encounter. But another, whose outward conduct for a time is no more commendable, is a patriot, who is ready, at every point and at every moment of peril, to throw his blood and life into the defences of the nation. Hearts! Hearts made right in the sight of God, — that is important. The uniform under which they may chance to beat is unimportant.

Thus conversion, in many instances, may not much change the outward conduct; that depends upon what the conduct has hitherto been. The employment may not be changed. The farmer, merchant, and fisherman, may remain the farmer, merchant, and fisherman still. But the heart-allegiance is changed. Conversion plants in the breast of every soldier the heart of a patriot — one that loves, serves, and will defend the celestial country and kingdom. God knows — we do not — whether all those who are professing to follow Christ, who are acknowledged as Christians, are such in fact. The principle upon which he makes his decision is not that there has been an artificial, superficial, or apparent change in the outward department merely. He requires a radical and thorough change of the heart. All that we can say is this: If the old life in the man has given place to the life from above; if the old man is put off, and the new man put on; if the soul is pervaded, illumined, swayed, exalted, empowered with that which will finally glorify it, and make the man a temple suitable for the spirit and truth of God; if the soul is seized with, or has come into quiet possession of, that kind of inspiration which causes the inclinations to run the way of its duty, so that the service and love of God have become natural; if the man has left the broad and dusty road, and entered the narrow and cool path which winds up among the hills of God to Paradise, — then he is born from above by the spirit, presence, and power of the Highest. He has entered upon the awful but glorious journey of a blissful immortality, and is leading, not a natural, but a supernatural life through a Redeemer.

Is this experience practically, as well as theoretically, possible? "One fact," Fox was accustomed to say, "is worth a thousand arguments." There lived in Jerusalem, during the early years of Christianity, a man who at first persecuted the doctrines of Christ with the greatest vehemence. He bound and put in prison both men and women for their belief, and by torture compelled many to blaspheme. Afterwards, however, this man was found preaching Christ with more ardor than any of the apostles, though for it he was tormented and cruelly persecuted, both by pagans and Jews. He exhibited, after a given day and hour, the most active and devoted Christian career which the world has ever seen, save one. He at last closed and crowned his eventful life by martyrdom, for the same cause he once persecuted. Who that has made himself familiar with the life of this man, Paul, can doubt that he had been converted, not in sentiment, not by development or self-culture, not by some scheme of ethics or social reorganization, but by a spiritual power, that regenerates and saves. Was it hypocrisy or enthusiasm, — was it a frantic fear of death, or a sentimental spiritualism, — which wrought this change? No; this was a case of evangelical conversion. That man was changed, entirely, radically, and instantly changed by the power of God. In this instance *development* plays no part; it is "crisis" throughout. But why pause to multiply illustrations? The world is full of them. They are not ideal pictures, but real events; not theoretical, or rhetorical, but practical experiences; not a representation of what may take place, but of what has taken place, and is taking place, throughout the world, daily. Men can actually love the scenes and associates which they once hated, and will do what they would once have thought themselves incapable of doing. Lawyers, judges, and senators, preaching Christ in our streets and churches, are noble and convincing illustrations. Men can be changed from selfish to benevolent men; from doing nothing to please God to doing everything to please him; from having nothing in common with Christ to having everything in common with him. If to-day a man is hard, unyielding, and uncharitable, he may to-morrow, through the grace of God, become kind, not easily provoked, bearing all things, enduring all things. And if he can become such, who will say he ought not? There is but one way, it is true, in which this can be accomplished. There must be some higher assistance, some guidance of God, or we fail. Every practical and serious desire of the soul for salvation is awakened from above. Regeneration is, in the broadest sense, a "birth from above." It can be accomplished, for God stands at every man's threshold. And accomplished it must be, or the kingdom of heaven is lost.

The new birth, as enjoined by our Saviour, is not only reasonable and possible, but, in case of every one who has come to years of accountability, and has wandered one step from the path of truth and duty, is absolutely necessary.

The supernatural life is supernaturally enjoined. It is not, Ye may be born again if ye choose, or if ye find it convenient, but, "Ye must be born again." "*Dei gennethenai*" (infinitive aorist) denotes a requirement more fixed and absolute than a direct imperative. It expresses a condition which admits of no question. It has all the force of a settled past fact. No alternative in its presence can stand for a moment. Our Saviour could not have employed such language, unless he meant that we shall be lost inevitably, without this second birth. But, you say, I am morally upright. My character is above reproach. Shall I suffer in the future life even if I do not become religious here? Will God stand on exact and rigid terms with me; is he not a Father? We will not stop to argue the case. Christ, in whom we find no disposition to hardness or harshness, who came directly from God, who knew the mind which is in God, who evidently understood what is necessary for man better than he does himself, that Being of such truthfulness, candor, and solicitude, says that the birth from above and the life supernatural are absolutely indispensable. Where, then, remains the ground for argument? Does not the entire claim against the necessity of conversion and a supernatural life either deny or ignore every word that fell from the lips of Christ on this subject? Is it not reckless beyond comparison thus to disregard his authority, especially when the exigencies of our condition were felt so keenly that he unhesitatingly died for us?

The truthful and solemn convictions of the human soul bear witness to the words of Christ. None are born Christians. New blood must be infused in all our veins. Every prince, peasant, master, slave; every rich and every poor man the world over; every one who stands with the multitude in the street; and every traveller, lonely and lost at night, with none but God near him, — feels the absolute necessity of conversion to a higher life. What stronger earthly claim can confront them? Reflection always results in a conviction that wherever heaven is, or whatever it is, it is not adapted to a natural heart and life. If one visits a regal palace, he clothes himself in his best attire. Rags are not admitted. No one thinks of presenting them. The most exalted condition of character possible is alone suitable to enter the firmest, the grandest, and the sublimest spot in the universe of God — the visible kingdom of heaven. Nay, that place sought for in many forbidden ways, sighed for by all amid the surrounding ills of life, — that resting-place, that embodiment of bliss and repose, that ideal of every heart never yet reached, that glorious home of God, — is felt to be absolutely beyond man's reach without a change of character. The change which is felt to be necessary is not a trivial one. It involves the work of a divine creation. It is a change which is equivalent to a resurrection from the dead. It requires the same omnipotent agency. "Can the Ethiopian change his skin, or the leopard his spots?" No! But the renewing agency of the Holy Ghost can do it.

When, therefore, the teachings of Christ, requiring that we be born of "water and the *Spirit*," are so positively confirmed by the deep and solemn intuitions of the soul, where is the chance for additional argument? Or, rather, what argument outweighs them? The giant hand, which is stretched forth into the joys and thoughts of life, which writes, with prophetic finger, upon the walls of every house, "Without this divine birth and life, weighed and found wanting," — that hand breaks in twain every iron link of logic forged to bind it, and in its freedom casts from itself all the silver chains of rhetoric that sceptics have thrown about it. The solemn declarations which were laid across the path of Nicodemus are laid across every path. If we move, we meet or pass them. This universal and obtrusive visitor is not easily dismissed. He is not partial. The hand that knocked at the door of that Jewish ruler's heart knocks at all hearts.

The more one studies this law of a new birth, the more will he see that it is an eternal principle. We cannot make it otherwise if we would. There is no power which can annul it. "If a retreating army," says some writer, "wants to cross a frozen river, the ice will not put off dissolving, but will run into the liquid state at a certain exact point of temperature. If a man wants to live, there is yet some diseased speck of matter, it may be in his brain or heart, which no microscope even could detect, and by that speck, or because of it, he will die at a certain exact time, which time will not be delayed for a day, simply because it is only a speck. Is, then, character a matter that God will treat more loosely? How certainly will any expectation of heaven, based on the looseness of God, and the confidence that he will stand for no very exact terms, issue in dreadful disappointment!"

Do not the advocates of a universal and indiscriminate heaven misapprehend the real character of God? Have they any ground for the belief that he is a free and easy, loose and careless being?* Is there anything loose in the realms about us, in the flying stars or rolling suns? Does not God weigh every atom, and fashion every rain and dew-drop with surprising care, and by the same eternal law with which he formed the sun and bound together the universe? Does not every particle under his care assume the

* Bushnell.

dignity of a world? His kingdom is order and law. There is no smuggling into place, or out of place. His police force is immense. He is kind, but exact; exact because he must be. The universe would be ground to powder were he not thus. Can his heaven, then, be an admixture of good and evil? a conglomerate formation of genuine Christians and heartless murderers, of devoted saints and debased sensualists? Must there not be a right hand, a left hand, a gulf, a definite line drawn? Will there not be those who are born from above and those who are not, those who are striving and those who are not, those who have followed the path seen by no vulture's eye and those who have followed the broad path thronged by many feet? Let us not be mistaken. The line is a broad one; there will be no difficulty in making a final separation. On the one hand, there will be a change of purpose — final, total, and sweeping; on the other, intentional disobedience; — on the one hand Nicodemus inquiring, "How can these things be?" and lingering in the presence of Christ until he speaks, and the difficulties vanish. On the other, Pilate inquiring, "What is truth?" and pausing only to shut and bolt the door against it. So far as man is concerned, it is a matter of willingness or unwillingness, of simple fitness or unfitness, of right or wrong. It is a turning from death to life. So far as God is concerned, it is an absolute requisition made upon his mercy to recreate a natural but willing heart. Both God and man must act, or there will be perpetual anarchy. If men are unyielding, they will be banished. If God withholds his assistance, he will be dethroned. Through a combined effort the impenitent man must become contrite, the proud humble, the unkind kind, the unfaithful faithful. The father, whose presence strikes terror into the hearts of his children, must become affectionate. In fine, sinful men must become Christians, or their exclusion from heaven is inevitable. It must be so. Christ knew it must be so, or he would have told us otherwise. Our part of the work is not difficult.

Say we will obey him, and the seed from heaven will fall into the heart — seed which ripens for immortality. The seed is ever upon the palm of the sower. No heart is so bad, so oppressed with sin, so care-worn, that it cannot be made cheerful as the blush of morning. If it is opened to the truth of God, the blood of Christ will bound through it in a new birth. We need not wait to ask how this can be done, whether chiefly by natural or gracious ability. We need not wait to comprehend the true theory of the atonement. God can implant gems and gold in the barren rock. He has done it. That is enough. When man is obedient, and has done all he can do, then he is to wait and see the salvation of God; an explanation of the theories will come afterwards. A supernatural life can only be discerned supernaturally. Only those of the fold know the voice. Without the fold is danger.

THE SUPERNATURAL LIFE

AS RELATED TO FAITH, WORKS, AND THE ATONEMENT OF CHRIST.

"For all have sinned, and come short of the glory of God.

"Where is boasting, then? It is excluded. By what law? of works? Nay, but by the law of faith.

"Therefore we conclude, that a man is justified by faith without the deeds of the law.

"Do we then make void the law through faith? God forbid: yea, we establish the law." *Romans* iii. 23, 27, 28, 31.

"Ye see, then, how that by works a man is justified, and not by faith only.

"Yea, a man may say, Thou hast faith, and I have works: show me thy faith without thy works, and I will show thee my faith by my works." *James* ii. 24, 18.

"That is the word of faith which we preach: That if thou shalt confess with thy mouth the Lord Jesus, and shalt believe in thine heart that God hath raised him from the dead, thou shalt be saved.

"For with the heart man believeth unto righteousness, and with the mouth confession is made unto salvation." *Romans* x. 8–10.

"If we wish to be just judges of all things, let us first persuade ourselves of this,—that there is not one of us without fault." SENECA.

II.

THE SUPERNATURAL LIFE

AS RELATED TO FAITH, WORKS, AND THE ATONEMENT OF CHRIST.

"The Lord wants reapers. O, mount up
Before night comes, and says, Too late!
Stay not for taking scrip or cup;
The Master hungers while ye wait." LOWELL.

THERE are various theories of salvation, all of which have able preachers to advocate, and influential societies to support them. Let us examine a few of the leading views, or rather some of the questions growing out of them.

Our definitions will be brief. Faith is believing with the heart unto righteousness; Works are the result of effort; and Salvation is man's deliverance from actual sin in this world, and from its consequences in the world to come.

Are men made religious, and finally saved, by virtue of believing? While mingling with Christian people, we frequently hear these expressions: "I wish to go to heaven by way of the cross;" "through the blood of Christ;" or, "by looking to Calvary." This is wonderful language. Originally, it implied the highest type of Christianity; but upon the lips of many it has become religious cant, and to the ears of many it bepseaks religious hypocrisy.

Examine the expressions separately for a moment. "By the way of the cross." The deep and essential meaning of the cross, in an evangelical sense, is not two pieces of wood crossed, but is a struggle towards a right life, which, in this world, is necessarily a cross-bearing life. One may look to the cross, in a physical or intellectual sense, until his hair is white and his eyes dim; he may talk eloquently about it until his lips are palsied or lifeless; it will avail nothing. Men must be willing to walk as well as talk — willing to walk the hard and flinty path with our Saviour. It is one thing to wear the form of the cross as an adorning about the neck, to place it on the steeples of churches, to handle it with hands, but quite another thing to display the spirit of it and of Christ in the life. Go to heaven "by the way of the cross," clinging to it with devotion, hailing it wherever met, though it costs self-sacrifice, agony, blood, and death. "The way of the cross" — what a world of meaning is involved in those few words! How far we are from apprehending its essential and majestic meaning!

Equally suggestive is the expression — "I wish to be saved through the blood of Christ." Bengel, who was somewhat in advance of many of his age, says, "The mere hearing and speaking of the wounds of

Jesus end in nought but words. There are those who only *name* Christ, and never *know* him. They make the blood of Christ an opiate to apply to conscience." The criticism of Mr. Emerson is just, though severe: "The thing Christ meant and willed when on earth is in essence more with them [certain infidels and atheists] than with those of their opponents who only wear and misrepresent the name of Christ; like the son of the vine-dresser in the gospel, who said, 'No,' and went, while the other said, 'Yea, and went not.'" Many who say "No." are laboring hard in the vineyard. Many who continually say, "I go, sir," are not found in the master's vineyard from one year's end to another. One may as well be an honest atheist as an unfaithful nominal Christian. "Whither of the twain did the will of his father?" inquired our Saviour. "They say unto him, The first. Jesus saith unto them, Verily I say unto you, that the publicans and the harlots go into the kingdom of God before you."

Men must learn to judge of their religion by their purpose to serve God, rather than by their emotions; by their spirit, rather than by their professions. It should never be overlooked, that to take Christ into homes and hearts, to clothe and feed him, though in the form of a weary stranger, is better than to say a thousand times, we love him. The supernatural life is not one of words, but of faith and deeds. Paul was saved himself, and believed others could be, but only by the blood applied. He was ready to live or die — ready for anything. That was a significant device on an ancient coin — a bullock between an altar and a plough, with the inscription underneath, "Ready for either"— ready for life or death, for service or sacrifice.

When one thinks of the blood of Christ, it should not be in such a manner as to make him feel, if impenitent, that he has taken a dose of opium, or inhaled chloroform. The gospel is not soporific, but is of the nature of a stirring and thrilling appeal, which sometimes cuts to the quick, like a sword double-edged. Christians dwell in the regions of principalities and powers, not of shadows and semblances. It is not the blood flowing on or from the cross that saves, unless it has also reached the individual, and unless he has added, or is ready to add, his own life-blood to the stream which washes away the sin of the world. It is not the cry, "Lord, Lord," that saves. Many, with that word upon their lips, shall be banished. A self-sacrificing spirit is the only one which can hope to be saved by the blood of the cross. Such is the life begotten of God. Where, then, it is asked, is faith? Much of it is dead! "It is vain; ye are yet in your sins," was Paul's decision. Such formality excludes spiritual vitality. Let the apostle's life interpret his theory and expound his meaning. "I die daily:" that is saving faith; that is showing faith by works. "I am crucified with Christ, and yet I live:" that is practical or New Testament Christianity. To die daily is immortality.

We pass to another phase: "I wish to be saved, or I expect to be saved, by looking to Calvary." This lenguage is also of solemn import. It should never be employed carelessly or heedlessly. It means infinitely more than remaining in the distance, and look ing at suffering, or looking upon Jesus hanging on Calvary. It is one thing to stand in the valley, gaze upon and go into ecstasies over a lofty mountain range, and quite another and different thing to clamber up its sides. The one is easy enough, the other costs something. The Christian religion does not consist in the exclamations of, "O, beautiful! O, glorious!" Is heaven thus secured? That would be an easy, and very convenient journey thither. The priest and Levite came and looked upon suffering — the suffering traveller by the way-side. Was there virtue in that? In that, rather, was guilt. It was the Samaritan, hastening to the side of the dying man, binding up his wounds, and bringing him to the inn, who was on the road to heaven by the way of Calvary. That is the piety Christ recognized. That is faith shown by works. A multitude of priests, scribes, and Levites, Jewish people and Roman soldiers, looked upon Calvary when Christ hung there. Was there virtue in that? No more, no less, than there is in all religion which ends in professions. Nominal Christians employ expedients and catch at shadows. They think they have the hidden life, but will not come to Christ that they might have it. The lofty claims of the life supernatural are never satisfied by receiving sentimental compliments and pleasant smiles. A Christian must look upon Calvary until he is transformed into it, in order to be saved by it.

Those thrilling and hope-inspiring expressions — "by the way of the cross," "through the blood of Christ," and the like — should come from the lips of those only who are struggling for a right life, and who are manifesting daily the spirit of Christ. They are eloquent pleadings only when heard from the lips of those who are consciously lost without the help of Christ, and who are seeking salvation through his atonement. If the expressions have become sentimentalized, let the church at once restore their majestic import. The mouth of the sceptic should no longer be fed by misrepresentations of evangelical Christianity. Let his voice be silenced by the earnest declarations of every Christian, that though justification rests solely on the broad principle of faith, still the conditions of human salvation do by no means stand upon imaginary or puerile foundations, but upon the absolute possession of the spirit of Christ — that spirit which ministers to the poor, which heals the sick, and feeds the hungry. That spirit which lays its hand upon him who has fallen among thieves, raises him up, heals, and comforts him. That spirit which seeks to save the world, which seeketh not her own, which suffereth long and is kind, which is Christ on earth again, but this time in the person of his follower. A spirit so simple that a little child may understand and practise it in the division of his apple to a destitute companion. A spirit which is old as eternity, and sublime as God, which has its home in His bosom. That spirit on which is based the religion of every inhabited planet and star in the universe, seen and unseen, far and near. Let that be the profession and the declaration of faith in the church, as it is the evident intention of all Christ said, and none can fail of its meaning, or object to its spirit.

There is another kind of spurious faith which

grows out of a perversion of certain other principles of the spiritual life. It is that in which belief is made to take the place of reality. As men think themselves, so they claim they are. Spiritual life is made imaginary. All things, without regard to actual condition or qualification, are as they are felt to be. Magnificent and gorgeous dreams are looked upon as a safe and good index of religious life and growth.

Though this is often a very enchanting, it is none the less a sophistical kind of faith. A man knows not whether he sleeps or wakes. But we doubt whether the belief changes the fact. We have little confidence in the man who is religious only when he feels like it. The history of God's children makes it doubtful whether they are most religious when they feel the best or the worst. A good dinner or a glass of brandy may make a man feel well, but is that religion? If the west and north winds make men feel better than the east, is religion, therefore, in the way the wind blows? Christ's religion is not. Good bread is better than poor; its effect is better; but men do not live by bread alone. The divine spiritual life exists, triumphs, and is most religious when its possessor is compelled to master his feelings. If pleasant, he makes them add speed to his flight; if oppressive, he grapples with and overcomes them. "Who shall ascend into the hill of the Lord? or who shall stand in his holy place?" He who dreams about it, or feels like it? "He that hath clean hands, and a pure heart; who hath not lifted up his soul unto vanity, nor sworn deceitfully. He shall receive the blessing from the

Lord, and righteousness from the God of his salvation." He is the one in whom the Holy Spirit finds his congenial home, and performs his appropriate work. "I am the way," says Christ. The way to walk, not to look at, he means. If the night is overcast, if we are anxious to accomplish a journey, and a friend should hail us in the darkness, saying, "I am the way," or "I will show you the way," we understand his meaning. We do not fold our hands and sleep. We rush into the night-darkness, follow the sound of his footfall, and try to be so near as to catch the pantings of his breath. We *follow*, as well as believe. Simple intellectual believing will never speed us on our journey, or bring us to a place of safety. So it is with Christ as the way of life. "Have I been so long time with you, and hast thou not known me, Philip?" are the mournful words that might be addressed to many a nominal professor. "None of his," and "I never knew you," were spoken to those who were expecting that heaven was theirs. How mistaken! Security *begins* in a renewed heart, and ends in a renewed life. Instead of being anything trivial, the gospel of Christ is the most startling appeal ever made to humanity. "Strive to enter in at the strait gate; for many, I say unto you, will seek to enter in, and shall not be able. When once the master of the house is risen up, and hath shut to the door, and ye begin to stand without, and to knock at the door, saying, Lord, Lord, open unto us, and he shall answer and say unto you, I know you not whence ye are: then shall ye begin to say, We have eaten and drunk in thy presence, and thou hast taught in our streets.

But he shall say, I tell you, I know you not whence ye are; depart from me, all ye workers of iniquity. And behold, there are last, which shall be first; and there are first, which shall be last." (*Luke* xiii. 24-27, 30.)

In what relation does an easily affected sentiment stand to these requirements of a divinely inspired life! Impulses, and agreeable impressions, which are often evanescent as summer clouds, are not the foundation on which Christians are to stand. True religion, the outgrowth of a supernatural life, is a living union with Christ. It is a believing, not with the head, but with the heart; not a believing at random, but unto righteousness. In case of the sinner, it is the casting behind him of everything human, a falling by faith into the arms of the divine, and an abiding there until the birth from above sends him forth again, not merely to talk sentimentally, and feel religiously, but to be *religious*, and evoke by his conduct the praises of the universe.

Are men made religious, and finally saved, by virtue of works? Theoretically, they are; practically, they are not. Perfect obedience, in deed and spirit, constitutes a divine life. The more one studies the nature of Christianity, the meaning of the atonement, and the cross of Christ, the more of a vital and earnest thing will it seem, to be a true evangelical Christian. Note a few distinctions involved in the question before us.

There has been much confusion in the church and the world respecting the relation of faith and works. Between Paul and James seems to lie an inexplicable paradox, but one in which we apprehend there is a crystallized truth, resplendent as sunlight. The formal Christian says, "I am saved by faith; I will do no work." That is faith without works, by which one should be frightened, sooner than invite it to his hearthstone. Paul rejects such faith. The professed moralist says, "I am saved by my works; I will have nothing to do with faith." That is works without faith, which is death. It is a corpse, which, after a while the owner will find to be destitute of the very life that gives it any value outside the dissecting-room or hall of exhibition. James rejects such works. What avails, then, justification by faith? A lawyer came to our Saviour, asking what he should do to inherit eternal life. He replied, "What is written in the law; how readest thou? And he answering, said, Thou shalt love the Lord thy God with all thy heart, and with all thy soul, and with all thy strength, and with all thy mind; and thy neighbor as thyself. And he said unto him, Thou hast answered right; this do, and thou shalt live." The meaning is this. If a man will love the Lord his God with all his heart, and with all his soul, and with all his strength, and with all his mind, and his neighbor as himself, with the understanding that his neighbor is the man who needs his help, and that his nearest neighbor is the one who needs it most, — if the man always has and always will thus comply, he shall be saved. That is a clear case. But if he has not, what then? If he has not given up the sins he knows he ought to forsake, if he has not shunned the company he ought to abandon, if in his dealings he has wronged any one, or falsified in anything; if he has not forgiven all his enemies, and sought their good; if, in fine, he has not always possessed the spirit of Christ, which is the embodiment of humility, of reverence, of sobriety, of gentleness, of charity, of forgiveness, of fortitude, of resignation, of faith, of active love, — the spirit which is one and all of these, — what then? Has he ground of hope by the law of works? Not in the least.

That lawyer blushed with shame when Christ made his reply; and it was well he did. But we hear it said, No man can reach such a standard. True; but that is the only standard that God's law and justice recognize: hence we say, *practically*, while men remain in the kingdom of God's law and justice, they await an inevitable death-blow. Taking the world as it is, no man can be saved by his own works. Were not salvation dependent upon a spiritual life, he might. The better one is, the more painful is his conscious unworthiness. The more he does, the more will he long to rest on something besides his own deeds. It is absolutely impossible for any one of Adam's descendants to pass, by his own efforts, from the natural to the supernatural life.

While objecting to a religion based upon sentimental prefessions, we purposely left the impression that deeds and endeavors were conditionally necessary. But there is another and deeper principle which underlies this, and to which we call attention for a moment.

There are two things involved in salvation: first, a groundwork; and second, certain conditions. The atonement of Christ forms the chief, nay, the sole groundwork of our salvation. It constitutes the only principle upon which God can justify any man, or vindicate his law to the universe. Without the atonement of Christ, no human being will or can be saved; rather, without the eternal principle which the atonement embodies. The infant and the idiot must be saved by the provisions of the atonement. The heathen, who have never heard of Christ as a Saviour; nominal Christians, who have no faith in Christ as divine; the moralist, who sees no virtue except in good deeds, — whoever, from either of these classes, is saved (some may be), must be saved by the atonement of Christ; for there is no other name given under heaven for that purpose. The provisions are ample; they are omnipotent as the arm of God; they stretch back to the beginning of time, and fold in their embrace the Antediluvian, as well as the last mortal who shall breathe on earth.

As one of the great principles of God's government, the atonement existed long before Jesus of Nazareth appeared. While looking, then, at the groundwork of salvation, the atonement stands before us in its majestic proportions, underlying every other thought and object in the universe. It stands alone. But the conditions upon which the atonement avails are none the less important. Without complying with them we are lost, in spite of the atonement, or any number of atonements. We advocate not an unconditional, but a conditional salvation, through the atonement. But what are the conditions? In general, it may be said, repentance, faith, an active Christian life, and conformity to the enjoined ordinances of the church. This, however, is an incomplete reply. No perfect and definite answer can be given. The conditions differ in every individual case throughout the world. They are graduated by the circumstances that surround us, by the providences of God which encompass, and by the constitutional peculiarities which characterize us.

The conditions required of infants and of idiots, if there be for them no future probation (?), are not those imposed upon an adult. Those required of savages and heathen, are not those placed upon men in civilized and Christianized lands. What the individual and particular conditions are, is made known, not to the world at large, but privately to every individual heart. God whispers them to all men: to this one, this specific thing; to that one, that specific thing. It is by obedience or disobedience respecting these special commands that a man stands or falls, is saved or lost; so that if a man accepts, by *practical* faith, the atonement of Christ, the whole code of laws in the new kingdom is fulfilled. Man is not merely pardoned by accepting Christ, but is justified also. Of this there can be no question. A multitude of voices testify to it. We discover, in this broad principle of salvation, an explanation of the favorite theme of Paul — "salvation without the deeds of the law." We are all lost, is his argument, unless there be such a salvation; for all have sinned and come short of the glory of God.

"But a tree," it is said, "is known by its fruits, and not by its leaves and branches." True; and yet all good trees are not fruit-bearers, in a worldly sense; that is, what is not fruit in one of these kingdoms of which we have been speaking is fruit in the other.

On one occasion our Saviour stood near the temple, and saw rich men casting their gifts into the treasury. Some, undoubtedly, were good men, and devoted. One gave his millions for the poor of the city; another swelled the treasury with thousands; others with hundreds. These offerings Christ did not despise; he honored them; they were well given. But "he saw also a certain poor widow casting in thither two mites." O, how contemptible! Two mites! What little fruit! what despicable fruit! Call the woodman; grind the axe; cut that tree down; put another in its place. Why cumbereth it the ground? But pause first. Christ knew what those two mites had cost the poor woman, and what toil had earned them. He knew that they were all her living; that her heart was right, though the offering of her hand was small. He overlooks nothing. In his judgment she had cast in, not more in *proportion*, but more in *fact*, than all the rest. That was salvation without the deeds of the law. Do Liberal Christians furnish a more liberal system of Christianity?

This principle may be urged still further. Though not a deed is wrought; though not a gift is bestowed, even of two-pence; though not a word is spoken for Christ; though the tongue is silent as the grave, because it cannot move, yet such a one may be already farthest advanced in the kingdom of God. The poorest and the lowest may reap as ample harvests as the richest and highest. One man may be just as devoted as another, rise just as high, come in possession of just as lordly a mansion as another, be he king or rag-picker.

The old heavens and the old earth pass away in this new economy, and all things are changed; sometimes in appearance, always in fact. We live in two realms. We may lead two lives; the one of which may, while the other may not, always conform to the will of the Father.

It is upon this principle of justification without the deeds of the law, so frequently set before us throughout the Scriptures, that we base the glory of the gospel of Christ. And also upon this same principle we base a conviction that the number of those finally saved will be greater than many dare believe. Not that we lower the standard, or destroy the terms of salvation, but we believe the terms are complied with oftener than we generally imagine. The books of the visible church on earth do not contain all the names of God's children. There are other church books than those we see and handle. Heaven is thronged with those who have not fulfilled the legal code. Indeed, there would be few there if the exact fulfilment were required.

The Jews thought Jehovah was their own exclusive right and property.* But the principle under discussion shows that he belongs no less to that large other world of men and nations. The Scriptures, though especially portraying the history of the Jews, are not silent respecting other nations. Now and then they

* See Robertson.

pass across the borders of Judea to find elsewhere some of the truest servants God has ever had on earth. We are told of Job, of Melchizedek, of Rahab. God has everywhere had his secret friends, at all times and in all nations; silent guests, ready at a critical moment to do his service. O, yes, there is a church on earth larger than our narrow hearts dare hope for. All those who are striving and groaning after God and his truth, after the universal Christ and his spirit, anywhere and everywhere, are its members. One has found what answers to the atonement without a preacher; another has walked by faith in heathen darkness; another has wrought for God valiantly; and all who have borne the cross found at their doors, are the children and friends of God.

Heaven is the place of the good. Many shall come from the east and the west. The Indian, whose faith in the Great Spirit made him a better man; the Hindoo, who believed in God, and did not forget works of benevolence and justice; the devoted Catholic, who despised all that was not pure and good in his creed; yes, and every man whose face has been set towards the light, and who has struggled towards it, — for God accepts human struggles, accounting them successes, — shall doubtless sit down with Abraham, Isaac, and Jacob in the kingdom of God. "This invisible church has passed through the centuries, absorbing silently into its bosom of all ages, of all nations, the good and the just."

"When saw we thee an hungered and fed thee?" and "Inasmuch as ye have done it unto one of the least of these my brethren," start a thousand pleasant questions in every generous and inquiring soul, and challenge the world to present a sublimer or more reasonable path to heaven.

Further inquiries respecting faith and works being unnecessary, we are led to the positive statement that —

Men are made religious, and are finally saved, through the atonement of Christ. Leaving behind us formal professions and human efforts, we now stand face to face with the grandest and sublimest reality in the universe — the Atonement of Christ. It is that upon which faith and works depend. Its work is not natural, but supernatural. One cannot explain it, more than he can explain other supernatural phenomena. We cannot explain God, because he is not a natural product. He is above the range of the natural. Why the atonement is made the groundwork of salvation no one knows. Men are charmed and perplexed in view of its efficacy. Likewise the angels. We can more easily show what it does than what it is.

Men have sinned. There is a difficulty in the way of forgiveness. Why, we may not know; the fact all feel. Repentance will not repair the evil done. No man can repair the positive damage that a single sin has done God's empire and love. The slightest dereliction has shocked the moral universe Darkness covers the guilty race like a pall. Humanity is baffled. All its efforts touch not the evil. "Pay that thou owest," thundered from the mountain, startles those hiding in the valley. It is at this crisis of terror that the atonement of Christ dissipates the darkness and implants immortal hopes. How? Why ask that question? We do not know. We know from experience that there is a connection between salvation and the atonement of Christ. Here we pause. Are we unreasonable? We drop the seed into the soil, cover it, and leave it. We do not see the connection between it and the beautiful flower that swells and blossoms above it; which kisses the atmosphere with its fragrance, and delights the eye which beholds it. But we have learned there is a connection: that is all; and that is enough. We sow and plant. Are we unreasonable?

Thus Christians have learned that there is a vital connection between spiritual knowledge and a practical belief in the atonement of Christ. They also have equal ground for denying the growth of the plant from the seed as for denying the connection between the atonement of Christ and the everlasting peace which it inspires in the hearts of men.

The atonement makes us one with God. All other difficulties vanish. The atonement shows men what they can become. They are gods fallen upon the earth. They are in distress and anguish. Through the atonement of Christ they rise; they extend their hands as upon his cross; they feel anguish like his; they feel the temporary loneliness of being forsaken of God; they assert, through Christ, their rights, their divinity, are born again, and are henceforth the redeemed sons of God.

Sin brought another world into this one. The atonement brings still another. It is above the natural We dwell in it, and are subjects of it, only through the agency of the supernatural life of the Redeemer.

The relation of the atonement to the salvation of the race manifestly involves a process which is both divine and human. The human steps are natural, the divine are supernatural. God and man alternate in the work. Each does what the other cannot. Each is helpless without the other. It is God's grace and human weakness cemented. It is a *co-working* which frees the soul from guilt, and lifts the world to heaven.

The atonement is of the nature of a perpetual benediction. The sufferings of Christ, upon which it is based, are not *as* those of guilty men, but are *for* guilty men. It is a smile of a Father, rather than a frown of the Almighty. The atonement is such a stroke of mercy that men are left, in consequence, to depend upon the love of God, as a child depends upon the affectionate embrace of his father.

Its effect upon the individual is miraculous. The man believes. His belief is not an opinion. Opinions are not sufficient to produce spiritual transformations. But the belief in the *atonement*, or in the *name*, or in the *necessity* of the atonement, is such that the Holy Spirit employs it as an agency through which he enters the soul and performs a re-creation. Old things pass away: all things become new.

Although it is as unreasonable to deny this transformation of the hearts of millions of our fellow-beings as it would be to deny the most manifest product of nature, yet it is as inexplicable as the nature and existence of God.

Multitudes there are who have not found the way. But if they are struggling for it, they are numbered by the court of heaven among those who are saved. They have faith in God and the right. The natural step is followed by the supernatural. It would be singular if among the varied human experiences some were not found who will struggle until death without the clear light of the other world bursting upon them. But it is enough to know that they are struggling towards Christ. If they do not reach a full understanding of him in this world, they will in the next. If the bud of that eternal life is in the heart, when the hinderances of the world fall off, and its ignorance is overcome by the revelations of the next, then, through the transformations of faith, the obedience of a filial love, and the renovation of the Holy Ghost, the undeveloped bud will burst forth into full and eternal bloom, fit to adorn the Paradise of God.

A SUPERNATURAL DESTINY FOR MAN.

"Death finds us 'midst our playthings; snatches us,
As a cross nurse might do a wayward child,
From all our toys and bawbles — the rough call
Unlooses all our favorite ties on earth;
And will if they are such as may be answered
In yonder world, when all is judged of truly."

SIR WALTER SCOTT.

"If a man die, shall he live again?" *Job* xiv. 14.

"Then shall he say also unto them on the left hand, Depart from me. . . . And these shall go away into everlasting punishment, but the righteous into life eternal." *Matthew* xxv. 41, 46.

"One question, more than others all,
From thoughtful minds implores reply;
It is, as breathed from star and pall,
What fate awaits us when we die?"

ALGER.

"'Tis Immortality deciphers man,
And opens all the mysteries of his make.
Without it, half his instincts are a riddle;
Without it, all his virtues are a dream."

YOUNG.

"Immortality o'ersweeps
All pains, all tears, all time, all fears; and peals,
Like the eternal thunders of the deep,
Into my ears this truth: Thou liv'st forever."

BYRON.

"Better, by far, laboriously to bear
A weight of woes, and breathe the vital air,
Slave to the meanest hind that begs his bread,
Than reign the sceptred monarch of the dead."

Odyssey.

I.

THE FUTURE EXISTENCE OF MAN.

THERE is a world of interest in the question of the sorrowing patriarch of Uz. No heart beats which has not, at times, paused with fixed attention before it. It involves the most thrilling inquiries of every earnest soul. It comes home to us. All that we hold dear on earth is, or will be, involved in it. All that we hope for in the future is, or will be, at stake upon its answer. As the distant and strange flight is taken by our friends, bereft and astonished nature has always, and will always, follow with the anxious thought struggling in the heart, or breaking from the lips, Have they gone — gone forever? or do they live beyond the horizon and above the clouds?

We briefly consider some of the common objections to the doctrine of man's future existence. Our doubts respecting the doctrine arise manifestly from three sources: *The magnitude of the subject*, *our ignorance respecting the method and possibility of a conscious existence hereafter*, and *our ignorance respecting the locality of the soul when separated from the body.*

But do not objections, from their magnitude, weigh equally against a multitude of relations in our present state? Will a candid man allow them to offset any direct argument in support of the doctrine under consideration? Or, should objections from the second source disturb our confidence, since the mode of operation and existence respecting everything is a mystery? Are the phenomena of talking and thinking, of memory and imagination, any less mysterious than the doctrine that this active, thinking, planning spirit of ours shall live forever?

Again: Should the fact that we cannot tell where the disembodied soul exists, lead us to deny its existence? We have looked to one and another of the myriad points of light that spangle the midnight heavens, inquiring, Is this star, or that, my home? and have received no answer. We have wondered whether an untold space intervenes between us and the departed, or only a thin partition of flesh and blood. We have inquired whether or not, if the dimness of our sight were removed, they of the other shore could be seen, as the servant of the prophet saw the armies of God on the mountain-side; and as yet we are in doubt.

But what if, for some good reason, God has not seen fit to reveal to us the precise place of our future existence, has he not disclosed to us enough? Heaven, the place of loyal hearts; hell, the place of disloyal hearts; the one the home of blessed, the other the home of doomed spirits, — are not those sufficiently definite revelations? Latitude and longitude add nothing. Who can tell where or how the essential soul of man exists even while in the body? It has been located, by different philosophers, all the way from the crown of the head to the soles of the feet. Shall we, therefore, disbelieve its existence? Must we in everything come down to that philosophy which will not reason except from matter up to spirit? Must we return to pagan mythology, and insist upon making the earth support the heavens? Are not the heavens and the truths of revealed religion self-supporting and self-illuminating? Why, then, attempt to make spirit depend upon matter — the eternal upon the temporal, the absolute upon the empirical? Is a thing unreal because invisible? Are the stars destroyed when the sky is overcast? Must everything become the object of sight and touch before we can be certain of its existence? Can we take no substitute for the "pound of flesh"? What is the power that moves the world, and makes "the crystal spheres ring out their silver chimes," — can we see it?

What is, where is, the substance of man's being, — can we tell? Or, how do we continue to live when we are asleep, — do we know? Let us say, then, that there is no law of gravitation: we die when we sleep, and the world is annihilated on a dark night, — why not? What a contracted view of immortality is this which depends upon keeping the soul within hailing distance of earth! Better continue plodding as we do, than inherit such immortality.

Truth and certainty, in their highest sense, belong not to this, but to the invisible world, — that world where God is, "where human thought ranges freest, where human feelings swell into a vastness like the deep and living ocean,"* through which men's affections soar away into eternity: that world of faith furnishes the most substantial basis upon which to build our hopes. Its data are more certain, its testimonies are more sure, its prospects more enchanting, its songs sweeter, its joys more abiding; and we are miserable if we have never heard or felt them.

We pass to the arguments which support the doctrine. They are from four distinct sources: the moral government of God, the spiritual nature of man, certain well-known phenomena, and Christian faith in an inspired revelation.

The Moral Government of God and the Future Existence of Man. — We live in a world where virtue and success are not always united. Sometimes innocent men are condemned; frequently guilty men escape. The most unprincipled sometimes prosper, and in all their business relations march from youth until death through fields of success, and of their own choice. On the other hand, moral and religious men are often distressed and baffled. Evils visit and revisit them — to-day in one form, to-morrow in another. Sometimes these two classes — the religious and irreligious — meet. Their interests clash, with every advantage on the one side, and every disadvantage on the other. The poor are ground into the dust, and gains are speculated out of their very destitution. With these aggravated and merciless transactions men often become thoroughly impatient, and feel that

* Shedd.

God does not do his duty, or he would hurl down these oppressors from their high places, and raise up those who are bowed in the dust. All persons feel that they could improve upon God's plan of operations, and correct, to advantage, his moral government. Could they not, so far as the present life is concerned?

This condition of things has been noticed through all history. Democritus put out his eyes, because he could not endure to see wicked men prosper and good men suffer. Mr. Hume says, "Such is the confusion and disorder of human affairs, that no perfect economy, or perfect distribution of happiness or misery, is ever, in this life, to be expected." The ancient Theists were persuaded that nothing less than the existence of all mankind hereafter, with a more exact distribution of rewards and punishments, could excuse present irregularities.

Ancient philosophers, to reconcile the inconsistencies in God's moral government, resorted to a multitude of expedients and theories. The familiar maxims, "The gods move slow, but sure;" "The mill of the gods grinds late, but fine,"—are merely excuses for divine delinquencies, and involve the expectation that the unrectified wrongs of this world will be righted in the next. Shall we be less thoughtful for the divine integrity than were the pagans? Or is Jehovah more insensible to the iniquities and irregularities of society than Jupiter? If so, hail, Jupiter!

Nay; but these wrongs will be righted—not here, but hereafter. If there is no hereafter, there is no just God in the universe. Ten thousand loyal hearts are beating and waiting for the sight; they will not see it until the curtain concealing another life is lifted: then they will see it. But this involves the future existence of the race.

The Skill of the Creator, and the Future Existence of Man.— A glance at the universe reveals the most marvellous and perfect adaptation of means to ends. Then is seen a fitness in all things. So wonderful is this adaptive power, that from it is inferred the existence and wisdom of a Creator. It is a remarkable fact, that all scientific professors — the chemist, the astronomer, the natural philosopher, the anatomist, and the natural historian — vie with one another in their praises of the skill of God. Each claims that his particular department of science proves it more conclusively than any other. Scarcely an object in creation but is sure to bear its testimony to the same truth. The decaying seed, bursting into life; the blade of grass, nodding to the breeze; the little dew-drops, held sparkling in the tiny cups of a woodland violet; the leaf of the forest, opening its palm to give and receive life; the ocean, with its heaving tides, its coral palaces, its submerged mountains; the giant cloud, tinged with fire; and the sun, wheeling his huge proportions from morning until evening through the vaulted sky, — disclose relations so beautiful and harmonious, that they have driven atheism and dualism, and all kindred theories, save speculative pantheism, from the world.

There is one solitary exception to this general principle — *man.* His harmony with this world is never complete. He is ever vibrating between trembling apprehensions and glowing aspirations. His heart throbs constantly with those unsatisfied desires with which God has crowded him, but which are so far, so infinitely far, from complete realization in any condition of life. Amid conscious infirmity, under sentence of death, there is ever a feeling after, if haply he may find his home. The race is homesick. It longs for a knowledge more satisfying, a voice of welcome more cordial, an approval more tranquillizing, and a resting-place more permanent, than earth can give.

No wonder that man is the most dissatisfied and fault-finding creature God has made. Viewed as to this life only, he has every reason to be. Created with a nature that no grasp of wealth, no attainments of knowledge, no sway of power can satisfy, then caged and fettered! Created the lord of earth, to whom the entire animal creation pays its homage, then left to be more miserable and unsatisfied than the creatures he rules!

The only beings on earth whom God has so created as to be satisfied with this life are brutes and fools. The lion, roaring and roving through the desert, mad and impatient for its prey, when his hunger and that of his young are satisfied, returns to his den with no higher thought or desire. The little sparrow longs not for the plumage of the bird of paradise to complete its happiness, but, when its few wants are satisfied, warbles forth its praises to God as if earth itself were Paradise. But man becomes more restless the more his wants are supplied. Grant his desires, and you multiply them. Deck him with kingly robes, and you are not so near satisfying him as if he were in tattered rags. Clothe him with righteousness as with a garment, and you have only increased his longing for a purer life — a resurrection in the likeness of his Redeemer.

The life of man has no meaning, there is no sense or reason in his creation, or in the creation of the world about him, if this throbbing nature of his ceases to live at death. Without the knowledge of a future existence in some men, and the dream of it in all, every man would "curse God, and die." Job's wife would have been justified in giving her advice, and Job in following it. But on the supposition that man is at present placed in an unnatural and temporal sphere, and that he will attain the end and object of his creation sometime and somewhere: on the supposition that every man, good and bad, will find his own place — he that loves God and his service a place suited to him; he that hates God and his service one adapted to him; naked or clothed upon, as the case may be: on the supposition that all may find what they hope for or expect — that which philosophy gropes after, that which apostles and prophets were inspired to proclaim, that which is given to faith, — then the riddles are explained. Man is no longer the "wretch" and the "fool" of creation, which the maxims of all nations have otherwise justly declared him to be. He is the subject of discipline, the object of God's tender solicitude; but the being whose true sphere is in eternity, above all principalities and powers. Is not the creation of man an unpardonable blunder, unless there be for him a future existence?

We pass to the third argument.

Certain well-known Facts and Phenomena indicate Man's Future Existence. — Sometimes it happens that an old man visits the scenes of his childhood. As he nears the place he once called home, and some familiar object meets his vision, his sluggish energies arouse a little, his form is more erect, his step is quicker, and his eye is brighter. In proportion to the increase of home scenes, increases also his strength and activity. When the familiar objects thicken along the pathway, and the memories of the past throng about him, his age is forgotten, his youth is renewed, and his eye flashes with all the fire of stalwart manhood. So it is sometimes with dying men. They appear to catch sight of familiar objects on their journey. As God's promises are realized, as the thrones above and the prepared mansions pass in review, their eyes light up as if they were windows through which they were looking into heaven; the tongue has been loosened, the voice strengthened, and songs of triumph have burst from lips that falter not, though they had trembled in an attempt to whisper an hour before. They are nearing home. Were the body not exhausted, every child of heaven would leave this world bearing upon his face the refulgence of the city of God.

Again: The activity which the spiritual nature of man displays in certain instances when it loses the partial or entire control of the body, is suggestive. The acuteness with which man hears. the clearness of his sight, the keenness of his perceptions, and the powers of his memory and conscience, all go to show that his conscious, spiritual activity does not depend upon a natural and healthy condition or union of it with the body, but that it may be greatly, even preternaturally, increased by an entire suspension of the harmonious union of spirit and body. There are instances on record where persons, to all outward appearances, have been dead. They have remained thus for hours and days. Not a pulse could be felt, not a breath was drawn; the lips were bloodless, and eyes sunken. Afterwards they have recovered their animation, and in many cases have borne testimony that, during all the time of this suspended animation, though they had lost entire muscular control over the body, as much so as if there had been a complete separation, yet a most perfect and vigorous consciousness of every passing event was retained. Every preparation for burial was noted; every word spoken was heard and remembered. Who can tell but every man attends his own funeral!

These cases of suspended animation do not demonstrate, but they certainly point in the direction of the spirit's entire independence of the body, so far as consciousness is concerned.

The same general phenomena occur in health. A person may be occupied in his room, and take no note of the ticking of a clock on the shelf. Upon leaving the room, he affirms he has not heard a single click. But if the ticking had ceased during his presence, his attention would have been instantly arrested. We may sleep soundly while carriages are thundering past our windows; yet an unusual noise in our apartment, though slight as a whisper, will bring us to our feet. Have we not often slept soundly until the minute we had previously resolved to wake? The principle involved is the same in each of these cases. There is a nature in man which does not — we may say which cannot — sleep. It is continually on the lookout. The moment anything unusual takes place it sounds the alarm. It shouts to one sense, pushes against another, and tugs at a third, until they are aroused, until the danger is past, until discouraged in its efforts, or until there is a fatal result. Is there not here an activity of the soul which is above any and all the senses? Does it any more depend upon them for its conscious activity, than does the eagle depend for its life upon the cage that confines it?

The same principle may be still further extended and illustrated. In the Life of Dr. Francis Wayland, recently published, we find the following incident: When, on a certain occasion, he was expected home from New York, after attending medical lectures there during the winter of 1814–15, Mrs. Wayland, his mother, who was sitting with her husband, suddenly walked the room in great agitation, saying, "Pray for my son; Francis is in danger." So urgent was her request, that her husband joined her in prayer for his deliverance from peril. At the expected time he returned. His mother at once asked, "What has taken place?" It appeared, at the time of her agitation, while coming up the North River on a sloop, that Francis had fallen overboard, and the sloop passed over him. He was an athletic swimmer, and readily kept himself afloat until he could be rescued.

A certain woman, the wife of a sea captain, started from her sleep at midnight, and exclaimed, "O God!

my husband is lost!" Subsequent facts showed that the ship on which her husband sailed went down in that storm and at that hour.

More than one mother, during the late war in this country, has described the precise spot where her son fell, the time of his death, and the character of his wounds, and this days before the news of his death had reached home from the distant southern field.

A friend of the author once narrated to him a vision of the death of an absent sister. He perceived the minutest transactions — the last look, the pressure of hands, the surrounding friends, the very moment death occurred, as denoted by the clock on the shelf, — and this while hundreds of miles away. Subsequently, the facts as they occurred and as seen by the brother, were found to be in perfect agreement.

We need not pause to multiply illustrations of this kind. Every household has its witness. The task before us is to ascertain, if possible, the basis of all these phenomena. What is it, and what its character? Spiritualism! But what is spiritualism? What can it do in such cases? This is a display of the activity of the spirits of the living, not of the dead. Wayland's mother was not dead, neither was her son Francis. Here is a phenomenon which the spiritualist seeks to ignore; a phenomenon also which passes entirely beyond the range of ordinary sensation. This is a conscious activity of man, which depends in no way, directly or indirectly, upon his hand, his ear, or his eye. Lock up or destroy every recognized sense, — still this mysterious power of apprehension is not touched or affected. It ranges over the world with the freedom of a king. Does it not look as though, that when the physical tabernacle falls, from it will merge this something, which is so entirely independent of a bodily organism for its knowledge, which overleaps all bounds, and which asks for no visible contact with that which it perceives? We go still farther. May not Wayland's mother have felt that there was danger, by being herself consciously near it? May not the mother who saw her son on the field of battle, and the brother who witnessed the death of his sister, have had a conscious activity hundreds of miles distant from their own physical or recognized presence?

The knowledge obtained in these cases was most certainly not from the spirit of the dead son coming to the mother, not from the spirit of the dead sister coming to her brother; but can we as confidently say that it was not obtained by the mother's own spirit, while visiting the boy in danger, or in death?

Does not the language of Paul go very far in proving the possibility of such an absent, conscious activity? "I knew," he says, "a man in Christ, above fourteen years ago, whether in the body I cannot tell; or whether out of the body I cannot tell: God knoweth; such a one caught up to the third heaven." (2 Cor. xii. 2.) Would Paul have employed such language had he not believed in the possibility of the thing supposed?

If it be admitted that the soul is capable of a conscious activity in one place, while the body is in another, — and ten thousand incidents of life demand such admission, — will it not sweep away every objection of the materialist to the doctrine of a future existence for the race?

Grant this principle of conscious activity apart from the body, as indicated in the phenomena of sleep, of suspended animation, and of premonitions, and we can easily admit the future existence of man in thus proving his independence of the body. The body might be annihilated before the return of that absent activity, and the full play of it would be unaffected. The natural body might be left in the grave forever, without preventing the conscious activity of man from rising to heaven, or from sinking, with all its powers unimpaired, into the dark abyss prepared for the lost. We advance a step farther.

These phenomena we are considering militate against the doctrine of the unconscious sleep of the dead in the intermediate state. They indicate that while death shuts one class of senses it opens another. From the spiritual activity sometimes manifested, it would appear that life is death, and death life. We live in two worlds; one is visible to us, both to the dead. The dead possess all the consciousness of the living, and much more. The dead are just out of our sight, — round the corner of the temple of nature. We dwell in the suburbs of the eternal city, they are in the kingly metropolis. We are in the basement, they are in the royal chambers of state. We are under clouds, they are in a light so radiant that if it should fall upon us at midday "the earth would seem to suffer an eclipse, and hang like a corpse in the midst of shadows." *

* Sears.

Christian Faith, based upon an Inspired Revelation, and the Future Existence of Man. — The argument from this source, though the most difficult to state, is nevertheless the only one which is *felt* to be entirely convincing. The prominence which the Scriptures give to this fact is truly surprising. So bold is the language, so impressive the imagery employed, that many sincere Christians, without distinguishing between a mere existence in the future and the healthy vitality of that existence, — between a cold, intellectual view of it, and the moving, abiding confidence which the doctrine inspires in a Christian heart, — have concluded that the Bible teaches that future existence, in any sense, is impossible without Christ, and that the wicked must, therefore, be annihilated at death. This, however, is a great mistake. A future existence no more depends upon faith than does the present existence. The simple existence of man in the future is not at all affected by his relations to Christ. Death cannot have the least effect upon the spiritual nature of man. Death can touch only materials organized. The command that could destroy even one spirit, or the law that could allow of such destruction, might also result in the destruction of all spiritual existence, good and bad, including the Creator. The annihilationist does not realize whither his doctrine leads him.

> "The soul, secure in her existence, smiles
> At the drawn dagger, and defies its point."

So far as the subject involves the question of reason or philosophy, but one conclusion can be reached:

that if future existence can be predicated of one human spirit, it must be of all, good and bad alike. But let us turn to the Scriptures. Fix the attention, for a moment, upon the single passage from our Saviour at the head of this discussion: "These shall go away into everlasting punishment, but the righteous into life eternal." The period here referred to is not at death, but long after death — at the final judgment of the world. The words here translated "everlasting" and "eternal" are in the original the same word, which, together with a similar one from the same root, constitute the common scriptural terms in use to express indefinite and also endless duration. The word before us is employed in the New Testament on sixty-six different occasions; in fifty-one of which it is used to express the duration of the happiness of the righteous; twice to express the duration of God's existence; in six other connections, where, all admit, it means eternity. There remain seven passages where the word is applied to the duration of the punishment of the wicked. Can any candid explanation of the use of this word, or any fair interpretation of the passage under consideration, in which the word is employed in the same connection to express both the duration of the happiness of the holy, and the duration of the woe of the lost, evade the conclusion that if we base our belief respecting the eternal existence of God, and the eternal felicity of holy men, upon the teachings of our Saviour, we must also, on the same ground, accept a belief as to the future, if not the endless, punishment of the finally impenitent sinner? We say *future* or *endless*, because the future existence of all men is the only question this discourse proposes to settle. But it is asked, How do you explain those passages which are claimed to teach that there is no future existence apart from Christ? Are there not passages which as unquestionably represent that there is no true life in this world without Christ? What is the stream without the fountain, — what the branches without the vine? "Without me, ye can do nothing." But does this language imply that all men are literally dead, like the severed branch, apart from Christ? Does it not rather mean that all true vitality is impossible without a union with Christ? In a sense, we admit, there is no immortality possible apart from a divine Saviour — in the same sense as there is no true life on earth possible without him. There is no future existence and no immortality without him which has real value. Without him a belief in the future state is little better than guess-work, and heaven is only a conjecture. A view of the future existence, without Christ, can evoke no smile from the human face. It may unfold the outside of human nature, but the hidden depths of our being will lie dormant until the forces of a spiritual and supernatural life through a Redeemer evolve them. "Never can the ocean tides of the human soul heave and swell until they are moved by what the Scriptures call 'the power of an endless life.'" This power descends only from the splendid city of God, and upon him only who is an heir of heaven through Christ. The second death, whenever it occurs, is the eternal separation of the soul from all that man holds dear. It is a condition from which restoration is absolutely impossible. This we believe to be the sense of the passages in question. They lose none of their pungent force by this interpretation; and the harmony of the Scriptures can be fairly maintained by no other explanation. In what perfect keeping, also, is this view with the experience of mankind! Ask him who has never been influenced by Christain faith, or by the spirit of Christ, though he has lived a hundred years. Has there been any real vitality to your life? He will tell you, no. Few men have known the world better, or shared more largely in its smiles, than Lord Chesterfield. One less fortunate would have pronounced his life full of reality and vitality. Hear his own confession:

"I have run the silly rounds of business and pleasure, and have done with them all. When I reflect on what I have seen, what I have heard, and what I have done, I can hardly persuade myself that all that frivolous hurry, and bustle, and pleasure of the world has any reality; but I look upon it all as one of those romantic dreams which opium occasions, and do by no means desire to repeat the dose for the sake of the dream. Shall I tell you that I bear this melancholy situation with the sustaining constancy and resignation of which others speak? No; I bear it because I must bear it, whether I will or no. I think of nothing but killing time, now it has become my enemy; and my resolution is to sleep in the carriage during the rest of the journey."

His experience is not an exceptional one. Is this doubted? Then let any man who is destitute of a Christian faith ask himself, "Shall I walk those golden streets? Shall I cool the feverish excitement of this life upon the shores of that river? Shall I see the city and the throne of God, and God Himself, face to face? — and he will learn how vague are his hopes, and how tantalizing are his fondest dreams. His only answer, if honest, will be, "I do not know." Or, let a mother who is destitute of Christian faith, but who is familiar with all else that can be advanced in support of this doctrine, and who desires it to be true above all things else, ask, "Will the bud that blossomed on my bosom, and fell into the earth, unfold itself, and send its sweetness out into another world? Will my own spirit make its journey good across the sea? Shall I behold the blossom, and press it whence it fell?" She will answer, if honest with herself, "I do not know."

William R. Alger is a good representative of this class. After canvassing the subject of the future life in all its bearings, he honestly concluded his work of more than six hundred pages with this cheerless language: "When we die, may the Spirit of truth, the Comforter of Christ, be our confessor; the last inhaled breath, our cup of absolution; the tears of some dear friend, our extreme unction; no complaint for past trials; but a grateful acknowledgment for all blessings, our parting word. And then, resigning ourselves to the universal Father, — assured that whatever ought to be, and is best to be, will be, — either absolute oblivion shall be welcome, or we will go forward to new destinies; whether with preserved identity or with transformed consciousness and powers being indifferent to us, since the will of God is done." Here is submission, but not one word of thrilling assurance.

There are bright stars which glitter and sparkle throughout his work, but, like those of pagan philosophers, they impart to the soul no warmth. He talks calmly about death, but removes not its sting. He plants the grave with the choicest flowers at human command, but it is not swallowed up in victory. What, then, avails talk or flowers? With what manifest propriety do the Scriptures represent that those who are destitute of Christ reach, at length, a species of practical annihilation! *Ad nihil* — traversing the universe to reach nothing! Certainly we shall be pardoned for judging a man by his own conclusions.

Nay, it is a heart possessing and rejoicing in an active evangelical Christian faith which alone can enable its possessor to rise above this sunless sky of rationalism, and break to the world its confident assurance in the voice of revelation — "For we know that if our earthly house of this tabernacle were *dissolved*, we have a building of God, a house not made with hands, eternal in the heavens." But Mr. Alger, and those with him, will say, "You do not know this." *We do know it.* May we not judge? With a Christian faith, which is the gift of God to penitent hearts seeking it, that future life is as certain and real as if our feet were already upon its pavements. Do you doubt this? Find Christ, abide with him, and anon you will doubt no more.

THE RESURRECTION OF MAN.

"I by no means accept the common idea of the resurrection. It is not rising again; it is rising up — a higher state."

JAMES FREEMAN CLARKE.

"Verily, verily, I say unto you, Except a corn of wheat fall into the ground and die, it abideth alone: but if it die, it bringeth forth much fruit." *John* xii. 24.

"But some man will say, How are the dead raised up? and with what body do they come?

"Thou fool, that which thou sowest is not quickened, except it die:

"And that which thou sowest, thou sowest not that body that shall be, but bare grain; it may chance of wheat, or of some other grain:

"But God giveth it a body as it hath pleased him, and to every seed his own body." 1 *Corinthians* xv. 35-38.

"Marvel not at this; for the hour is coming in the which all that are in their graves shall hear his voice,

"And shall come forth; they that have done good, unto the resurrection of life; and they that have done evil, unto the resurrection of damnation." *John* v. 28, 29.

"And when they heard of the resurrection of the dead, some mocked; and others said, We will hear thee again of this matter." *Acts* xvii. 23.

"For each one body that i' th' earth is sown,
There's an uprising but of one for one;
But for each grain that in the ground is thrown,
Threescore or fourscore spring up thence for one;
So that the wonder is not half so great
Of ours, as is the rising of the wheat." HERRICK.

"An angel's arm can't snatch me from the grave;
Legions of angels can't confine me there." YOUNG.

II.

THE RESURRECTION OF MAN.

THE subject of the resurrection of the dead meets mankind everywhere. It is a doctrine inwrought with the laws of our being. Dismiss it if we will, it is sure to revisit us. It comes, bidden or unbidden, as naturally as our memories of the past. The thought of death standing at our own door and knocking — the death and resurrection of Christ, together with a score of religious themes — reproduce it. Whenever we lay our friends in the tomb, or kneel at their graves to weep and pray, we involuntarily ask, though perhaps silently, "*How will they come forth?*"

Though the question of the resurrection of the body is one of perplexity; though we may have had frequent occasion to review and change our previous conclusions; though we have often vacillated between belief and disbelief, between indifference and disquietude; though we have sometimes felt, with the "Country Parson," that the doctrine is one that it is not wise to scrutinize too minutely, and that the day of wonders can alone disclose the whole truth, — still we have, with the most natural and the best of reasons, continued to dwell upon the subject, and enter upon new fields of investigation, that we might search into the grounds of a rational faith, and the more so as we have seen the day approaching.

The Scriptural Theory of the Resurrection of the Body. — In the time of the apostle Paul there arose violent discussions in the church at Corinth upon this general subject, involving both the resurrection of Christ and the future personal resurrection of all men. The Corinthian congregation was composed of persons who had gathered from every existing school of philosophy. Their previous intellectual opinions seem, for a long time, to have been cherished with jealous devotion. Christianity corrects the heart first, the head afterwards.

The two most prominent and opposing theories entertained by this celebrated church were Gnosticism and Stoicism. The first taught that sin could be predicated of the body only, never of the soul: consequently, when the soul is freed from the body, sin will no longer exist, and man will no longer be held accountable for it. Stoicism, on the other hand, contended that sin must be conquered by the force of one's will, both in the soul and in the body. This conquest, it was claimed, constitutes a resurrection to a new life, and the only resurrection possible. Very naturally did those opposing classes of mind, when brought into the same church, clash in their interpretations and expositions of the doctrine of the resurrection. The controversy was prolonged; and we infer from the spirit of the Epistle that it was, on the part of some, unchristian-like.

At length, to settle these discussions, and restore harmony to the church, some leading member or members wrote or sent to the apostle Paul, to know, among other things, what was true on the subject, and what was not; how far it was safe to believe, and how far to disbelieve, the theories then in dispute. Here, then, we have, for a definite purpose, a direct and specific question, requiring a direct and specific answer; so that, of all else in the Bible upon the doctrine of the resurrection of the dead, this letter of Paul to the Corinthian church affords the surest foundation for our belief. Our theory of the question must here be established. All other passages must be interpreted by it, and be made to harmonize with it; for this one was given for the special purpose of disclosing to us the doctrine, and is the only passage of any length in the Bible which has been given expressly and avowedly for that purpose. Ascertain its exact meaning, granting its inspiration, and there need be no further difficulty. We may know to-day, and know to-day precisely as well as when the world shall end, what will *then* be our condition.

In the examination of this and confirmatory passages, we shall be governed by the following principles of scriptural interpretation; that it is not our duty to seek to find difficulties, but to remove them; that we should not seek to *make* contradictions, but should try to discover the truth; that we should not believe the most *improbable*, but the most *probable* of two possible interpretations; and that the most simple and natural interpretation, other things equal, should guide us to our conclusions. What, then, is the least objectionable, the most probable, and the most natural interpretation of the passages before us, concerning the resurrection of the dead.

The Embodiment of the Soul in the Future.—The "resurrection unto life," and the "resurrection unto damnation," would seem to be meaningless in the lips of Christ, were not the human soul at some future time to come in possession of a body, in which it shall live and through which it will act. We cannot fail to notice, also, that there is scarcely a verse in this entire chapter to the Corinthians which does not directly or indirectly disclose the same fact. It is made particularly clear in the following expressions: "But God giveth it a body." "There are bodies celestial and bodies terrestrial." "It is sown a natural body, and raised a spiritual body." "There is a natural body, and there is a spiritual body." No one, we think, can honestly deny that these expressions teach the existence of a future body, in which the immortal spirit shall live and reign.

The Future Body to differ from the Present.—An examination of the passage before us will lead, also, to the conclusion, that the apostle designed explicitly to state that the future body will be free from all gross materials, such as enter into its present structure, and that, in this respect, it will be unlike the present body. What other interpretation can possibly be put upon the following expressions: "It is sown in corruption, it is raised in incorruption." "It is sown in dishonor, it is raised in glory." "It is sown in weakness, it is raised in power." The only obvious impression is, that the body is now mortal; it will then be immortal; now natural, then spiritual; now one thing, then another. "All flesh," continues the apostle, "is not the same flesh; but there is one kind of flesh of men, another flesh of beasts, another of fishes, and another of birds. There are also celestial bodies, and bodies terrestrial; but the glory of the celestial is one, and the glory of the terrestrial is another. There is one glory of the sun, and another glory of the moon, and another glory of the stars; for one star differeth from another star in glory.

"So also is the resurrection of the dead. It is sown in corruption, it is raised in incorruption. . . . Now this I say, brethren, that flesh and blood cannot inherit the kingdom of God; neither doth corruption inherit incorruption." We are not able to see on what principles of interpretation these passages can be made to harmonize with a theory of the resurrection which calls for the restoration of the old body, particle for particle, as it was constituted when it returned to the dust.

Must it not be conceded, if we rely upon the language employed, that the materials of the new body will be unlike those of the present, and that the new body will differ from the old one as the glory and brightness of the sun differ from the glory and brightness of a star; as much as things celestial differ from things terrestrial; as much as the spiritual differs from the natural?

Must we not conclude that the resurrection body is to be etherealized and spiritualized; that it is to be of such a character that a volition, perhaps, will be able to send it to the stars, as it now sends thither our thoughts; that this image of the earthy is to give place to the image of the heavenly; that the dew of perpetual youth, the vigor of eternal manhood, the glow of perfect health, is ever to rest upon that new body, to increase its strength, to enhance its beauty, and to enable it to defy death and live forever? Is not something else besides exactly our old organism to encircle us? Is not the diseased blood, which is now freighted with fever and death, which courses languidly through the veins, which cannot, according to the apostle, inherit the kingdom of heaven, to give place to that which will paint an eternal rose upon the cheek, and impart to the faded eye the splendors of another world? Move on, O son of man, and conquer! The dead are the only people who do not sicken and grow old. "Sown in weakness, raised in power!" Carry out the apostle's illustration. "Thou sowest," he says, "not that body that shall be, but bare grain, it may chance of wheat, or of some other grain; but God giveth it a body as it hath pleased him, and to every seed his own body." Call to mind the field on the hill-side. The seed that was sown disappeared. In its place, and springing from it, was waving, for a time, the tender blade, painting the field with life and beauty. Later stood the ripened grain, and then the sheaf, ready for the garner. Is all this the material which was sown? It has come from the material that was sown. True; and we call it, in freedom of speech, the grain that was sown. But is it, in fact, *the identical grain* that was sown? Has not the old material, in part at least, disappeared? Is not this which we see something new and more beautiful?

But let us look more closely. The springing grain is our authorized commentary. We must patiently consult it while interpreting this illustration given both by Christ and by Paul. The seed contains in itself two opposing forces — one conservative, the other formative. The tendency of the one is to *in*fold, that of the other to *un*fold. While the seed is safely stored in the garner, the conservative force predominates, and the shell is master. But under other influences the formative force predominates; the shell is broken, the essential life comes forth, the crust is thrown away, true progression commences, and perfection follows. Apply the illustration to the future body, and what is the inevitable conclusion? Is it that the same body, in fact, which goes into the grave, is to come out of it, and that the old material is to be the identical material of the new body? Is not the simple and natural meaning of the passage this — that the old body gives place to a new one, though the essential forces remain?

If we die wasted with consumption; if we die with limbs and features swollen and distorted with dropsy; if we die on the battle-field, with limbs mangled and broken; if we die of old age, full of weakness and decrepitude; or if we die with intellect shrouded with delirium, so that friends can scarcely recognize the one beloved; — if these, and a multitude of other divers accidents befall us, are we to enter those worn-out, diseased bodies again, and bear them through eternity? Nay, this "vile body" is to be changed, "that it may be fashioned like unto Christ's most glorious body." As we have "borne the image of the earthy," we are also to "bear the image of the heavenly." If so, we can triumph. "O death, where is thy sting! O grave, where is thy victory!" The grave, with such a resurrection, has already conceded to mortals the victory.

We pause at this point to consider briefly those passages which are claimed to teach a literal resurrection *of*, instead of the resurrection *from*, the old body. The first passage we notice is from Ezekiel's vision of the valley of dry bones.

"The hand of the Lord was upon me, and carried me out in the Spirit of the Lord, and set me down in the midst of the valley which was full of bones; and caused me to pass by them round about; and, behold, there were very many in the open valley; and, lo, they were very dry. And he said unto me, Son of man, can these bones live? And I answered, O Lord God, thou knowest. Again he said unto me, Prophesy upon these bones, and say unto them, O ye dry bones, hear the word of the Lord. Thus saith the Lord God unto these bones: Behold, I will cause breath to enter into you, and ye shall live; and I will lay sinews upon you, and will bring up flesh upon you, and cover you with skin, and put breath in you, and ye shall live; and ye shall know that I am the Lord. So I prophesied, as I was commanded; and as I prophesied, there was a noise, and behold, a shaking, and the bones came together, bone to his bone. And when I beheld, lo, the sinews and the flesh came up upon them, and the skin covered them above; but there was no breath in them. Then said he unto me, Prophesy unto the wind, prophesy, son of man, and say to the wind, Thus saith the Lord God: Come from the four winds, O breath, and breathe upon these slain, that they may live. So I prophesied, as he commanded me, and the breath came into them, and they lived, and stood up upon their feet, an exceeding great army. Then he said unto me, Son of man, these bones are the whole house of Israel; behold, they say, Our bones are dried, and our hope is lost; we are cut off for our parts. Therefore prophesy and say unto them, Thus saith the Lord God: Behold, O my people, I will open your graves, and cause you to come up out of your graves, and bring you into the land of Israel. And ye shall know that I am the Lord, when I have opened your graves, O my people, and brought you up out of your graves; and shall put my Spirit in you, and ye shall live, and I shall place you in your own land; then shall ye know that I the Lord have spoken it, and performed it, saith the Lord." (Ezekiel xxxvii. 1–15.)

This passage is a startling representation of something; but is that something the literal resurrection of the dead? On that barren field bone came to bone, sinew to sinew, the flesh was formed, the breath came, a great and mighty army stood before the prophet, perfect as life, and of veritable flesh and blood, bone and sinew. "Then said he unto me, Son of man, these bones are"—what?—a representation of the final resurrection? There is not the slightest reference to it; but "these bones," said the voice, "are the whole house of Israel." The principle, then, here taught, is, that when the Jewish nation, whose moral and spiritual state resembled the lifeless condition of dried bones, shall turn to God, and do works of repentance, it will rise to a new spiritual and moral life, receiving honor again from the people of the earth.

It is a national resurrection which is here taught, and one that has nothing whatever to do with a personal resurrection of man. Let the Jewish nation but repent and acknowledge Christ to-day, and the original manhood and splendor of the children of Israel, as they were in the days of David and Solomon, would return upon them. The prophecy of Ezekiel would be literally fulfilled, and the Lord would bring them and place them again in their own land, in the bosom of the green hills of Judea.

Another passage frequently quoted by the advocates of a literal resurrection of the body, is from the Book of Job. "And though," says the patriarch, "after my skin worms destroy my body, yet in my flesh shall I see God." The true meaning of this passage is easily discovered, if we embrace in our view the whole drift of the afflicted man's argument. He had been repeatedly charged with a want of integrity. His friends and enemies had told him that his sins were the cause of his misfortunes. In his heart Job knew this was false. He had faith that his past course would soon receive a vindication, and that his integrity would be proved and acknowledged. The harmony of the entire Book of Job depends upon taking this view. The passage, then, may be paraphrased thus, representing Job as speaking to his friends, and saying, "You suppose I am forsaken of God on account of my sins. It is not true. To be sure I have not the means at present to disprove your position, or establish mine; but I believe that, though I am now suffering, and though I may suffer still more, even until the worms eat my skin, and then eat into my body, yet in my flesh, on the earth, and before I die, I shall see, and you will see, my vindication." We need not add that his faith, that particular faith, was rewarded. God did appear; he reproved his enemies, approved Job, and blessed him; so that "the last days of Job were better than the first."

The argument for the resurrection of the old body, particle for particle, is also supported, it is claimed, by the fact that Christ's natural body was the one raised from the tomb.

Two suppositions are legitimately deduced from Christ's literal resurrection: either that it was designed to be a seal of his commission, a manifest miracle, to confirm to the world his divinity, to reassure the wavering faith of the disciples, and, being witnessed by more than five hundred different persons, to have vast influence in spreading Christianity during the first century; or else it was designed to be an exact type of our own resurrection.

Which of these two suppositions is the more reasonable? Do the Scriptures, by word or hint, suggest that Christ's resurrection was a type of ours? Can his resurrection in any proper sense be an exact type? Were the most important conditions of such a resurrection fulfilled by him? He was but three days in the grave, while we may slumber there for ages. He did not see corruption, while we are to become dust and ashes. But even if this difficulty could be removed, — though it cannot, — would it not seem far more reasonable, and infinitely more grand, to look upon our Saviour's resurrection as the seal of his divinity, and the first fruits, not of the resurrection, but "of them that slept"? Where, then, is Christ's physical body? it may be asked. Did it not ascend to heaven? Did not the disciples witness its ascension? Is he not there to-day? Flesh and blood are not there! "Five *bleeding* wounds he bears," is Watts's poetry, not Paul's Epistle to the Corinthians. Christ's glorified body was not the body shown to Thomas; save at the transfiguration, it was not seen by any of his disciples until after his ascension. It was then seen. Stephen saw it, crowned with dazzling splendor, on the day of his martyrdom; Paul saw it, above the glory of the sun, on the road to Damascus; John saw it in Patmos; great multitudes of dying Christians have seen it. Nay, we believe the *valley* is dark and lonely to him only who knows not Christ. But this glorious body is not precisely the one which walked to Emmaus, or met Mary at the tomb. Where is that body? We do not know where it is. The record says nothing about it; and beyond the record we cannot go. We might say that the fleshy covering was annihilated, or that it underwent a gradual transformation, or was cast off, and the gross materials flung back to earth. But it is only *safe* to say that He has a glorious body, which is now the type of our resurrection body, without flesh, without blood, without spot, without blemish; the embodiment of beauty, the home of truth, the splendid tabernacle of the Holy Ghost, the perfect manifestation of the Godhead, and the likeness of every child that is born into the kingdom of heaven. With a hope based upon such a view, we are not of all men most miserable, for through this fact, as through the gospel of Christ, life and immortality are brought to light. May we not, then, conclude that Christ's resurrection was designed for a seal of his ministry, rather than an exact type of our resurrection; that it furnishes for us the hope that as he lived after death, so also shall we live after death; and that our resurrection body will not be the present, but one like his — infinitely better than the present, of infinitely greater capacity, and of sublimer beauty?

This interpretation of the passages in question relieves us at once from the necessity of employing in our reconstruction the old particles of matter which have lost their identity, which have been organized and reorganized again and again, which have entered into other bodies, into the vegetable and animal kingdoms, into the atmosphere, and the clouds that float above us. These old particles, that have become diseased, and worn out, and cast off, if our interpretation be correct, are not the material which shall constitute the body that is to be, but new particles of a new material, which is capable of bestowing surprising activity and marvellous endurance, will enter into the resurrection organism, and render it subject to none of the ills or accidents of life.

The Connection between the Present and the Fu

ture Bodies.—Another fact, clearly brought out by the apostle, and supported by the figure employed by our Saviour, is, that though the present and future bodies differ in certain respects, there exists, nevertheless, an important connection between them. Unless we admit this, the force of the illustration, which implies a vital connection between the seed and the plant, is lost. The kernel of grain, as it falls into the earth, looks as hard and lifeless as a pebble in the street. But, by resting in the soil, moistened by showers, and warmed by the sun, it sends forth its shoots, its blade, its flower, and then other fruit like itself. "Except," said our Saviour, "a corn of wheat fall into the ground and die, it abideth alone; but if it die, it bringeth forth much fruit." Why death is ordinarily necessary to develop this connection, or what the connection is, we cannot tell. We know the facts, and here we rest.

Take another illustration. The grub which is to-day stripping the tree of its verdure, feeding upon the most ordinary kind of food, creeping slowly from limb to limb, or crawling upon the ground, to-morrow will enter a state of seeming death; will wind itself up in a kind of shroud, be concealed as in a coffin, and buried in the earth. A month later, it will come forth from its sepulchre, no longer to lie on the earth, or crawl upon the branch. Clad in beauty, it will traverse the fields of air and light, feed upon the sweetest flowers that bloom by the wayside, fluttering in our path, and sipping nectar as from the hand of God. The connection which exists between that torpor of death and subsequent life we do not see.

We only know that this seeming death is necessary in order to develop the connection between the old life and the new one. The seed and the grub both follow the laws of their being — a law which is universal. Organized matter in one form, becoming disorganized, is reorganized into other forms, which exist under new conditions. In view of such a law, it is by no means difficult to admit the fact, that if the old body has in it the germ of a new one, — and the apostle and our Saviour both teach that it has, — then from the old body, at the command of God, will develop a new one; whether the old one be buried in the sea or on the land, it matters not. We must bear in mind, however, that this will not be, strictly speaking, a resurrection *of* the old body, though the expression may be allowed, but is, more properly, a resurrection *from* the old body. The term "resurrection of the body" never occurs in the Scriptures, and the term "resurrection *from* the dead" is more frequently employed than "resurrection *of* the dead." These expressions are suggestive, and call for something more than a casual examination of the point under consideration. We dwell upon it a moment longer.

Some physiologists tell us that the materials of the human body change every seven years. Others say they change several times yearly. The periods are thus made to vary from a few months to several years. But are there not certain facts which go to qualify or correct both estimates? Is there not something in the body which men have overlooked; something, perhaps, which the dissecting knife has not yet found, nor the skilful microscope detected? May not a particle of vaccine virus, or a score of different contagious diseases, produce such an alteration in our physical organization, that no number of physiological changes can destroy their effect? Is it not true that the bite of a rabid dog may not result in hydrophobia for twenty years, and then terminate fatally? May not a mother bear a child which in youth appears to be in perfect health, but who, perhaps, at twenty years of age, dies of some disease inherited from the mother, of which she herself may subsequently die? From these and other facts we conclude that there remains an essential substance in man, which does not appear and then disappear, like the gross material of the body, but which remains undisturbed through life. The anatomical autocrat must again wipe his spectacles. There are other substances than skin and bones. The world is awaiting a new and improved science of physiology. But in the mean time is it unreasonable to assume that this abiding essence is to the physical body what the vital germ is to the wheat? May there not be in the human body formative, or progressive, or unfolding energies, as in the kernel of corn? May there not be, inwrapped in this inner mantle of our unchanging and adhering physical identity, forces, which, under certain favorable conditions, as in case of the seed, shall predominate over the conservative powers of the body, and develop a future spiritual organization? Does not the existence of forces presuppose organism? Do not the formative forces sometimes show themselves in the grain while standing in the field? Are there not blades which appear on the ripened stalk, under the influence of heat and moisture, before the sickle has done its work? If so, there is nothing unreasonable in the belief that the dead of the earth and of the sea, and that those who are alive upon the earth in the last day, shall be clad in the new garments God shall give them.

> "The wonder is not half so great
> Of ours, as is the rising of the wheat."

Such, then, is the scriptural doctrine of the resurrection from the dead, as it is especially set forth in this important passage from Corinthians. Whatever may be the difficulties surrounding the subject, however mysterious the questions that spring from it, we are to accept it, not because it is difficult, not because it is mysterious, but because God says it is true; and that is enough. Whatever the Bible teaches on this or any other doctrine is true — true yesterday, true to-day, and forever true. The believing Christian standing upon this rock is stronger than the whole world standing upon any other foundation. The unbelieving world is, to-day, unstable as the sea. The needle must point to an inspired revelation, as to its only star of hope. When it does, the mariner is safe, though the clouds and night are dark.

Is the Scriptural Theory of the Resurrection rational? — The intuitive demands of the soul underlie all true and all known theories of philosophy. That we must ultimately be guided in our investigations and conclusions by inner and hidden impulses and desires, if not by special inspiration, is a principle admitted by the rationalism of Germany, as well as by the radicalism of America. With this admitted principle of investigation before us,—nay, *furnished* us,—we may apply it to the subject in hand.

Can there be found anything in human desires, instincts, or reason, which opposes the first deduction from the passage under discussion—that the soul is to be embodied in the future world? Is it not true that there is an instinctive and positive demand, in every human nature, for a body to dwell in? Who can think of the future life with pleasure, without thinking of it as organized? The idea of a purely spiritual existence, unembodied, thus to last forever, and complete its destiny in the universe of God, is painful and repulsive. The sceptic, whatever his views of revelation may be, unconsciously clings to the union of soul and body. The natural idea we have of a disembodied spirit is that of a wandering, restless ghost. As naturally as we breathe, we seize upon the idea of a home for, and an embodiment of, the soul—one that is perfect, and under complete control. Such a condition, during our future existence, can alone satisfy our desires. Any other condition would never have been dreamed of, but for enmity to the truth, and a false interpretation of the Scriptures.

But more than this: human nature, to be complete, must have some kind of organism. Human nature is the necessary union of both body and spirit.

All believe that the highest possible happiness is in store for some part, at least, of the human family. That condition cannot be attained, in any case, without an embodiment. Our future perfection and happiness do not depend upo the change of our nature into something unlike itself, not upon its absorption into the Deity, not upon its development into divinities, but simply upon its completion. Revelation entertains no other view. Perfect humanity, or human nature, and our happiness, is secured, and in that way only. Thus, upon high and strictly rational grounds, we may assert that a bodily organism in the future life is a positive necessity of our nature. It is a revelation, not from the Bible alone, but from every human soul. Those who go back of the Hebrew for an original text will find this doctrine a transcript of the divine mind. It is as vital to our growth and perfect development as the exercise of any other law of our being. The application of this principle can be carried a step farther. Not merely *a* body, but a *new* body, is desired. The old one will not answer. We intuitively demand a body which shall be free from the gross materials of the present. We instinctively look for an improvement, and could not feel satisfied if we thought the same accidents awaited us in the future life which throng our path in this. We would change tenements rather than be at the trouble and expense of moving out only to move back again. The passion of the race runs to repairs — to new and better buildings. We look for a body in which no hidden disease, as in the present one, shall lurk, or can lurk. We expect to be free from anxiety lest death shall spring upon us at every unguarded moment. We desire a body which the heat of summer and the cold of winter are alike powerless in affecting; one which can withstand the encroachments of chill and fever, of weakness and age; one which shall continue upon an endless and deathless journey without pain or weariness.

An Organism between Death and the Resurrection. — This involves an inquiry which does not necessarily belong to this subject, but which deserves attention. If the soul demands an organism in which to dwell, if it does not lose its consciousness at death, and if the resurrection does not take place until the end of the world, what is man's condition in this intermediate period or state? Various theories are advocated. Some writers resort to an unconscious intermediate state. Others claim that the resurrection takes place at death; others, again, that the soul is conscious, but is reduced to "pure essence," or a "metaphysical entity;" a "substance uncompounded, without parts and without place." The first and second class of views are unscriptural. We cannot, therefore, entertain them. The third is unsatisfactory and meaningless.

Those philosophical terms, to most men, denote nothing but nonsense. If they mean anything, it is, that the soul, at death, goes nowhere, and becomes nothing. We reject all this. The soul is either nothing or something. If it is something, and not infinite, it must have a definite location. If it has location, and if it is the centre of natural or supernatural forces, it must have a definite natural or supernatural organism. The material is unimportant. Furnish us with that substance which results from the correlation of galvanic forces, and we can produce from it a galvanic man who can walk. Let God breathe into him a soul, and he is complete.

The spiritualistic notion of "circles" of dead friends revolving over us in some kind of gassy media is intolerable.

How refreshing it is to turn to the Scriptures! The impression they leave is, that the condition of the dead is purely objective. There is nothing unreal or spectral. Dreamy and shadowy phantoms find no place in the Scriptures. The organisms of the dead in the intermediate state are as real as those of angels. We are no less organized after than before the resurrection. Let us have done with spiritualistic and anti-scriptural notions, which reduce the universe to gas, and our deceased friends to atmospheric phenomena. We are not to become ghosts and nothings. Such representations are hideous. We escape from them as from shadows at nightfall. When we die we shall see friends, and know them as certainly before as after the resurrection.

Is not this statement confirmed by the strongest evidence which the subject can possibly receive? When the eyes of mortals are closing in death, do they not frequently seem to open upon sweet and well-known faces? Do not dear and familiar names sometimes break from their closing lips? The welcome of friends long since dead is heard in the heavenly world before the farewells are hushed in this. There is a moment when the physical organisms of this world are seen in company with the spiritual organisms of the other world, and where the blending voices of both worlds are audible.

But if this spiritual organism be so complete, why the need of new resurrection bodies? What if we do not know? God says we are to have them; that is enough. We take his word for it. It may be that the dead can better communicate (impressionally) with the living by means of the intermediate organism. The resurrection body might preclude this happy ministry. But the communication among the dead may be more perfect through a resurrection body. Until that is received, the dead may remain in an anteroom, listening to the splendid music of the inner and larger hall, without fully participating in its realities. They are consciously happy or consciously miserable. The only question is one of degree and relation. But when probation ends, when the dead are no longer needed as ministering or tempting spirits, when the roll of human history shall be completed, then human nature will receive this additional completion. The instinctive demands of the soul will be fully gratified. This will take place in the general resurrection, at the end of the world. Science interposes no objections to these views. It is our friend. In its more recent deductions respecting the correlation and conservation of forces, it kneels before revelation and embraces it. Science does not claim that the only *substances* are those which are seen and handled. There is something besides rocks and gravel-beds. There are bodies terrestrial and bodies celestial. There are bodies natural, bodies spiritual, and bodies spiritualized. These may or may not have the properties of matter, and yet be the most tangible substances in the universe. On scientific grounds we may not be able fully to solve these wonderful questions. The facts they involve none can deny. Revelation discloses them. Upon this we plant our feet, and await, in joyful expectation, the "day and hour."

The Connection between the Natural and the Spiritual Body, Rational. There is a deep philosophy underlying the impulse that prompts us to visit the resting-place of departed friends. We have embodied the true theory in our word *cemetery*, meaning a sleeping-place. We instinctively feel that there is a value in the old body above its visible associations. No other piece of clay is like that which has encircled a dear friend. There is something which underlies these human impulses and sentiments. We desire a pleasant lot in the graveyard. We are choice in its decorations. It seems fitting to have the church and the graveyard identical. We feel that it is a kind of misfortune to have our friends buried in the sea, where we cannot sit by their graves. At the prospect of our own death, we select the spot for our burial. "I should like," says Burke, "that my dust should mingle with *kindred* dust; the good old expression, *family burying-ground*, has something pleasing in it." These natural desires and expressions of the soul, and the elegant decorations of our cemeteries, contain more deep and pure philosophy, on the subject of the resurrection, than all the unbelieving professors of Cambridge, on this or the other side of the sea, ever dreamed of.

"There's a narrow ridge in the graveyard
  Would scarce stay a child in his race;
But to me and my thought it is wider
  Than the star-sown vague of space."

But why, unless there exists a connection, though an inexplicable one, between the "sleeping-ground" and our future existence? Unless the germ and treasure of another life lies hidden beneath the sod, or slumbers within the tomb, the entire school of Renan may as well drop their pens and seal their lips; for the most sublime and the most reliable foundation of all truth and philosophy set forth by them has no basis whatever.

But how satisfying, as well as inspiring, is it to find in the book of God so pleasing a doctrine so fully and beautifully disclosed! Is not this doctrine satisfactory in its details even? Think you we shall fail in a desire, at last, to revisit this old, gray world, just before its final conflagration? It has witnessed our trials and our tears, our pleasures and joys. Here have been our birthplace, the home of our childhood, the fields where we have labored for Christ, and met the hard discipline of life. This is the world which holds our bodies and those of our friends. How can this earth, wherever in the universe we may have wandered, fail of exciting our interest? Would it not be a pleasant experience, as well as a dictate of philosophy, if, in the graveyard of ourselves and friends, our spirits should at last meet to bid an eternal and ever-present welcome to each other, and a final farewell to the crumbling world and the crumbling body? Would it not be well, as the old world passes away, and the new Jerusalem descends from God out of heaven upon the earth, prepared as a bride adorned for her husband, if we together shall triumphantly awake in the bodily likeness of our Redeemer, and enter upon a destiny ever-glorious, never-ending? The response of every heart must be, "Amen, so let it be."

> "Awake, thou wintry earth:
> Fling off thy sadness!
> Fair vernal flowers, laugh forth
> Your ancient gladness.
> We sleep, we rise."

The Future Body will be the Perfect Expression of the Character formed in the Present Life. — In the language of revelation, "God giveth it a body as it hath pleased him, and to every seed *his own*," or appropriate "body." The body is to be perfectly adapted to the character. This condition involves a very simple principle of our being. The present body, if we may be allowed the language, constantly seeks to give expression to the soul that inhabits it. The formative energy within us, which is an attribute of the soul, taking the food we eat, by laws of digestion, circulation, and secretion, forms a body which resembles the inner man. It is a natural and mechanical adjustment of principles and parts. A good man looks like a good man, and a bad man looks like a bad man. This is the tendency. In process of time, the tendency is sure to show itself. Persons thrown much in one another's society, who remain on terms of intimacy and harmony, as, for instance, a husband and wife, will come to be alike, and then to look alike. These tendencies of expression must be very active and powerful, for the soul appears in and stamps itself upon every feature of the face, and upon every member of the body. It not only flashes from the eye, but shows itself in the foot and on the hand. The shape of the finger, to a detective, will indicate the pickpocket. The shape of the nose decided Napoleon in the selection of his generals. These are the laws of our physical organization. Is it not rational to believe that these same laws will, in the future life, give to every seed its own and appropriate body? God has few laws that are dead letters. Our characters will eternally and inevitably impress themselves upon everything with which they come in contact. The whole man will appear. Every thought he has cherished, as well as every governing principle of his life, will show itself, must show itself, as the soul takes to itself the spiritualized and etherealized matter, and builds up, out of the seed sown, the new and eternal tabernacle. We shall know and we shall be known. The whole story of life will be told, whether we will or not, and whether we are good or bad. The best man will look like the best; the worst man will look like the worst. If we are the children of God, that fact will be stamped upon the future body in characters of living light and beauty. All who have the image of Christ in the heart will have their new bodies fashioned after Christ's most glorious body. Every child of heaven must, from the necessity of things, in the metropolis of God, have Christ's name written on the forehead. He will have his stamp of royalty, his insignia of office, this ancient coat-of-arms of God's family. He is in the line of kings and priests. These laws of natural development will not be impeded by disease, accident, premature death, or old age, as in this life. The bodies of all the redeemed, old and young, perfect or deformed, in this world, will in the future life be completed. "But the prattling child, whose life was nipped in the bud, may I not see it as it was," asks the fond mother? The question is well. But what of the youthful mother, who dies and leaves a child who lives to old age? Is it the infant, or the bent and gray old man, who is to meet and call her mother? A husband dies at five and twenty, and leaves his fair young wife, who lives on five and fifty years. Will he call that weary, wrinkled woman, whose whitened locks bespeak years enough to be his grandam, wife? Completion and perfection will be the law. Through all these years that wife has talked of their meeting in another world, as if her husband were dead but yesterday; and separated from her former self, she has ever been thinking of the happiness of that comely girl who seemed to have died with him. It is *completion* in every instance which will give most joy in heaven. The impeded laws and undeveloped tendencies will then bring forth perfect fruit. The dwarf and infant will grow to manhood. The healing power of Christ will make the lame walk, the blind see, and the old young. The deranged mind will be clothed, as in earlier days, with love and innocence. Every one will retain his own and old identity. Upon every feature of those who are redeemed will glow the radiance and serenity of heaven. Each will wear the full and perfect image and superscription of the Master of the Feast.

But another principle is equally true. The character of the wicked will be written upon his features with startling distinctness. There will then be no cloak to cover him. He will be destitute of the power of a deceptive smile, and of that false pretence which now subserves his selfish purposes. All the hate, all the remorse, all the disgrace, and all the crafty cunning of the soul will find, must find, perfect expression. The wretch will look like a wretch. The vicious will look vicious. The sensual and devilish man in this world will look like a sensual and devilish man in the next world. He could not help it if he would. The judgment books are fully written, and in a legible hand. They are open to the most public inspection. Between the sheep and the goats a child will be able to distinguish. The man without the wedding garment may, will, be speechless. Conceit and bluster will have no place there. Judgment will begin in the bodily tabernacle. Over all will brood the sorrow, which at last "biteth like a serpent and stingeth like an adder." All know the refuge: let all accept it.

THE NATURE AND OPERATIONS OF CONSCIENCE.

"And when Herod would have brought him forth, the same night Peter was *sleeping* between two soldiers, bound with two chains; and the keepers before the door kept the prison." *Acts* xii. 6.

"At that time Herod the tetrarch heard of the fame of Jesus, and said unto his servants, This is John the Baptist; he is risen from the dead." *Matthew* xiv. 1, 2.

"Yet still there whispers the small voice within,
  Heard through gain's silence, and o'er glory's din;
Whatever creed be taught, or land be trod,
  Man's conscience is the oracle of God."

BYRON.

"O treacherous Conscience! while she seems to sleep
On rose and myrtle, lulled with siren song,
. . . . . .
The sly informer minutes every fault,
And her dread diary with horror fills;
. . . . . .
Unnoted notes each moment misapplied;
In leaves more durable than leaves of brass
Writes our whole history; which Death shall read
In every pale delinquent's private ear,
And Judgment publish; publish to more worlds
Than this; and endless age in groans resound."

YOUNG.

"We cannot shake off the conviction that there is a divine, as well as human, element in conscience."

JAMES WALKER.

"The divine image in man may be burned, but cannot be burned out." ST. BERNARD.

III.

THE NATURE AND OPERATIONS OF CONSCIENCE.

SOME philologist has remarked that "a language is often wiser, not merely than the vulgar, but even than the wisest of those who speak it; being like amber in its efficacy to circulate the electric spirit of truth, it is like amber in embalming the relics of ancient wisdom." Granting that language is a divine gift to men, these embalmed treasures become invaluable. Every primitive root holds the germ of a God-given truth.

Nature of Conscience. — Applying the above principle to "conscience," some writers * have placed it among the most solemn words in the English language. That which it represents is seen to be something more than an ordinary faculty of the mind. It has to do with what every other faculty overlooks, and is linked in its operations with something outside and entirely independent of the human soul.

Before developing this thought, we may note certain

* Among whom is Trench.

verbal definitions which have grown out of an observation of the workings of conscience, and which may aid us in arriving at a correct understanding of it.

"Conscience," says John Foster, "communicates with something mysteriously great, which is without the soul, and above it, and everywhere." Chatfield calls it "Heaven's silent oracle." Young speaks of it as "a God in man." Dr. South says, "It is the eye of the soul." Robert Burton describes it as "an epitomy of hell." The Egyptians represent it in their hieroglyphics by a mill which grinds our souls with the remembrance of past sin. Ammianus, a Greek epigrammatist, describes it as the queen of causes and moderator of things, which pulls down the proud, raises up and encourages the good. The ancient poets universally call it Nemesis — the avenging fate which sooner or later overtakes the guilty and brings them back to justice. These definitions, which attach to conscience something outside of man, accord with those operations of our own souls which inevitably result from the consciousness of a right or a wrong action. All men feel, when condemned by the conscience, that they are more than self-condemned. No one can say that conscience is anything less than the normal working of an attribute of the soul, put into operation by the presence or approach of the Infinite Judge. It is the representative of an invisible ruler. It furnishes alarms and apprehensions which, on natural grounds, are unaccountable. "It is a dark unknown,"* which threatens men with death when they have done evil.

* Blair.

There is a controlling element involved in the conscience, which we can neither see nor resist. Guilty men are met by an omnipresent danger. They find in every object something to dread. They hate solitudes and midnights. There is no other faculty which compels man to recognize God; no other faculty beholds in him the avenger of guilt. In the conscience God seems to walk the earth in his splendor and purity. No man thinks of approving himself on account of the sublime and blameless decisions of his conscience. They result from no virtue in him — at least so he feels. This is remarkable, unless the verdicts of conscience are not man's, but God's.

Though there were a thousand divine voices heard within men, urging to obedience, they might, for all that, be a thousand-fold the children of evil, and have nothing to indicate that their spiritual ruin from the fall was not complete from turret to lowest foundation. If, however, there exists this duplex character in our spiritual being, if that which seems to speak so well for us, and which has led some to suppose that our ruin was only partial, be the divine voice, then all phenomenal and perplexing questions disappear. Our fall is as entire as if the voice were never heard. If this be true, the age of patriarchs returns. The voice which spoke to Adam in the garden, and to Cain in the field, continues to communicate with us, as distinctly, though not as audibly, as with them. The "*sun*" of "*suncidesis*" and the "*con*" of "*conscire*" become, not a knowing with one's self, but a knowing with some one else outside one's self. All feel, if there be such another "*knower*," that he is

God. If conscience is that faculty through which the soul holds direct communications with the divine, as it communicates with the past through memory, and with the present through the senses (which none deny), then may we not assume that those feelings of approval or disapproval which follow the decision of the judgment, that we have intended to do a right or a wrong action, result chiefly or solely from the direct approval or disapproval of the omniscient One? Certainly no other hypothesis can harmonize so many existing discrepancies respecting our moral sentiments and faculties. What else except this union of the divine and human in the conscience could exercise such dreadful power? Admit this union, and no wonder that society is made a terror and solitude a hell to wicked men. How kingly and supreme is conscience! No condition can depose it, nor bars bolt it out. It is able to pierce through an armed battalion, make discordant the sweetest music, tear off any mask, and dash every smile from the face. It instantly comprehends any and every point of law; asks no authority, but is itself authority. Its accusations are never noisy, but always terrible. It plants a girdle of thorns about a man's heart, and holds it there. It can make what Byron calls "a hell in man." All the opiates in the world cannot quiet it. It breaks up the harmony of the social circle in man by waging a civil war. It can silence all outside congratulations, and drown all friendly adulations. No king can look it out of countenance, or warrior conquer it. How accurately and impartially it judges! It masters completely the man of guilt, holding him down, grinding him down, overawing and overwhelming him.

Can this wonderful principle in man be merely a sentiment of the soul, or nothing but the normal operation of an intellectual faculty? That which gives such awful force to the word, and such overwhelming effect to the operations of conscience; which prompts the entire race to do right, and restrains them from the wrong; which bestows such perfect peace upon the innocent, and sends such fearful agitation and condemnation into the hearts of the guilty, — is no mental or mortal power: that startling voice we hear, is God's.

The Universality and Constancy of Conscience. — If an omnipresent spirit and the most ordinary degree of intelligence are the only prerequisite conditions upon which an act of conscience necessarily depends, its universality and constancy must become at once a necessity. These characteristics of conscience are also attributed to it by all speculative views, and by universal experience.

Some nations have been in possession of what others have not. Savages are often destitute of taste, refinement, and even of the rudiments of civilization; but no nation, and no individual of any nation, have ever yet been found destitute of conscience. Like death, it assails the civilized and uncivilized; monarchs as well as peasants. Among all classes it makes its clear distinction between just and unjust, between duty and crime. It is coeval with human nature. The brethren of Joseph, three thousand five hundred years ago, were affected concerning their conduct by the same feelings as those of which we are now conscious. "And they said one to another, We are verily guilty concerning our brother, in that we saw the anguish of his soul, when he besought us, and we would not hear; therefore is this distress come upon us. And Reuben answered them, saying, Spake I not unto you, saying, Do not sin against the child; and ye would not hear? therefore behold also his blood is required." (Gen. xlii. 21, 22.) Cicero gave the world one of the best descriptions of conscience ever written. It is from his "De Republica." "There exists a true law, pervading all minds. . . . This law cannot be annulled or overruled; no senate can loose us from it; no jurist can explain it away. It is not one law at Athens and another at Rome, one at present and another hereafter, but one law perpetual and immutable."

How forcibly this voice of two thousand years ago, from the corrupt court of Rome, confirms the words of the apostle, "They that have not the law are a law unto themselves." That is, with or without a written revelation, there is a divine law — rather a divine *lawgiver* — in the breast of every responsible agent; one who approves if we obey, who condemns if we disobey. It is a law which is equally binding upon Greek and Roman, Jew and Gentile, Barbarian, Scythian, bond and free.

Its universality, though more apparent, is no more certain, than the *constancy* or *unintermittency* of its action. No act passes unnoticed by conscience. Sooner or later, human conduct receives its sanction or condemnation. We know that many men appear never to be troubled by conscience, who evidently ought to be. These are only apparent exceptions to the constancy of conscience, which so often meet and deceive us. There is a world of indifference about us, which is only affectation. There is a world of mirth, which is only art. There is music without harmony, and laughter without joy. There is a frivolous life, a turbulent state of society, which seems to carry upon its surface confidence and contentment, but which is only a "fearful looking forward to a fiery indignation." When least serious and most indifferent, many men could best express their heart-feelings in the words of Dryden, —

> "Here, here it lies: a lump of lead by day,
> And in my short, distracted slumbers,
> The hag that haunts my dreams."

We often say that men stupefy their consciences, or sear them as with a hot iron. Some very wicked men seem to go round their conscience, hide from it, laugh and sleep in spite of it. But such lulls do not last forever. The soldier misses his camp-companion most when the tumult of battle is over. Like a judicious parent, it is God's way to reserve the worst punishment until after all excitement is past. There is an awful power in a calm but temporary reserve. When business is driven the hardest, conscience keeps on posting her books all the same; every item is noted; and on a quiet day they are thrown open for inspection. "I have my serious hours," is every honest man's confession. "The wind bloweth where (and when) it listeth; thou canst not tell whence it cometh and whither it goeth." These occasional — sometimes distant, sometimes indistinct — movements of the conscience-faculty are just as real and positive remonstrances of the Holy Ghost, delivered to the soul against a sinful course of life, as if spoken from the sky in a voice of thunder.

One element of conscience is the consciousness of moral action. It must therefore be intensely and constantly alive to every moral intention. Though seared, it has its quick. The Infinite One speaks, and the crust is broken. Solomon calls conscience, for this reason, "the candle of the Lord." When lighted, no human act can extinguish it, though it be put for a time under a bed or in a measure. There is for man no solitude in the universe. Man cannot hide from himself or from the Holy Spirit. Conscience is like the eye of a good portrait: it will follow us wherever we go. It is an eye-witness, in the words of the apostle, "ever bearing witness." Unless there is a change of life, it will at last become the full, clear, intense, resplendent, and piercing eye of the Godhead.

Conscience the Universal and Ultimate Rule of Human Action.— That our conduct must, in all cases, conform to the dictates of conscience, is a principle admitted by all, and one which is necessarily implied in the view we have taken of its nature. If it is the direct command and decision of the Holy Spirit to the soul, there can, of course, be nothing beyond, though there may be something parallel with it.

The conscience is plainly distinguishable from the moral sense, or faculty. It is not the educator of the race. Our education comes from experience, from men, and from books. Conscience never presumes to tell a man what is right, or what is wrong, in the abstract. It is not supposed even to recognize any distinction respecting what is right, or what is wrong, in themselves considered. It presupposes, on the other hand, that every man knows himself what is right and what is wrong. Its plea, and its only plea, to man is, "Try to do what you think is right." Its only condemnation is, "You have not tried to do what you believe to be right." Guilt can be charged upon us only at that point. At that point it is charged upon us. So far, then, as the ultimate rule of action is concerned, it makes no difference how ignorant or how wise we are. It is immaterial whether we are in heathen or Christian lands; with or without the law; devotees to the pope, or Mahomet. Paul has clearly expressed the correct view: "For there is no respect of persons with God. For as many as have sinned without law shall also perish without law; and as many as have sinned in the law shall be judged by the law (for not the hearers of the law are just before God, but the doers of the law shall be justified. For when the Gentiles, which have not the law, do by nature the things contained in the law, these, having not the law, are a law unto themselves. Which show the work of the law written in their hearts, their conscience also bearing witness, and their thoughts the meanwhile accusing, or else excusing one another), in the day when God shall judge the secrets of men by Jesus Christ according to my gospel." (Rom. ii. 11–17.)

Independent of the Bible, then, conscience, so far

as our conduct is concerned, echoes the oracle of the God-Spirit. Independent of the apostles, it binds and it frees us. Many admit this, but pervert it. They assert that man has in conscience all that is necessary for his guidance, and that a written revelation is, therefore, superfluous. So far as the moral quality of our conduct is concerned, it is true we have, without a written revelation, all that is necessary. We have within us the universal and *ultimate rule of action;* but we have not within us the *ultimate rule or standard of right.* We can discover the moral quality of our action through this union of the divine and human understanding in the soul of man; but our knowledge of what is absolutely right, in itself considered, must be decided upon and disclosed by the Spirit Divine, independent of our co operation. This is a knowledge which we cannot discern, and which God has never whispered to the race save through inspired men. The telling us to do right is not the telling of what is right. How wisely these things are ordered! No one can say that the Creator has required overmuch, or that he has burdened the soul with complicated questions.

A sinless life has not the least embarrassment in the divine economy. If we follow conscience, we shall not sin, though we may do what is in itself wrong; we may do wrong conscientiously, not knowing that it is wrong; but that is not sin.

It is at this point we discover we have need, for our highest good, of something besides a universal and ultimate rule of action; that is, a universal and ultimate rule of right also. The perfection of the race requires both conscience and a written revelation. Remove the controlling power of conscience, and we undermine the foundation on which revelation builds its power of commanding the heart. Remove revelation, and we are left in darkness. When men follow both these voices, or both combined in one, then they cease to sin, and cease to do wrong likewise. When the apostle was arguing that "if the Gentiles do by nature the things contained in the law, they are a law unto themselves," he anticipated the very question that would be asked, and answered at the same time all the objections of those who see no necessity for a written revelation. "What advantage, then, hath the Jew?" is the question he expected would be asked, and the one that is often asked. Thus he answered it: "Much every way; chiefly because that unto them were committed the oracles of God." That is, they who have the Scriptures have the ultimate standard of right. They have this in addition to the universal and ultimate rule of action, which is the conscience.

It is sometimes asked, Why send missionaries to the heathen? What advantage is gained? Will they sin less? May be not. May there not be as much sin in nominally Christian as in pagan lands? Possibly—perhaps *more*. What advantage then? Much every way; chiefly this: that when men obey conscience, or when they try not to sin, with an open Bible in their hands, they will do right, as well as not sin. It saves the experience of burning the hand to a crisp, in order to learn that fire is hot. Conscience simply leaves the man on trial to do what he *thinks* is right.

Revelation puts him on trial to do what is right. Conscience is God's school-*master*, whose mission is to frown or smile. Revelation is his school-*instructor*.

Give the Bible to the world, and the Spartan mother would no longer teach her son to steal, that he might become a more strategic warrior, but would teach him the love of patriotism, based upon pure and high principles. It would teach the Hindoo mother that it is rather her duty to educate her female infant, than throw it into the Ganges. It would teach Paul that the suppression of heresy is right, but that it must be done in the spirit of charity, and with a bloodless battle, — with the sword of the Spirit, rather than the sword of Damascus dripping with innocent blood. It would doubtless add to their responsibilities, but it would add to their intelligence also. Were all men fools, there would be no sin. But would that condition be a satisfactory gain? The real gain to the heathen in possessing the Bible is this — they would know how to banish from their lands ignorance, superstition, and corruption. They would plant in their places the principles, or the germs, of the purest freedom and civilization. Yes, this neglected Bible brings much, every way, with it of good and of blessing to the wandering, suffering race of man.

Theodore Parker has honestly and well remarked that we can "trace its path across the world, from the day of Pentecost to this day. As a river springs up in the heart of a sandy continent, having its father in the skies, and its birthplace in distant, unknown mountains, — as the stream rolls on, enlarging itself, making in that arid waste a belt of verdure, wherever it turns its way, creating palm groves and fertile plains, where the smoke of the cottager curls up at eventide, and marble cities send the gleam of their splendor far into the sky, — such has been the course of the Bible on the earth. . . . There is not a boy on all the hills of New England; not a girl born in the filthiest cellar which disgraces a capital in Europe, and cries to God against the barbarism of modern civilization; not a boy nor a girl in all Christendom through, but their lot is made better by that great book."

Let other lands feel its refreshing and saving influences! A good and desirable, as well as an innocent condition of society results not necessarily from a high state of civilization, not from thorough scholastic training, not from an active conscience even, but from acquaintance with and obedience to the written word of inspiration. Observe, this statement does not detract in the least from the former. As a rule of action, the conscience remains supreme. Between it and the Bible there never has been, and never can be, a pitched battle, except in the brain of a lunatic. We must conclude, therefore, that with revelation or without it, all men are innocent or guilty. When they pass from this world to the next, they pass with absolute innocence or under absolute guilt, as they have obeyed or disobeyed their consciences. Before this tribunal we are to stand. This book contains our life or death sentence.

The Normal Operations of Conscience. — It was midnight. Arrangements had been made to execute an eminent apostle of Christ. He himself had every reason to believe that his last night had come. The strong guard, the delay until after the Passover, the previous execution of James, the delight it occasioned the Jews, and the popularity it gave to Herod,—all pointed in the same fatal direction. There were scenes of excitement throughout Jerusalem. Herod was congratulating himself upon the opportunity of securing additional popularity. The Jews were rejoicing that one of their ablest opponents was to be overthrown. The Christians of the city were gathered together, praying and bewailing the fate of their leader. Summerville has graphically represented that the upper and lower worlds were filled with intensest interest. But the doomed man, where was he? Tossing from one side of his couch to the other? O, no. Rushing about his cell screeching with agony; clinging to the bars and looking from the grated windows? O, no. He was sleeping as soundly as he was wont during a tranquil night in his fishing-boat on the Sea of Galilee. At the usual hour he had laid off his outer garments, loosened his girdle, put off his sandals from his feet, composed his mind, and was awaiting God's pleasure. It was not stolid indifference, but divine composure; a representation in statuary of the prayer, "Thy will be done." It was not a fitful sleep, but the sound repose of childhood. The bright light did not wake him, nor the presence of the angel. Not until the strange visitant touched his side, nay, smote upon it, did he awake to consciousness. Must not such presence of mind, such composure, have had the most substantial basis in the universe? It had. The Holy Ghost, through the conscience, always speaks peace into the hearts of God's children, when he bids them go, and do, and suffer. He it is who is with them, not as a sentiment, but as a fact. There ought to return to men that earnest religious spirit of the Hebrew scripture which saw the work of the Lord God in the lily, which felt the Spirit's presence directly in the heart, and heard his voice distinctly in the conscience. With such a *con*-science we need not be surprised that when men are naked they are clothed, that when they possess nothing they possess all things. It is not *nerve* that is bravest, but man and God made friends, and dwelling together in harmony. If a man has, in this strange compartment of the soul, a happy social circle, no matter how the storm howls without. Such men become heroes. The voice of the loudest slander is drowned. The dove lays at their feet the olive leaf. The peace of heaven descends upon them though seated amid the ruins and desolations of death.

But this picture has its reverse. Herod, the murderer of John the Baptist, was distinguished as the founder of the city of Tiberius, and as the temporal sovereign of our Saviour. He was a conqueror and a statesman. He was surrounded by all the wealth and splendor of an Oriental court. He was a Sadducee. In theory he rejected the doctrine of the resurrection, and regarded the future life as visionary. Invested with such circumstances, and possessing such faith, what could disturb him? The protection of his court, the blandishments of his queen, the annihilation of the dead, — what more could be asked? How securely such a man must rest at night! How complacently walk the streets, and rule his kingdom!

But Herod did not. Look at him! The name of an obscure person sends terror into his heart at every step. He forsakes his court and flees to the company of his servants. He discloses to them his apprehensions. How unkingly his conduct! When he heard of the fame of Jesus, these are the words which escape from his pallid lips: "This is John the Baptist; he is risen from the dead." He trembles like a scourged slave. If he enters a darkened room, he is sure to meet the mangled corpse of John the Baptist. If he starts from his sleep at night, it is because he hears a dying groan echoed from the gloomy cell of John the Baptist. The rustling of a leaf is his breath; a footfall is his approach. Every floating rumor is associated with the hideous phantom of the mutilated dead man. Every look means mischief. Every cloak conceals a dagger, trembling to leap into his heart. The very atmosphere is loaded with poison. His realm is in rebellion, and his palace crowded with murderers. What! is Herod insane? O, no, not insane; he is laboring under a fit of superstition. We object. Why not call things by their right names? There is something more at work in his soul than superstitions or sentiments. What is it then? Pardon a delay of the answer for a moment. An English king is represented by one who knew the power of an enraged conscience as exclaiming, —

> "O, coward conscience, how dost thou afflict me!
> Cold, fearful drops stand on my trembling flesh.
> Is there a murderer here? . . .
> Then fly. What from? Myself?
> My conscience has a thousand tongues . . .

> (They) Throng to the bar, crying all, Guilty! Guilty!
> . . . Shadows to-night
> Have struck more terror to the soul of Richard
> Than can the substance of ten thousand soldiers." *

Do we condemn the representation as overwrought? Was that king insane, or superstitious, merely? When Booth, the assassinator of President Lincoln, was lying in the agony of death, lifting his trembling hands, and fixing his glassy eyes upon them, he exclaimed, "Blood! blood!" Yes, the innocent blood of a beloved and murdered president was upon them. He had washed them, and they were white as marble; but to him they were not clean; they were stained blood-red.

> "What hands are here! Ha! they pluck out mine eyes.
> Will all great Neptune's ocean wash this blood
> Clean from my hand? No! this my hand will rather
> The multitudinous seas incarnardine,
> Making the green — one red."

Was J. Wilkes Booth merely insane or superstitious? No! It was the Holy Ghost saying to him, as he said to Cain, "What hast thou done? The voice of thy brother's blood crieth unto me from the ground."

The Future Peace or Misery of the Human Soul intimately connected with Conscience. — It is reasonable to conclude that the divine administration will proceed upon the same general principles in the future as in the present. The unperfected here will be com-

* Richard III.

pleted hereafter. Consummation and incompleteness are the opposite representations of mortality and immortality. If, then, the conscience is that faculty through which the Spirit Divine discloses to man what is the judgment of Heaven respecting his course of life, our future happiness or misery must necessarily be involved in its untrammelled and perfected decisions. There is no escape from these positions. The future destruction of conscience can afford no relief. God must die with the death of conscience. The lapse of time cannot diminish its activity. A deathless spirit is in possession of a deathless conscience. Deprive the race of the power to discern moral distinctions, and the universe is deprived of heaven as well as hell. Consider the thought practically. Had not Herod slept soundly, many a night after the murder of John the Baptist, before the public appearance of Christ alarmed him? Had the lapse of time removed his terror?

Mr. Webster, in the trial of the Knapps, described not the extraordinary, but the normal and ordinary workings of conscience in all ages, and for all crimes. "He had done the murder. No eye has seen him, no ear has heard him. The secret is his own, and it is safe. Ah, gentlemen, that was a dreadful mistake. Such a secret can be safe nowhere. The whole creation of God has neither nook nor corner where the guilty can bestow it and say it is safe. . . . True, it is, that, generally speaking, 'murder will out.' Every murderer, like the first one, feels that every man's hand is against him. The guilty soul cannot keep its own secret. He feels it beating at his heart, rising to his throat, and demanding disclosure. He thinks the whole world sees it in his face, reads it in his eyes, and almost hears its workings in the very silence of his thoughts. It must be confessed. It will be confessed. There is no refuge from confession but suicide, and suicide is confession."

Mr. Webster did not commit that murder; yet he knew something of the human heart and the power of a guilty conscience.

"With us," continued Mr. Webster, "these convictions are with us in this life, will be with us at its close, and in that scene of inconceivable solemnity which lies yet farther onward, we shall still find ourselves surrounded by the consciousness of duty, to pain us wherever it has been violated, and to console us so far as God may have given us grace to perform it."

What is there in the nature of time or eternity which can lessen the overwhelming force of moral convictions? They are a constituted part of the universe. This law, which is not one at Rome and another at Athens, is also not one on earth and another in heaven, but one universal and unalterable. There is no evasion of it. Why do not unbelievers defend the invariableness of this law, as they do that of the laws of nature when we speak of miracles? There are religious teachers who claim, not that God is a good, but that he is a "goodish" sort of being; that he is inclined to wink at all kinds of evil, or call it right. They tell us that the sinner is as much in God's service, and meets his approval as surely, as the most devoted Christian; that his deathbed will be as soft and his reward as sure. But what will these men do with the nature and operations of conscience? If our senses affirm that God is good; if the smiling field and fragrant rose breathe his love; if the gifts of his mercy declare his fatherhood, do not the lashings of an enraged conscience, in the hour of death, demonstrate as unquestionably his severity and justice?

Whatever be our theories of the nature of conscience, no one can deny the facts of its operations. The man who tries to do right is approved. There is no deviation from this law; it is eternal and universal. The man who does not try to do as he feels he ought, is condemned; this law, also, is eternal and universal. If God is immutable, there is no *natural* counter-law, in heaven or out of it, which can change these conditions. The closer a man draws to the future world, the greater is the joy or the anguish of his soul. Were not men stupefied with drugs, or weakened by disease, every death-bed would be terrible or glorious. Let those who scoff at future punishment first be able to extract this sting of conscience from the heart of guilt. Unless its power be removed, annihilation or future and endless anguish is inevitable. Group these statements, and associate with them existing facts.

It is one of the most inevitable laws of our being, that when men are most depressed in consequence of guilt, and are grappling with death, the latent energy of this tremendous faculty is quickened. During the very hour when, of all others in a man's life, his condition calls most loudly for compassion, then his conscience returns from its wanderings with augmented pungency. In the hour of physical dissolution, the Infinite Spirit and the soul meet together in the conscience more closely than ever before. They see together, know together, and have an understanding together, more perfectly than ever before. No anguish is mitigated. The embankments which Satan, the world, and the human will have thrown up between the soul and the clear sky are broken down. In that hour God takes the helm and steers the agitated bark into an unknown port, through frightful and turbulent waters, growing constantly more dark and fearful. He gives such an expression of his displeasure to the guilty man as to make him screech for very anguish. Such men feel that death, nay, that a thousand deaths, would be more desirable than their present agonizing condition, if continued.

Where, then, in the name of reason, is there any future escape for the guilty soul? O, but men are not guilty. Men are guilty. They know it. They ever and anon feel the deep and dark malignity of sin pressing upon them. Every sinner feels that he must bear the whole weight of his own guilt. So far as any natural law is concerned, his scarlet sins must remain scarlet, his crimson sins crimson. There is no radiance to light his lonely pathway. But is there not a remedy? Not in nature, or the natural. But is there none elsewhere? Yes. God pity the race if there were not. Man can look conscience out of countenance. Its terrible power may become harmless, unmanned, and unarmed. Man's crimson sins may become white as snow. Not by a slow process of social development, but sometimes instantly. The experiences of eighteen hundred years prove it. But how? Must not sin always rebuke the sinner? Yes. Must not the Law-giving Father always hate sin with perfect hatred? Yes. Can the man who has committed sin escape the frightful operations of conscience, here or hereafter? No. Where, then, is heaven? In what consists salvation? Where is pardon? There are laws which pass beyond the range of the natural. They are supernatural. The natural and supernatural do not clash. One is above the other. The Father makes salvation possible, by giving us the opportunity of becoming in Christ Jesus new creatures — other men than what we are. That old man who was under the law remains there, the eternal object of rebuke; he is excluded; agony and remorse unite in casting him into outer darkness. But this new man is something and somebody else.* He is Christ's brother. At his approach, the broad gates above swing open; shouts of welcome on every hand are heard. The crown is placed on his brow; the spotless robe covers him. The man who enters heaven is faultless. Conscience cannot harm a faultless man. What more can be asked?

"Love, sad and strong, appeared, asking of earth, Why weepest thou?"

* Noyes.

THE NATURE AND OPERATIONS OF MEMORY.

"But Abraham said, Son, remember that thou in thy lifetime receivedst thy good things, and likewise Lazarus evil things; but now he is comforted, and thou art tormented." *Luke* xvi. 25.

"Still o'er these scenes my memory wakes,
And fondly broods with miser care;
Time but the impression deeper makes,
And streams their channels deeper wear."

BURNS.

"And slight withal may be the things which bring
Back on the heart the weight which it would fling
Aside forever; it may be a wound,
A tone of music, summer's eve, or spring,
A flower, the wind, the ocean, which shall wound,
Striking th' electric chain wherewith we're darkly bound.
And how, and why, we know not, nor can trace
Home to its cloud this lightning of the mind,
But feel the shock renewed, nor can efface
The blight and blackening which it leaves behind."

BYRON.

IV.

THE NATURE AND OPERATIONS OF MEMORY.

THE vital point in the parable of "The Rich Man and Lazarus" involves the future operation of one of the most astonishing faculties of the human soul. This faculty, and its relation to the future life, especially in case of the finally impenitent, furnish us with a wonderful subject for discussion.

The Nature of Memory.— The faculty called memory has interested speculative minds in all ages. As would be expected, it has led to many and curious speculations respecting its nature and operations. The more recent scientific deductions are, that memory is not so much a special faculty of the mind, as the action and result of the "self-energy of the soul." * This soul-power, while in the body, displays itself through the organs of the body. It sees through the eye, hears through the ear, feels through the hand, and remembers through the brain. Let the soul escape from the body, and it would not need the eye to see, the

* Hamilton.

ear to hear, the hand to feel, or the brain to remember. These activities of the soul, by the means of intuitions, would then accomplish their work, without the intervention of organs. No natural organ can assist the soul in its operations. It is, at most, only an outlet indicating barriers elsewhere. The soul, freed from the body, would be like the city of God, whose gates "shall not be shut at all by day; for there shall be no night there." Keeping this thought in mind, we are prepared for a closer analysis of the faculty under consideration. In order not to burden our minds with numerous definitions, we employ but two terms; namely, *retention*, by which is meant that power of the soul through which it retains the knowledge which it has acquired, and *mental reproduction*, by which is meant that power of the soul through which it recalls, at a given moment, as in recollection or reminiscence, the knowledge it has in possession. It is one of the most fully established principles of psychology, and one which is attested by an experience almost universal, that we live and move amid all our past experiences. Our knowledge, active or passive, immediate or distant, the knowledge of every item that has been seen or thought, felt or done, by the soul, is like the Deity, ever present with it, though, like the Deity, it is not always recognized. It is not only treasured up by the soul, but has become a part of it. Hence one person has as good retentive power as another. Retention is a constitutional part of the soul, and depends for its full power simply upon the soul's existence. In this respect all men are alike.

On the other hand, there is, perhaps, no mental

operation in which such extreme differences appear as in the reproductive faculty. Its power is largely accidental, and dependent upon the cultivation, health, and natural play of the faculties. There are some persons who possess this power almost miraculously. Themistocles, the Athenian statesman, could call the names of the twenty thousand citizens of Athens. Hortensius, next to Cicero the greatest orator of Rome, after sitting a whole day at a public sale, enumerated correctly, from memory, the multitude of articles sold, their prices, and the names of the purchasers. Seneca, the rhetorician, could repeat two thousand names read to him in the order in which they had been spoken. In 1581, a Corsican youth repeated accurately thirty-six thousand words after once hearing them. It is said of Grotius and Pascal, that they could recall, at will, all they had ever thought or read. Ben Jonson tells us that he could repeat all he had ever written, and whole books that he had reviewed. Macaulay in a short time committed to memory and repeated the whole of Paradise Lost. It is said of Humboldt that he was never known to forget anything. Some years ago, a traveller, who had then recently returned from Jerusalem, discovered, in conversation with Humboldt, that he was as thoroughly conversant with the streets and houses of Jerusalem as he himself was; whereupon he asked the aged philosopher how long it had been since he visited Jerusalem. He replied, "I have never been there, but I expected to go sixty years since, and prepared myself."

Again, some persons have the power of recalling,

with the greatest facility, certain things, and appear utterly destitute of it in other respects. One can recall events easily; another, faces; one names, another dates. In a single family this diversity may often be discovered. In the narration of a story, there will be an appeal to this one for dates, to that one for names, to a third for a description of places. In the mouth of the two or three witnesses every word is established. This has, doubtless, given rise to the suggestive and familiar expression, "Let us put our heads together." Again, there are those who, at times, are not able to recall the most familiar facts. There are many authentic cases where men have forgotten, for the time, their own names and the names of their children. In these several instances, the retention, we should say, is equally good. The persons differ in their recollection only. It is folly to say that the man did not retain his own, or his son's name, though he could not reproduce it at a given moment. At this point we may also discover the precise difference between what is termed a good and a poor memory; the one can reproduce his knowledge at will, the other cannot. So one man may know as much as another, and yet be unable to express anything clearly. There is a familiar expression, heard alike from the lips of the school-boy attempting in vain to recollect his lesson, and from the feeble old man endeavoring to answer your question, which embodies the true philosophy of memory, — "I know, but I cannot think;" "I have it, but I cannot recall it just now." Old age furnishes us with a double example, both of an impaired faculty, that cannot recall, at times, an event of yesterday, but which remembers with perfect distinctness scenes that transpired in days of earliest childhood. Old age lives more in the past than in the present. Who has not seen an old man pause suddenly, and lean on his staff, with his eyes fixed, or filled with tears, and he motionless as a statue? Who has not seen an aged matron, who had outlived her generation, pause, and let the work of her fingers drop nervelessly into her lap, as if she had forgotten the present while recalling the past? Something had suggested other places, other times, and other faces — faces they had loved, but could see no more on earth.

The effect of disease upon the mental powers is also an overwhelming argument respecting the retentive power of the soul. Some of the most unaccountable freaks are played upon the memory by disease. Instances are common and various. After certain diseases a partial loss of memory often takes place. The patient appears to have lost his entire previous stock of knowledge. Whatever may have been his former acquirements, he must now begin anew his alphabet. Perhaps he has lost his power to recall words, but retains that of recollecting things. In some instances persons are so affected that they can recall any noun, but not a single verb. What is still more marvellous, "and of no very unfrequent occurrence," says Sir William Hamilton, "one language, in the case of persons familiar with several, has been taken neatly out of his recollection, without affecting in the least his remembrance of the others." In all these instances, it usually results that after a time, of a sudden the entire previous stock of knowledge glides back into the mind.

The power of reproducing it returns. The knowledge was retained all the same and all the while, but for a time it was latent.

On the other hand, there are cases where diseases, especially nervous affections, have increased almost miraculously this power of mental reproduction. We call attention to but one illustration, and to this because it is both very remarkable and authentic. It is the case cited by Samuel Taylor Coleridge. It occurred in Gottingen, Germany, a year or two before his visit to that city, and had not then ceased to be a frequent subject of conversation. A young woman of four or five and twenty, who could neither read nor write, was seized with a nervous fever, during which she continued incessantly talking Latin, Greek, and Hebrew, in very pompous tones, and with the most distinct enunciation. The case attracted the attention of a young physician, and by his statement of it many eminent physiologists and psychologists visited the town, and cross-examined the patient on the spot. Sheets full of her ravings (as they are called) were taken down, and were found to consist of sentences coherent and intelligible, each for itself, but with little or no connection with one another. All trick or conspiracy was out of the question. The young woman was a harmless and simple creature. No solution of the case presented itself. The young physician determined, however, to trace her past life, step by step. He succeeded in discovering the place where her parents had lived, made the acquaintance of a surviving uncle, and from him learned that the patient had been taken by an old Protestant pastor, at nine years of age, and had remained with him until his death. After much search, the young medical philosopher discovered a niece of the pastor, who had lived with him as housekeeper, and had inherited his effects. She well remembered the girl. Anxious inquiries were then made concerning the pastor's habits of study, and the solution of the phenomenon was soon obtained. It appeared that it had been the pastor's custom for years to walk up and down a passage of his house, into which the kitchen door opened, and to read to himself, in a loud tone, out of his favorite books. In his library was found a collection of Rabbinical writings, together with several of the Greek and Latin fathers. The physician succeeded in identifying so many passages with those taken down at the young woman's bedside, that no doubt could remain concerning the true origin of the impressions made upon her mind, and reproduced by the action of a nervous disease. How singular, that words and sentences, tones and accents, only heard, not understood, and for years forgotten, should have been so faithfully kept by the soul! that under the influence of a peculiar disease they should be brought forth again with, if possible, more than their original freshness! This and a multitude of similar cases force us to the conclusion that every impression made upon the soul, early and late, momentary or protracted, remains with it in all its original freshness, even though the impression, at the time it is made, be as gentle as the notes of an Æolian harp at eventide, though it be but the reflex of an idle word, or the return of an idle thought, which had been cherished in the heart. It would seem, then, that if our power to recall the past were as perfect as our retention of it, all men would be able to station themselves anywhere, at any time, and, like a conjurer with his wand, call about themselves the mighty spirit of their past experience, with the vividness of present realities. These would come without calling. The wonder is, not that we remember, but that we can forget. It is most fortunate, however, that it is thus; for no material organism on earth could endure the natural and full play of these energies of the soul.

They would destroy the body as an unthrottled locomotive would destroy itself. If our past history, with its painful and pleasing details, should always be pressing itself upon us, it would, of itself, in a little time, entirely exhaust our physical energy. We should break down under it long before one half our threescore years had expired. While children, we are left to think as children. Other things, like God and heaven, are wisely shrouded. Now we see in part, but the time comes when that which is in part shall be done away.

The Action of Memory in the Future Life. — If we admit a future existence, and grant the positions already advanced, it follows that the soul, after death, is to be brought into perpetual contact with its entire earthly history. Judging from our present experience and the nature of a spiritual existence, there can be no reasonable doubt that the soul will be continually and deeply affected by its memories, either for happiness or misery. Every one knows how the activities of the soul are impeded or clogged by an unhealthy or depressed physical condition. This is especially true of the powers of memory. There are times when the same person can reproduce the past easily; there are other times when he can do so only with great difficulty. At one time we cannot recall what we desire; at other times it comes unbidden. There are moments when a name, or a face, not thought of for years, will unaccountably spring in upon us out of the darkness of the past. On the other hand, we sometimes lose our power of recalling what is most recent and familiar in our history. We are about to introduce two persons whose names are perfectly familiar; but just at the wrong instant, with the name almost on the lips, it slips from us. We hesitate, blush, and stammer; but to no purpose: we are left to the mortifying expedient of asking an old friend for his name. The difficulty is a physical one. A momentary perturbation has thrown an over-quantity of blood to the brain. The reproductive faculty will not do its work, or, rather, will not allow the soul to work through it.

In the next life such disturbing causes will be removed. Flesh and blood will not inherit that kingdom. The imperfect organisms which at present surround us, shut us in, clog us, will not then cramp the mighty energies of the soul. The caged eagle, impatient for its immortal freedom, darting through and above the clouds, will look at the sun.

The future spiritual state is to be one of intensest activity. From the nature of spirit it must be the embodiment of activity. An approach to this condition is sometimes experienced in this life, as, for instance, at those times when the energies of the soul, from one cause or another, are unusually aroused. All are familiar with the effect produced upon the mental faculties under such circumstances. There are emergencies under which the soul seems to rise above the body and into its normal sphere. Then it is that all, or nearly all, the past life is seen at a single glance, not as something strange and novel, but as old and familiar. It becomes a portrait, from which time has effaced not a feature. We seem to enter that mysterious labyrinth, which leads us onward until we come in immediate contact with much that was supposed to be lost, but which had only strayed. All things return at last to each and every man, as the spirit returns to God after its life's work is done and the body has gone to dust.

Mr. Webster, in his reply to Hayne, upon the floor of Congress, furnishes an illustration. He informs us that during the moments of his highest mental inspiration, on that occasion, everything he had ever seen or heard, read or thought, stood before him in perfect order. His only effort was leisurely to select from this accumulation of facts and thoughts, and give to his audience. The experience of Mr. Webster, on that occasion, will be universal when the natural gives place to the spiritual, and the mortal to the immortal.

The same phenomena have been experienced by various persons in other and peculiar positions in life. The testimony of a multitude of persons who have been resuscitated from drowning cannot be disregarded. They tell us that during those moments when the approach was nearest to the spiritual state, when the soul was struggling with all its marvellous energies to keep its hold upon life, then the entire past was distinctly seen. The startling call in that dread crisis made all past events stand in awful grandeur before the soul. "Each terrified thought of life rushed, for the moment, to its ashy window, to behold itself."

Such an experience is not a passing in review, — a "frightful cavalcade," thundering through the soul, — but the past becomes present. It is more than a reminiscence; it is a present unity, an overwhelming, comprehensive grasp of all experiences. It is co-extensive, co-present, and linked forever to the absolute self that has produced or received impressions.

It would be more possible for heaven and earth to pass away, than for a single act, a single word, or a single thought, to be lost or loosened hereafter from that living chain of causes which has gone, or does go, daily, to make us what we are, and what we shall be. Give the soul an organism which is appropriate to it, — the body celestial instead of the body terrestrial; the body incorruptible instead of the body corruptible; the body immortal instead of the body mortal; the body spiritual instead of the body natural, — and the combined experience of the entire past history of every human soul, like a living reality, would start up before it without cloud or shadow, for its happiness or its misery. The judgment book of God could then be dispensed with. An exact copy of each life has been transcribed, and is preserved. All things are stereotyped. It may be that this etentive power of the soul is the dread book itself, or rather a copy of it, "in whose mysterious hieroglyphics every idle word is recorded." *

All the mighty physical displays that are crowded into the judgment day by poet and preacher, to increase its impressiveness, are feeble in comparison with the view that simply individualizes the vast assembly, making each solitary human soul stand, face, and be answerable for, its entire past life.

The soul's review of a well-spent or a misspent life, through which a glorious destiny is secured, or lost, will produce the most thrilling drama of the universe. What sadder or wider contrasts can be presented than between a rich and selfish man on the one side, pale and speechless, without the wedding garment, and a poor but faithful man on the other, who has come up out of great tribulation, having washed his robes and made them white in the blood of the Lamb? What transaction will more surely meet the approval of heaven than that which leaves a man to deck himself in his own garment, cut from the web he has been weaving through life? Is not the robe we weave, warp and woof, the robe we *ought* to wear? If there is justice anywhere, is not the spiritual path a man travels while in this life the path he ought hereafter to follow, step by step, straight or deviating, world without end?

The Operations of Memory, especially in Case of the finally impenitent. — The popular pantheistic notions of the nineteenth century are so well armed, and aimed so directly against the doctrine of future

* Coleridge.

punishment, that we pause to consider the positions advocated in the light of the general subject before us. The whole theory of modern pantheism may be summed up thus: All men and things are God. The man acting right, or wrong, as well as the tree growing from the soil, is only God acting through the man, or the tree. The man and the tree are alike irresponsible, and have nothing to answer for here or hereafter. But if there be anything taught by the faculty called memory, regarding it in whatever light we may, it is that a man is not a tree; that each man is an individual, who stands or falls, lives or dies, and answers for himself alone.

Nothing that enters into human consciousness, or comes within the range of human experience, can be in more direct antagonism to pantheism than the facts and existence of memory. Though the anatomist carefully dissects the body, though he traces every nerve to its origin, though he cannot find the locality of this unchanging and independent part of man, and doubts scientifically its existence, yet let him but recall a day or an hour of his childhood, and the illusion vanishes. Though we do not look like the children we were of ten summers, we know that there is something within which is unchanged. Whenever a rock, a brook, a face, or a voice brings strangely to mind another rock, or brook, a face, or voice, and shuts down to the groove the flood-gates of life, they leave us no longer the men we are, but make us the children we were. Whatever have been the sweeping alterations around us, or whatever have been the modifications of character within us, our personal identity has remained unchanged through all these years. The child and man are always self-same.

It is true there is very much in the habits of modern society which has a tendency to make pantheists of all men. The corporations in which men labor, the copartnerships which absorb the individuals, the general proneness to shrink from the use of those words, "I," and "You," which impart personality to whatever they touch, and the universal demand "not to be personal," contribute to this; but still God has left his witness in the world that man is an individual and responsible agent. This is felt to be the case the instant Memory lays her finger upon any spring that bolts her windows.

Can the pantheist have met, anywhere in his distant migrations, the full visage of his own soul, and have staid with it alone, still, attentive, and not have felt that his past history has singled him out from all others in the universe? Where can he have been, not to have felt this lasting, undivided, startling, awful, and adhering personal identity! It is clearly written upon every act of memory, as it floats up from the past, bearing upon its very forehead the proof of our continued identity and responsibility, not through the last day or hour of life, but through every moment of our conscious activity. The facts of memory preclude the possibility of the absorption of the individual into the divine nature. Make a combination of the two by a miracle, if you choose; but can a miraculous combination extinguish the man or the God? Identical they never have been; identical they never can be.

The time is not far distant when science will recognize these truths, and when the present pantheistic notions of Germany, England, and America will be looked upon as the idlest talk, and when the teachings of the Bible, in which pantheism has no place, and which on every page fastens personality and responsibility upon every conscious member of the race, will be universally recognized as the basis of all theoretical, as it now is of all practical philosophy.

We return to the main argument. If the many transgressions of life, which, at present, lie concealed at our doors, should at last appear under the active reproductive energy of the soul in perfect clearness, would they not load us with misery? In the silence of our thoughts, and in the occasional vivid reproduction of the past, even in this life, have we not felt momentarily the sense of remembered, or even partially forgotten, guilt rushing over the troubled spirit with a sentence which has made us dread the future and wish to hide from God? Most men are not guilty of flagrant crimes. Judas, Herod, and Nero are the exceptions. Yet, if the multitude of deeds and thoughts now slumbering, if the duties to God and humanity, which have been neglected or carelessly pushed aside, should be vividly brought before the best of men under the light of God's countenance, they would be shocked by their number, if not by their flagrancy. The remembrance of them would vitiate the perfume of every flower, and dim the brightest sky that ever smiled upon the earth. The rich man in the parable did not think his conduct very sinful while living. He looked upon himself as a respectable man, and was so regarded by others. Our Saviour did not speak of him in severe terms. Of what did he accuse him? Of any breach of the law? Did he say he was a calumniator, an oppressor of the poor, a persecutor, or a robber? Nothing like it. This was all he said: "There was a certain rich man;" and this was his crime; not that he was rich, but that a suffering poor man was lying at his gate, and lying unrelieved. The rich man did not abuse him or order him away, but most likely allowed him the fragments of his sumptuous meal. Yet he was a criminal. Christ so regarded him, for he had not done by the poor man as he would be done by. He had not listened to Moses and the prophets. His heart refused instruction, and his memory clung, with hooks of steel, to the fact that a poor beggar had suffered within his reach, and had suffered unrelieved. One drama had ended, another had begun. Under the remembrance of that unfaithfulness his head throbbed, his tongue burned, and his cry for a drop of water was heard far and near. That was a small boon to ask. Could his tongue have been cooled by so small a gift, it would have been ignoble in Abraham not to have furnished it. But such a thirst, excited by the memories of the past haunting him, could not be cooled by a drop of water, nor by all the waters of the frozen seas. Not flagrant crimes, not the guilt only which is appalling in the eyes of the world, but simple unfaithfulness towards God and his claims, towards humanity and its wants, kindles a fire which no possible external agency can quench. Such a troubled soul could not find repose even upon the bosom of God. It could find no pleasure if instated amid the regal splendors of the groves of Paradise. The trouble is deep and within. The scorching sun is upon the plain, and there is no shelter for such a traveller.

If this be true of a *respectable* (?) sinner, what of the soul stained with acknowledged guilt? Who says that such a one has no punishment in store? Will the angel who whets not his sword in vain, even in this life, be conquered in the next? "O, if I could forget!" is the wailing cry that has gone up from more than one earth-born heart. "I will forget! I will die, and thus escape my memories!"

> "Poor, foolish mortal, thou hadst better live!
> Then thou mayst snatch the respite of a moment;
> In death thou canst not;
> Oblivion is the dream of fools;
> Men sleep in life, in death they wake."

"*Remember!*" that was the word which tore off the purple robe of this life, and placed upon the shoulders of the rich man a robe of fire. That solitary word, "Remember!" rang the death-knell of his latest hope. A misdemeanor had sprung up to the sky, had cut the hair, and the suspended sword fell — upon his heart. The bitter complaint of Byron was his —

> "My solitude is solitude no more,
> But peopled with the Furies.
> I have prayed for madness as a blessing; 'tis denied me.
> I have affronted death, the cold hand
> Of an all-pitiless demon held me back,
> Back by a single hair — which would not break.

In imagination I plunged deep,
But like an ebbing wave it dashed me back
Into the gulf of my unfathomed thought.
I dwell in my despair,
And live. And thus I live forever."

But there is something more than the ordinary operations of memory which will involve the soul in the future; something more than the clear, spiritual presentation to one's self of crimes; something more than the reproving eye of conscience looking in upon our misdeeds; something more than the accusations of Satan. It is the publication of all that is past to God and the universe which will overwhelm us. There are many, who in this world, without apparent emotion, can bear their own secret thoughts, but would hide in shame and confusion if the contents of their hearts and their past history should be published upon the house-tops and to the multitude. The hand would tremble, the foot falter, the tongue stammer, and death would be a boon. But published all this is to be. We are painting daily our own portraits, to be worn as about the neck, to be hung as upon parlor walls, and to remain forever before our own and the eyes of the universe. We are putting into that picture every deed, word, and thought of life. Who does not feel the blood mount his cheek? The day of judgment will be a day of universal and overwhelming surprise. Are there not those who would, sooner than have their children and friends know them thus, pray to be banished from their presence forever? Tom Moore never blushed at his own immoral pages until told that his daughter had been reading them. Those who demand the companionship of earthly friends in the future, irrespective of the character formed, know not what they ask. Final separation and endless punishment will not lose a single unfortunate victim, even if the redeemed are gratified by having near them every earthly friend they may desire on the day of the general judgment. We now see through a glass darkly, then face to face. God shall bring every work into judgment, with every secret thing. This will make a world of difference with our views and demands. "Whatsoever a man sows, that shall he also reap." Chaff or wheat, calm or tempest, wind or whirlwind. The present life witnesses the gain or loss of everything. As we are, as we make ourselves, as our memories present or report us, so we go into the next life — and thus remain. "He that is filthy, let him he filthy still; he that is righteous, let him be righteous still. As the tree inclines, let it fall: as it falls, let it lie. The picture we paint is the picture we shall have. But is there no destroying it? No. Cannot we deface it? No. Must the world see it, and examine it, as in the sunlight? Yes. What, no escape from all that we have said or done in the past? No. "O, wretched man that I am, who shall deliver me from the body of this death? I thank God, through our Lord Jesus Christ." How through him? By destroying the picture? No. By effacing it? No. How then? Simply by painting Him upon the canvas also. Let but the most guilty man of earth find Christ, and make him a part of his own character and history, and he will not tremble that his picture is to be hung out to the universe, though bearing every misdeed. He will delight to have his children gaze upon it, for about those faults and sins of his life will linger the thrilling radiance of a manly and heroic struggle, which is bathed in the love of Christ. It will show that he has burst the fetters of sin, and has been made an obedient child of heaven. Such an adorning about the blackest picture of sinful humanity will give it a welcome anywhere and everywhere in the universe. Angels will be enraptured before it, and Christ will delight to own it.

In effect, it will be as if God had gently borne the soul above the bitter remembrance of the past; and thus his word represents it. In effect, it will be as if the purple robe of fire had been washed of every spot and made white in the blood of the Lamb; and thus his word represents it. This is the redemption of the soul through Christ. Without Christ there is a great gulf between the soul and heaven; it is impassable. Seize his hand and cross the gulf.

THE THRALDOM OF CHARACTER.

"From depraved influences arise, first, familiarity, then, nature." QUINTILIAN.

"Ephraim is joined to idols: let him alone." *Hosea* iv. 17.

"Therefore I say unto you, All manner of sin and of blasphemy shall be forgiven unto men; but the blasphemy against the Holy Ghost shall not be forgiven unto men.

"And whosoever speaketh a word against the Son of man, it shall be forgiven him; but whosoever speaketh against the Holy Ghost, it shall not be forgiven him, neither in this world, neither in the world to come." *Matthew* xii. 31, 32.

"For it is impossible for those who were once enlightened, and have tasted of the heavenly gift, and were made partakers of the Holy Ghost, and have tasted the good word of God, and the powers of the world to come, if they shall fall away, to renew them again unto repentance; seeing they crucify to themselves the Son of God afresh, and put him to an open shame." *Hebrews* vi. 4-6.

"But the fearful, and unbelieving, and the abominable, and murderers, and whoremongers, and sorcerers, and idolaters, and all liars, shall have their part in the lake which burneth with fire and brimstone: which is the second death." *Revelation* xxi. 8.

"One sinless with infernals might do well;
But sin would make of heaven a very hell.
Look to thyself then, keep it out of door;
Lest it get in and never leave thee more."

BUNYAN.

V.

THE THRALDOM OF CHARACTER.

THE Scriptures convey the impression that there are some sins for which there is no pardon, and some sinners for whom there is no reprieve. Such fatal conditions justify patient investigations.

The Scriptural Statements respecting the Thraldom of Character. — We avail ourselves of the light which is reflected upon the subject of an unpardonable sin, from the circumstances attending its original announcement by our Saviour. Accompanied by his disciples, he had made a circuit through Galilee, and had just returned to Capernaum. Here the people brought unto him, among others, a most unfortunate case of disease — that of one possessed of a devil, also dumb and blind. In presence of the rulers and the multitude, Christ healed him, "insomuch that the blind and dumb both spake and saw; and all the people were amazed, and said, Is not this the Son of David" — the Christ that was to come? "But," continues the narrative, "when the Pharisees heard it, they said, This fellow doth not cast out devils, but by Beelzebub, the prince of devils." It was this sentence, together with the spirit that prompted it, which called from the lips of Christ the announcement of the possibility of committing an unpardonable sin.

It is reasonable to infer either that these Pharisees had already committed it, or that they were in extreme danger of its commission. The conduct they manifested on the occasion in question should be our exposition of the subject, should receive our patient and honest investigation, and should remain to the world a solemn and perpetual warning.

The healing of diseases by divine help was not a new thing in the Jewish nation. Some of the old prophets, in God's name (never in their own), had wrought miracles of cure, and had dispossessed the afflicted demoniac. But the ability to exercise such remarkable power had ever been regarded as peculiarly the mark of God's Spirit and presence. It was an endowment which had always been looked upon as wholly opposed to satanic influence, and as subversive of the kingdom of the prince of darkness. Had any other personage, on the day in question, wrought that stupendous cure, these very Pharisees would have looked upon the deed, not as giving evidence that the agent was in league with Satan, but that he possessed unmistakably the gift of divine authority. Mark the course of events. When the deed was wrought by our Saviour, — whose progress among his countrymen the rulers and Pharisees had determined to arrest, and to arrest because they did not like him, or the way in which he came, — when the excited and honest mass of the people inquired if the person doing such a deed must not be the predicted Son of David —

the Son of God, then the Pharisees exclaimed, in language of supreme contempt, rejecting all their past admissions, though compelled to submit to the demonstration of power in the miracle wrought, "This fellow does not cast out devils, but by Beelzebub, the prince of devils."

We may note, then, without difficulty, that the general characteristic of the sin of which these rulers were guilty, and the one for which we have every reason to believe there is no pardon, is not a sin, or a course of sinning, committed ignorantly, but knowingly. It is not a careless, but a wilful and presumptuous rejection of that which is good and true. These Pharisees were not ignorant men; they were not the men to be led away by superstition, or to be blinded by mere fanaticism. They were, on the contrary, the most polished and educated classes of Judea. They knew what they were doing. They had in mind a definite purpose, for which they worked day and night, to which they bent every energy and turned every event. They had seen the miracles of Christ, they had heard his preaching, they had witnessed nothing but purity in his life, they had every reason to believe in him; and yet, because they did not like him, or his teachings, and because they loved their evil deeds, against which he spoke, they charged him with every crime imaginable. They scandalized his familiarity with the poor and sinful; they called him a wine-bibber, a glutton, a Sabbath-breaker, a conspirator against Cæsar, and affirmed, in the present instance, that he was a co-worker on earth with the devil.

The sin of these men had not been committed in a

moment. It was not a sin against the humble personage who came from Nazareth; but their sin was the persistent rejection of love, proof, and remonstrance. They had rejected Christ step by step, — in his deeds of charity, in his life of purity, by violence and deceit, — until they had reached a settled determination, against the most solemn convictions of truth, to destroy him at all hazards. We submit to any one if there is not something fearful, nay, frightful, in such a cool and deliberate banishment of the light.

A paraphrase of the text, written fifteen hundred years ago by Chrysostom, will, perhaps, illustrate more fully the same thought. Putting the language into the lips of Christ, he represents him as speaking to the rulers thus: "You call me a deceiver and an enemy of God. I forgive this reproach, for you have stumbled at my flesh, with which you see me clothed. You do not know who I am; this I forgive. But can you be ignorant of the fact that the casting out of devils is the work of the Holy Ghost?" At this point our Saviour fixed their guilt. And from this point his enemies took their final departure. After the day the Pharisees falsely charged Christ with casting out devils by Beelzebub, he never invited them into his kingdom, or even pointed them to the way of life. A remarkable change took place in the method, as well as in the substance, of his teachings. Previously, his style had been plain and simple; for example, the sermons on the Mount and at Nazareth. Up to the date in question, never a parable, or an intentionally obscure saying, had fallen from his lips; but "from henceforth," says the evangelist, "without a parable spake he not unto them." The disciples, at the announcement of his first parable, were naturally surprised, and immediately inquired, "Why speakest thou unto them in parables?" "Therefore," said our Saviour, "speak I to them in parables, because they seeing, see not, and hearing, they hear not, neither do they understand."

Mark states the case still more forcibly, thus: "But unto them that are without, all these things are done in parables; that seeing, they may see and not perceive, and hearing, they may hear and not understand, lest at any time they should be converted, and their sins should be forgiven them." The meaning is, that these men had hardened their hearts so that they could not understand. They had closed their ears, and our Saviour closed his lips. God's Spirit was withdrawn. The door was locked and bolted. They were abandoned and left forever outside the gates of the city.

We thus discover that the design of some of our Lord's parables was to make the truth dark and incomprehensible to the spiritually blind. But when he was with the disciples and the honest people, he *interpreted* to them the parables that he only announced before the wilfully blinded rulers. "And when they were alone," writes Mark, "he expounded all things to his disciples." The parable explained made the truth clearer.

The rulers in this abandonment were not left absolutely free to do whatever they desired; that would not have been safe. But while their volitions and intentions were perfectly free, their outward acts were controlled and overruled, as by fate. They desired to kill Christ, and tried to do so before his time, but were prevented. They had committed the sin all the same. Sin is not in the outward act, but in the heart. To hate a brother with a murderous intention *is* murder. The lustful glance of the eye with an intention or desire cherished *is* crime.

If the rulers had not been abandoned in this restricted sense, if their hearts had not been hardened into rock, would they have taken the course they did, and have rejected the wonderful miracles which Christ wrought in their presence? Would not his mildness or his warnings, his eye of compassion or his solemn denunciations, his unwearied forbearance or something he had done or said in the past, have softened their sullen hearts, or checked their persistent malignity? Unless their hearts had been closed, and unless God had taken his final departure, would they have continued to send officers to arrest our Saviour, when the first had returned, saying, "Never man spake like this man"? Would they have instigated Pilate to a capital sentence against him, when he could find "no fault at all in the man"? Would they have remained unmoved at those startling appearances which drew from the centurion, and the multitude with him, the exclamation, "Truly this was the Son of God"? Would they have closed the awful drama by fabricating such extravagant and unnatural falsehoods to cover up the facts of his resurrection?

Look at these men. They yielded not, they saw not, they heard not, but persisted in their rebellion even unto death. There was no pause, no misgiving, no forgiveness. But what! Did not Christ pray at the last that these men might be forgiven? No. "*Father*, *forgive them, for they know not what they do*," was not said of the Pharisees and rulers. Lost men, they knew what they were doing — that they were doing wrong. But the *multitude*, deceived, instigated, and led on by the rulers, did it ignorantly. It was malice, not ignorance, that prompted the rulers to say, "This is done by Beelzebub:" it was ignorance and blindness, not malice, that led the populace to follow the rulers, crying, "Crucify him!" And because these did it ignorantly, like Paul, they were forgiven. The prayer of Christ in their behalf was heard, and prevailed. The common people saw their mistake, repented, and left the city, to the number of forty thousand, after the siege under Titus had commenced: for these people Christ had prayed. But the priests, and rulers, and unrepentant Jews remained. And there ended the manifestation of God's kingdom to the Jewish state. The fatal line had been passed; beyond it was the death-struggle between Jew and Gentile, with the Jew conquered. The end of the old world was followed by the beginning of the new. It was begun amid the far-spreading light of burning Jerusalem, under whose trembling and falling walls were buried alike the hopes and lives of the Spirit-abandoned enemies of the cross. This was and is to be their eternal condemnation — that light had come into the world, and they had wilfully and presumptuously chosen darkness in its stead. The reason is significant — "*because* their deeds were evil."

In view of these facts, are we not justified in saying that the spirit they displayed, wherever found, in Judea or elsewhere, is the spirit that bears in its bosom the sin for which there is no pardon on earth or in heaven? If this statement needs clearer explanation, or broader application, it may be deduced from the Epistle to the Hebrews, sixth chapter: "For it is impossible," says the inspired writer, "for those who were once enlightened, *and* have tasted of the heavenly gift, *and* were made partakers of the Holy Ghost, *and* have tasted the good word of God, *and* the powers of the world to come, if they shall fall away, to renew them again unto repentance; seeing they crucify to themselves the Son of God afresh, and put him to an open shame." There is a regular gradation, you will notice, in this entire passage. Those whom the apostle here describes had been instructed in the doctrines of Christianity; they had enjoyed the blessings which the new religion afforded; various gifts had been bestowed upon them by the Spirit; they had cherished the hopes which the gospel inspires; they had been in possession of the fullest evidence, internal and external, of the truth and divinity of Christianity. "Now, if any of this class," continues the apostle, "shall apostatize, it is impossible" — "*adunaton*" — not, very difficult, — Paul never uses the word in that sense, — but it is *absolutely* "*impossible* to renew them." Note the reason: "seeing they crucify the Son of God afresh." These apostates would have done precisely what the rulers and Pharisees did, if the opportunity had presented itself; and were equally guilty. The principle involved is precisely the same as in the former instance. The Scriptures throughout are harmonious respecting this crime, and as explicit as its nature will allow.

The Thraldom of Character viewed psychologically.—A wilful suppression of evidence, and a rejection of known truth, signalize it. There is formed a resolution to escape from light into darkness. It is not a careless, heedless, or thoughtless backsliding; not such a transgression as that of David, whose ungoverned passions hurled him suddenly into crime, but who was brought to his knees by a single word from the prophet; it is not such a transgression as that of Peter, whose fear and impulsiveness drove him blindly on to the denial, but whose heart was well nigh broken by a single look from the eye of his Master: this extempore kind of sinning is not the falling away that is meant, but sin persisted in when known to be sin, and when felt to be displeasing to Heaven. It is a surrender of the soul to the enemy, with full knowledge of the truth of the Christian religion; it is a trampling under foot of the rational convictions of the soul; it is taking upon the lips, or cherishing in the heart, those anathemas against Christ which his enemies required of apostates; it is a mortal man in terrible encounter with immortal truth, and overcome by it; it is another crucifixion of Christ. The man committing this sin has, in the process of his sinning, formed a character completed at a given point, so fixed, so fatal, that he feels he cannot *will* to serve God, or resist evil. He has gone so far that he not only will not, but to all intents and purposes he cannot, be pardoned or blessed. The doctrine of perseverance is philosophical. An aged saint's perseverance in a path of virtue, and an aged sinner's perseverance in rebellion, are morally certain.

Is it said that this statement destroys the Fatherhood of God, and makes of him a monster of cruelty? But is it not true that this principle involves no new discovery, and is it not applicable to every department of divine law? Are there not certain physical shocks which so affect the nervous system that a recovery is impossible? May not a man do such violence to his moral susceptibilities that he no longer feels the force of moral distinctions? If God has made such laws, is he not in consequence a monster? If we decide otherwise in these cases, can we not as easily preserve the divine integrity, though we admit that there is a terrible sin, or a certain violent state of sinning, which leaves a man dead, until death brings him to life again?

Is it not a remarkable fact, in support of this view, that those of our fellow-men, who have gone the farthest in their unnatural rebellion, when brought to the bed of death, or led to the scaffold, with striking uniformity, point back to some definite deed that stands before the soul with astonishing clearness, as the turning-point in their lives, after which good influences were withdrawn, and no return to the path of virtue was attempted?

This is a principle which meets us everywhere, and in a variety of forms. To move is to meet it, and to move too far in any direction, *physically*, *mentally*, *morally*, or *spiritually*, is to cross a line we cannot recross. There is before every man this universal Rubicon, from which he may retreat, or over which he may pass. There is nothing dark, then, or mysteri ous, hanging over this subject. It is as clear as the sin is fatal. The consequences are as inevitable as human existence. The sin against the Holy Ghost is not some "awful, irrevocable deed," around which a disordered fancy has thrown an impending doom, but something no more unnatural than the commission of any sin is unnatural.

It is probable that this transgression is so common, that all lost men, at or just before death, become blasphemers against the Holy Ghost. The simple event of death can be regarded only as a spiritual crisis, in the sense that all impenitent men, who have rejected the truth for a length of time without blasphemy, are left, in the last moments of life, under a final and vivid presentation, to which they may yield, thereby escaping from destruction, "as by fire," or which they may reject, thereby adding this fatal sin to the rest that have been accumulating against them. The blasphemer against the Holy Ghost, after rejecting God for a time, simply retires into the inner apartment, that he may hear no longer the hand knocking at the gateway. The door is then closed by another, and allowed to rust upon its hinges. The cheering voice saying, "Come unto me," may have been but recently heard sounding its friendly warning in his ears with a plaintiveness and earnestness never before experienced, and which, prior to this, might have evoked tears from his eyes, joy from his heart, and smiles from his face; but it now makes no more impression upon him than upon a dead man. An awful suicide has been planned and committed by such a transgressor. It is as when a man retires by himself, and then removes, deliberately, every obstacle, and then feels for the pulsations of his own heart, and then steadily and coolly fixes the point of his own dagger, and then, when every preparation has been made, and every energy of his being has been called into requisition to accomplish the purpose, without, perhaps, fully realizing what he is doing, knowing only that he is taking some awful and defiant step, then — he gives the fatal stab, and all the help in the universe cannot restore him.

The Spirit of God, like the breath of life, departs. The candlestick is removed out of its place. The talent is taken away, and given to another. The soul of that man has silently and forever closed itself against God and heaven. The gentle voice that once hailed and cheered him will be heard no more.

It is worthy of remark, also, that the approach to this condition is often gradual, though none the less fatal. Though it is sadder than would be the crash of worlds, yet this condition of character may be formed more noiselessly than the whisper of a falling leaf. The descent in this secret way, from which "universal nature recoils," is not always by a sudden plunge; not always at once; not from the full lustre of truth into profound darkness, as the flashing, disappearing light of a falling star, but is more frequently like the slow and stealthy approach of a serpent, or a concealed enemy.

Nature even lends her hand to perfect the concealment. She covers with carpets and flowers an earth full of fire. The thickest and most luxuriant plots are oftenest those that conceal the dead. No criminal, it is said, is ever led to the scaffold who does not have a glimmering hope, even when the death-cap is drawn over the eyes, and the noose adjusted about the neck, that the whole transaction is not a reality, but a dream, or something like it. He is quite confident there is concealed a reprieve for him somewhere in the hands of the jailer. It is a wise provision that we are so constituted as not to realize the most weighty experiences of life. They are hidden from us. We may feel pain from a slight blow, and be unconscious of the one that takes the life — conscious only of the shock. We may not, and do not, know the hour of our natural death. It is well that we are thus left, and still better if we are always ready. It is well that nature has provided an opiate for the one who has passed the line of probation, and a friendly veil for the eyes of those about him. This is a merciful, but withal a terrible, condition of uncertainty — merciful, that we do not know the hand when we touch it, the face when we see it, or the voice when we hear it; else we should start back as from one who has committed a double suicide.

But let us not be deceived by the deceptive character of the sin, the friendships of nature, or our own natural blindness.

> "Let no man trust the first false step
> Of guilt; it hangs upon a precipice,
> Whose steep descent in last perdition ends."

The inthralment, then, of a man's character is complete with the commission of the unpardonable sin. It *consists* in the suicide of the higher spiritual nature. It is *accomplished* by slow degrees, followed by a definite rejection of the truth, either in word, deed, or thought. It *results* in the withdrawal of the Holy Spirit from the heart, and *constitutes* a crime which God does not forgive, neither in this world nor in the world to come.

Is the Thraldom of Character possible in the Present Age? — There is nothing in the nature of this sin that terminates so fatally, which would prevent its commission by any one, at any time, and anywhere. There is no reason why men who walk daily in our midst may not be trembling upon the verge of this precipice, and there is much in the spirit and conduct of men which indicates, in modern society, the presence and victims of the second death.

During an extensive revival in an American college some years ago, a company of students met, and, as if led on by Satan himself, pierced veins in each other's arms, mingled their blood, and with it signed a formal resolve that they would resist forever God's Spirit and the religion of Christ. Their convictions ceased, though the religious interest for a time continued. Not one of the number referred to was converted. Subsequently, one by one they died, in despair, with the gloom of future and eternal ruin hanging over them. The crime of these young men was probably blasphemy against the Holy Ghost. They sinned knowingly, despised evidences of the truth knowingly. It was malice prepense. They made their own record, took great pains to make a sure record, and in this they approached the awful point of departure. The soul in such an effort is strained, if we may be allowed the expression. It is strained until there is a break, a dislocation, between it and the God-Spirit forever. This is not a solitary illustration.

If we go among men, talk with them, and examine the motives that govern them, we shall find, in some cases, that their hands are coolly and deliberately raised against God — raised and held. We shall find that there are men who, in daylight, *intend* never to change from their course of sin; men who reject Christ, with convictions in his favor; who say that the apostles were "moved on and instigated by the spirit of the devil," and who feel that what they are saying is not true. We shall find men who assert that Christianity is a humbug, and who know better. There are men who, like the most brilliant and most worthless of foreign infidels, have the heart to conclude their letters with the well-known and horrible blasphemy, "Crush the wretch!" There are men in New England, who cordially responded to the following announcement, publicly made at a *religious* (?) meeting of spiritualists, held only a few miles from Boston: "I am not Jesus Christ, nor Paul, but I am a damned sight better than either of them." When men can deliberately do and say such things, it looks as though blasphemy against the Holy Ghost, and thraldom of character, are as possible in the nineteenth as they were in the first century. There are offences less violent and impious, which, in this connection, demand our attention. There are men who have religious convictions, and are trying to banish them. There are men in whose ears the calls of mercy are growing yearly less and less audible and direct, upon whose hearts the arguments of the preacher and the entreaties of friends fall like idle whispers. There are men who are in the habit of justifying a wrong course, that they may continue in it. Some there are who do not know on which roll their names are written, and who do not much care. There are others who do not feel the tender drawing of the Divine Spirit, as they were wont in earlier life. The disposition they once had to become Christians is lost, in part, or altogether. There are still others, to whom the present, past, and future have lost, or are losing, their meaning; upon whom the surrounding providences of the overruling Father leave no abiding impression, and to whom they speak nothing plainly, but in parables, as Christ spoke to the rulers. Whoever has but one such experience is in danger. He has committed, or is in the way of committing, a crime, not in unbelief, not in ignorance, not against man, not against the Son of man, not without clear light, not by a single act, but with deliberation, and against the Holy Ghost. He is struggling upon, or near, remediless disaster. If he falls, can he blame any but himself?

The Thraldom of Character as related to God.— It is often asked if it is consistent with the character of God to refuse forgiveness to this sin, and, if so, on what grounds. All men instinctively recoil from the thought that any human being will pass into the next world, there to remain forever, under the oppressive sense of unrepented and unforgiven guilt. There is no Christian heart on earth that would not rejoice in the announcement that all men will finally be forgiven and saved, if such announcement can be safely made. There is no one who does not prefer to think of God as a loving and merciful Father, rather than a Judge of crime and guilt. But should our preferences conceal the truth? Must not men be blind and deaf who fail to see and acknowledge that the God-Father in revelation, providence, and nature is not all smiles? There is the frowning of a midnight tempest, as well as the smiling of a June morning. There are the bursting of a mountain, a stream of fire, and a burning sea on the very spot where, yesterday, was the blooming of an Italian garden. God is love; penitent hearts find him thus. God is a consuming fire, and impenitent hearts feel him to be such. No one can study his providences in the world without discovering the very principle embodied in the text — the unyielding justice that forgives not, but holds the impenitent and self-hardened victim aloof forever. God is immutable, whether in the smiling morning or in the midnight tempest; whether in the garden blooming or in the garden desolate. But he is not so immutable as to make it all the same with him whether men sin or are holy; whether they transgress innocently or knowingly, carelessly or maliciously. Indifference is not immutability. Electricity is the same, but it appears quite differently when traversing the electric wire, or bearing our message to a friend, and when crashing through our dwelling and killing its inmates. Fire is the same, but it appears quite differently when warming the trembling child of poverty before the hearth, and when sweeping away the wealth and dwellings of a great city. God is the same; but are we not blind, stone blind, like the Pharisees of Jerusalem, if we say that he has the same feelings towards the penitent child and towards the wilful sinner? He cannot look upon *unrepented* sin with the leas allow ance. God is merciful, but sin is hateful to him. He would save the sinner if he could reasonably do so. The *finally* impenitent sinner destroys himself, and puts himself *beyond* the forgiveness of God. There is something which shocks the very foundation of God's government, in this cool, deliberate banishment of the light. The Holy Spirit, who is otherwise and at other times a personal friend of man, and who communicates the divine will and promise to the race, is grieved beyond measure by such conduct. He resents the towering insult, not "capriciously or arbitrarily, but with full and perfect measurement of the deed done." Then, with solemn formality and infinite regret, he takes his leave of the sinner. The conduct of God towards the finally impenitent has been wonderfully considerate and patient. He has shown his love and mercy to him in a thousand ways. The cheer that comes from his word, speaking forgiveness for sin and amnesty for the sinner, is enough, one would think, to win any heart. The extensive and astonishing plan of pardon which he has furnished, the providential care that orders all things for our good, his readiness to forgive, and his plenteousness of mercy, are written, as upon the clear blue of heaven, with starlight and sunlight. Under the incentives and encouragements of such proclamations, let honest and penitent hearts rejoice; let the bowed head be lifted, and the tearful eye brighten. In the very passages before us there is a wonderful expression of God's readiness to forgive. Listen. "All manner of sin shall be forgiven." Sins of ignorance, though terrible; the blind and ignorant transgressions of conscientious heathen, though appalling; their deceits, their thefts, and their murders, "shall be forgiven." "I obtained mercy," exclaimed Paul, the blasphemer and persecutor, "because I did it ignorantly." Our Saviour, sometimes, sets no conditions. They shall be forgiven, we think he means, through repentance and the provisions of the atonement. Sins of unbelief shall be forgiven. Sins of ignorance are usually directed against God, his existence, wisdom, or goodness; while sins of unbelief are usually directed against Christ, his divinity, his union with the Father, and his present official relations. When Christ, therefore, is spoken against because he is not understood, it shall be forgiven. "Whosoever speaketh a word against the Son of man, it shall be forgiven him." Not only "all sin," but even *blasphemy*, shall be forgiven, provided it does not progress until it becomes blasphemy against the Holy Ghost. Blasphemy is defamation of what is good and holy, or a disposition to despise it. It forms the climax of ordinary transgression. But even this towering sin shall be forgiven unto men. How sweeping, and far-reaching, and overshadowing are the mercies of God! The soul that asks for more than this is not an honest soul. The sinner, then, is destroyed in spite of God's forbearance. No man falls until the Infinite Father makes concession after concession to him; until the Logos appears to him and dies for him; until after the Holy Ghost has often spoken to him, as Christ spoke over Jerusalem — "I would," "Ye would not." No man falls until he has crushed his religious sensibilities, voluntarily, in his own hand. No one will finally perish whom the Godhead has not guarded as the apple of his eye, only not destroying his freedom. No man has been left alone, but Christ has, time and again, offered his presence and assistance. In the words of the "New Birth,"* "The fallen man's steps have been thronged by pleading spirits The cross of Christ has blocked his wayward course more impassably than if it had been a flaming sword. Intercessions have been made for him in heaven with hands uplifted, in which were the prints of nails. His history has been one long struggle against obstacles, with a wilful repugnance to holy restraints: with an adroit suspense of conscience, that he might fraternize with sin, he has sought out, and discovered, and selected, and seized upon, and made sure of his own way over, and around, and through these obstacles to the world of despair. He has done it, — he, and not another." The parable represents the lost soul as speechless. Is it a matter of surprise that it should be thus?

Recurs the question — Is it evidence that God is not merciful, if he does not save such sinners? The worst sinners are they who might be the most successful Christians. They have natural abilities denied others. May not God set a dreadful and eternal mark of distinction upon a transgressor who is exiled because he chooses to be exiled; whose name is on the black roll, and there because he himself persists in writing it with his own hand and in his own blood;

* Phelps.

whose God-like endowments, with all the "unmitigated and unrelenting forces" of his soul and will, have been concentrated in the choice to be and remain sinful? Is not God merciful unless he reverses all the principles of our moral character, crushes out our free moral agency, and introduces in its place absolute necessity or a blind fatality? Can he not be allowed to make any distinction between loyal and disloyal men? Nay, God's mercy and the well-being of the universe, require that man should be left free, but held responsible; free, but free to enslave himself when his character has been established and found to be dangerous to the interests of society. States are in rebellion. There is an appeal to authority, and then to arms. The states are conquered, but certain leading rebels are not. Would not that be a puerile humanity, a philanthropy run wild, let loose, which bids that government take serpents into its bosom? But what is true of a civil government is true of God's, and what is true of its subjects is true of his. *Impenitent* rebels, wherever found, are outlaws. No policy can be offered, or is safe, which does not regard them thus.

Those who oppose the doctrine of future punishment, future chains and darkness, are accustomed to say they cannot believe that God will take pleasure in forever punishing the sinner. They claim that he will provide some expedient, either annihilation at death, universal salvation, or restoration. But does he take pleasure in witnessing the terrible woe and pain which sin entails upon its victims in this world? Does he take pleasure in seeing the inebriate and the sensualist irredeemably enslaved to their appetites and passions? And yet they are enslaved. In consequence of these things, men suffer. The world is full of misery. Why does He not prevent it? Are antecedent probabilities valid in opposition to facts? All believe that it will not be any personal gratification for God to withhold forgiveness from the finally impenitent, merely for the sake of withholding it. That would not be God-like. But may not some other motives influence him? We know, from the very best authority, that sin is to be an eternal fact in the universe of God. As such, must it not have its own awful and isolated development, its own awful and isolated history? * The majesty of God's natural laws requires that violations of them shall be followed by the infliction of penalties. An eye for an eye, a tooth for a tooth. Are his moral and spiritual laws less important? Would it be safe to admit certain characters into a place of which one of the primal ideas is security? Does not the peace of heaven demand that those who are selfish, and have not the spirit of Christ, which alone destroys selfishness; that those who are impenitent, unmerciful, and unforgiving beyond recovery; that those who choose darkness rather than light, because they have continued to love evil deeds, until they have learned to love nothing better, — does not safety require that such men be allowed to chain themselves outside the gates of the city? Lax administration towards such a class will work the ruin of any government. Heaven is no

* Shedd.

exception. Do not God's providence and revelation justify the conclusion that he is too wise and decisive to follow the pusillanimous course of a people who fail in a just conception of what treason means? Will he not make it odious throughout his domains? Will he not put such a stamp upon sin and treason that they will be known anywhere? To do it, is it not his duty? Will the righteous verdict of the universe excuse him for not vindicating his broken laws by the enslavement of wilful and hardened traitors? Are not the traitors of his government those who deliberately and wilfully reject and resist him? Sin is treason. It is of no use to say such traitors do not exist; they do exist. Mix well with the world, and you will see them. God's object in the punishment, the self-imposed punishment, of the sinner is not personal gratification or vindictiveness, but is resorted to as an extreme measure. It is a plan by which to prevent another catastrophe in his kingdom. One such is enough, full enough. The heart sickens at the thought of another. Loyalty throughout his vast empire, henceforth, is his grand design. The safety of an ever-progressive and ever-increasing kingdom is the problem. Extreme measures, which now exist, but which were not at command before Satan fell, and before sin entered the universe, can effect this. Shall God employ them, or not? They are in process of execution already: shall he arrest their normal action? Shall the event of death reverse all law, and make treason glorious? Shall an impenitent Satan be reinstated in Paradise? Shall the lights of heaven be reintrusted to his bloody and deathly hand? Universal and eternal interests hang trembling upon the answer. "Yes," and "Farewell, heaven," must be spoken in the same breath. Many earthly governments have stood for centuries, which would have had an early extinction but for their salutary and vigorous enactments against treason. Ostracism or loyalty, chains and granite walls or obedience, are the right and left ventricles of a nation's heart. The future, if our conclusions be correct, lies between one hell and one heaven, or two hells and no heaven.

"And thou, Lord, in the beginning hast laid the foundation of the earth; and the heavens are the work of thine hands: they shall perish, but thou remainest; and they all shall wax old as doth a garment; and as a vesture shalt thou fold them up, and they shall be changed; but thou art the same, and thy years shall not fail." *Hebrews* i. 10-12.

"Knowing this first, that there shall come in the last days scoffers, walking after their own lusts, and saying, Where is the promise of his coming? for since the fathers fell asleep, all things continue as they were from the beginning of the creation. For this they willingly are ignorant of, that by the word of God the heavens were of old, and the earth standing out of the water and in the water: but the heavens and the earth, which are now, by the same word are kept in store, reserved unto fire against the day of judgment and perdition of ungodly men. But the day of the Lord will come as a thief in the night; in the which the heavens shall pass away with a great noise, and the elements shall melt with fervent heat; the earth also, and the works that are therein, shall be burnt up. Seeing, then, that all these things shall be dissolved, what manner of persons ought ye to be in all holy conversation and godliness, looking for and hasting unto the coming of the day of God, wherein the heavens, being on fire, shall be dissolved, and the elements shall melt with fervent heat? Nevertheless, we, according to his promise, look for new heavens and a new earth, wherein dwelleth righteousness." 2 *Peter* iii. 3-5, 7, 10-13

"And I saw a new heaven and a new earth: for the first heaven and the first earth were passed away; and there was no more sea. And I John saw the holy city, new Jerusalem, coming down from God out of heaven, prepared as a bride adorned for her husband. And I heard a great voice out of heaven, saying, Behold, the tabernacle of God is with men, and he will dwell with them, and they shall be his people, and God himself shall be with them, and be their God. And God shall wipe away all tears from their eyes; and there shall be no more death, neither sorrow, nor crying, neither shall there be any more pain: for the former things are passed away." *Revelation* xxi. 1–4.

"Let not your heart be troubled: ye believe in God, believe also in me. In my Father's house are many mansions; if it were not so I would have told you. I go to prepare a place for you. And if I go and prepare a place for you, I will come again, and receive you unto myself; that where I am, there ye may be also." *John* xiv. 1–3.

"But, as it is written, Eye hath not seen, nor ear heard, neither have entered into the heart of man, the things which God hath prepared for them that love him." 1 *Corinthians* ii. 9.

"For we know that if our earthly house of this tabernacle were dissolved, we have a building of God, a house not made with hands, eternal in the heavens. For in this we groan, earnestly desiring to be clothed upon with our house which is from heaven." 2 *Corinthians* v. 1, 2.

"Far out of sight, while yet the flesh infolds us,
Lies the fair country where our hearts abide;
And of its bliss is nought more wondrous told us,
Than these few words: 'I shall be satisfied.'"

VI.

THE OLD HEAVENS AND EARTH DISPLACED BY THE NEW.

THE entire drift of revelation regards the present existence of the human race as temporary and disciplinary. The question before us is, whether or not, apart from revelation, there is direct or indirect evidence sufficient for the establishment of a reasonable and intelligent belief respecting the end of the present order of things, and the ushering in of a new and entirely different order.

Argument from Biblical, Traditional, and Secular History.—After the final preparation of the earth, we read that man was formed from the dust of the ground. God breathed into his nostrils the breath of life, and he became a living soul. It is a fact worthy of remark, that the most careful analysis of the human body discovers in its formation no chemical ingredient of any kind which is not a part of the soil beneath our feet. The account of the formation of Eve is brief and beautiful. God took a rib from the side of Adam, then closed up the wound, and developed from the bone the woman Eve. No greater difficulty attends such a formation than would attend a corresponding development from the dust of the earth. It is infinitely more illustrative of the ordained union of husband and wife. It involves a principle which lies at the foundation of all modern civilization. "This is now bone of my bones and flesh of my flesh: she shall be called Woman, because she was taken out of man. Therefore shall a man leave his father and his mother, and cleave unto his wife; and they shall be one flesh." (Gen. ii. 23, 24.)

Subsequently the new-formed pair were placed in a beautiful spot, which was adapted, every way, to their condition and happiness. There is a vast plain in Asia, lying between the thirtieth and fiftieth state north latitude, and between the ninetieth and one hundred and tenth degrees east longitude, which now produces plants, animals, and man in the highest state of perfection. No spot on earth surpasses it in natural advantages, and no spot so much deserves to be called the Garden of Paradise, or the Pleasant Land. Here, in this charming region, the modern Cashmere, graced by a perpetual summer, in all probability is to be found the cradle of the human race. At least tradition and history point in this direction.

Sacred history informs us that the earliest condition of man was not a state of barbarism, but of the highest civilization and refinement. The sacredness of the family relations and the worship of God were both recognized. The skilful use of language, the discernment of the nature of different animals, and the gift of appropriate names to each as they came before him, show that Adam was not a whit behind the modern masters of science — Cuvier and Agassiz.

It cannot be shown that a single nation or individual existed in an uncivilized and savage state on earth, prior to the building of the Tower of Babel. All history proves that, though from a civilized state nations may easily lapse into barbarism, it is impossible for a savage nation, without foreign aid, to rise into a state of civilization. The inhabitants of New Guinea, of the islands of Andaman and New Zealand, — in fact, every savage race on the globe, — are existing proofs. The monkey theory has no foundation in history or fact.

For a time after the formation of Adam and Eve all was well. The thorn was seen on the rose-bush, and was there to warn against danger, but was guarded so as to prevent injury. Monuments of death could be found in the earth, and seen upon its surface, to warn the early pair that Paradise, though in their possession, might be lost. But though a "thousand should fall at their side, and ten thousand at their right hand, it would not come nigh them." Heaven, but for the fall, would have been reached, not through death, but by a chariot of God.

At length followed the reverse of this enchanting picture. There were a temptation and a fall. Henceforth anxiety was written on the brow of man. Distress followed the mother of the race. And the loosened silver cord, the golden bowl broken, the pitcher dashed in fragments at the fountain, the wheel that should have drawn endless supplies of immortality crushed at the cistern, and the teeming fountains of the race flowing on, but emptying all their waters into the gulf of death, are the lessons of every hour that the early death sentence is not revoked, and that the knowledge of good *and* evil, which was gotten so easily, has cost most dearly.

During the sixteen hundred years of antediluvian history succeeding the fall, we may note the death of Abel and the exile of Cain. The descendants of Cain developed the various branches of art and science, cultivated literature and poetry, built their houses, and walled their cities, but were guilty also of all those gigantic crimes which ever attend a high but unchristianized state of civilization. The descendants of Seth, on the other hand, cultivated astronomy, agriculture, and horticulture. They recognized the rights of property and marriage. They exhibited extraordinary virtues and piety. Subsequently, however, upon the increase of the two races, the sons of Seth — called very properly "the sons of God" — were attracted by the graces and embellishments, the music, the songs, and the sparkling wit of the daughters of the enterprising Cainites, and formed with them unholy alliances. (Gen. vi. 1–5.) This struck the death-knell to the further developments of purity and true religion among the race of mortals. Subsequently violence and crime filled the earth, and not until after God had given repeated warnings — not until after he had entreated and expostulated through many years — did he sweep the earth of its rebellious inhabitants by the deluge of Noah, preserving, to repopulate it, the only family which had continued to serve him, and which alone could be trusted to hand down the knowledge of the true Jehovah to succeeding races. Of this deluge the voice of tradition is full and emphatic. Whether it were local or universal respecting the earth, the Scriptures do not say; but respecting man, they do say that it was universal. The theory of Hitchcock, respecting the deluge, so well accords with certain facts that we introduce the substance of it. The physical character of the country supposed to have been inhabited by the antediluvians, after their expulsion from Paradise, shows that it would have been easily overflowed by the sea, if but small changes of level had been introduced. In Western Asia, extending even to Russia, there is a territory nearly as large as Europe, the most of which is beneath the ocean's level. The Caspian Sea is eighty-four feet below the Black, the steppe of Astrachan has an average level of thirty feet below the Baltic, and the Dead Sea is thirteen hundred and twelve feet below the Mediterranean.

Now, if the low barrier between the Caspian and Baltic were depressed, a torrent of water would inevitably flow in and overwhelm this region. A large portion of Western Asia shows evidences of volcanic eruptions even in historic times, and of abundant eruptions in the later Tertiary period. Such convulsions, and also rapid oscillations, of the earth's surface are commonly accompanied by torrents of rain. Such phenomena are not altogether wanting in recent history. In 1819, two thousand square miles of the delta of the Indus were suddenly depressed. The waters of the ocean immediately rolled in, and covered everything, save the tops of the houses. With a few variations of the earth's surface at the time of the flood in these regions, where we know, from scientific researches, there have been such changes in comparatively recent times, an extent of more than two millions square miles of country would have been deluged. The fountains of the great deep would have been broken up, drenching rains would have fallen, every object within view from the ark would have been concealed from sight as effectually as if the ark had been sailing upon mid-ocean. Nothing having the breath of life, throughout that entire region, man or beast, could have survived, save the family of Noah and the domesticated animals taken with him into the ark. It accords with geological observation that a great oscillation in one direction is followed by another in the opposite direction. Granting this to have been the case, after the forty days of depression and storms, the rains would have ceased, the waters would have flowed back into the seas, the ark and dove would have found resting-places, and the representative family of the earth would have begun its new journey and history. The evidence is entirely satisfactory that the descendants of Noah, in the course of a few score of years, passed down into and overspread the rich and luxuriant valleys of the Tigris — ancient Babylonia. While the story of the flood was fresh in mind, they commenced to build a tower which should reach to the skies, that they might be independent of the interference of God in case of another flood.

To remove this feeling of independence, and the proud conceit of mortals, God, in accordance with his usual providence, checked their proceedings, and scattered the people over the earth. We read that "the whole land was of one lip and of one stock of words," and that God "confounded their lip, that they could not understand each other's lip." *

Language is a stock of words and the power of expressing them. The stock of words was not changed by this providential interference; but the organs of speech were so affected, that, when the people attempted to enunciate from the old stock of words, a peculiar sound was given, which could not be understood, save by that part of the people similarly affected.

Probably the three or four great divisions of language then commenced their development — the Shemitic, the Indo-Germanic, or European, the Egyptian, and the monosyllabic languages, if a separate classification be required for them.

All philological phenomena can be reconciled with this general fact and classification. As would be expected, a separation of those who spoke the different tongues into distinct communities soon followed, together with subdivisions of those families of the original descendants of Noah who had intermarried. The body of the Japhetic family overspread Europe. The Hametic overspread Africa, and the Shemitic passed to the south and east of Asia. Since the dispersion, secular history notes the rise and fall of the ponderous civilizations of Babylon, Nineveh, Egypt, Greece, and Rome; also the liberty, intelligence, and industry of modern times.

* Hebrew Bible.

The religious history includes the call of Abraham; the singular choice of the children of Israel as the peculiar people of God; the development and decay of the vast religious systems of Asia, Persia, and Egypt; the development of Platonism under the successive labors of the finest minds that ever dawned upon Greece, and its subsequent extinction; the birth of Jesus of Nazareth, and the triumphs of his gospel; the waxing and waning Crescent on the desert; the pope established and trembling on his throne; the scholastic Deism of England; the wild infidelity of France; the development of Hegelanism under the united efforts of the profoundest intellects of Germany, and its subsequent desertion; and the more recent, but ineffectual attacks of infidelity upon the doctrine and views of the evangelical church, — these events bring the religious history and controversies of the world to our own doors.

We may observe, also, that the direction of these movements has been westward, excepting the counter wave that sent some of the inhabitants of Asia across to the western shores of America, which has since given way before the mighty westerly tides that are soon to ingulf the last remains of the old Indian tribes of the new world. Here we pause.

As we glance at this vast field of history, and then towards the future, — as we examine these civil and religious movements in general or in detail, — can we fail of the impression that the whole is entirely meaningless, improvident, chaotic, is it not wild as a whirlwind, and mad as a storm throughout, unless the journey of humanity has been tempoı ıry and disciplinary? But what is the race to do next? Is not its onward march soon to be checked by the shores of the Pacific, and will there follow a rebound from west to east, over the world? Impossible! Is it to span the Pacific, strike the Asiatic coast, and begin its journey over again, whence it commenced? Improbable! Is it to stay where it is? Impracticable! Can the race continue to multiply as it has been doing in the past, and room be found on the earth's surface for the increasing millions? Certainly not.

Nay, every chapter of geology, every page of history, every providence of God, every deep conviction of the human soul, points with an index finger inflexible as steel, not to a repetition of the old story, but to its conclusion, and to the development of what eye hath not seen or ear heard.

Scientific Evidences of the Close of the Existing Order of Things. — Had we looked in the direction of the constellation of the Northern Crown in May, 1866, we should have seen a star suddenly burst forth with extraordinary brilliancy. Twelve days after this event, we should have observed that it had declined from the second to the eighth magnitude. But one explanation of the phenomenon has been presented. There is, perhaps, no question in the minds of scientific men that this outburst of light was a star suddenly inwrapped in the flames of a burning atmosphere. It is probable it was a central sun of some planetary system, which, having accomplished its destiny, disappeared. There are many other instances. This is noted only because it is so near us in point of time. Astronomers tell us of new stars in every direction, which appear and then disappear. Astronomical charts are dotted with important stars that have been lost from the heavens. What is there to prevent a similar catastrophe on this earth of ours? No one dares say that such an event is impossible, unless he would dare say anything.

On the other hand, will not familiarity with a certain class of facts force all to the conclusion that such an event is, in every way, probable? There are movements in progress in the planetary system, which, if continued, must inevitably result in its destruction Other destructive agencies exist. It is not claimed that the fisherman Peter was a scientific man; but suppose, for any reason, there should be intense heat developed on the surface of this planet; would not certain gases by chemical necessity be developed? Would not the hydrogen of the atmosphere be suddenly liberated? Would it not enter into new relations with the oxygen, forming explosive combinations? And is there any known power, excepting the divine, which could prevent a sudden and fatal explosion, in which the world would be on fire, and the atmosphere pass away with a great noise?

The shape of the earth is by no means fixed. It yields to its own revolutions, and to all outside attractions. It is slightly flattened at the poles, but is so pliable that the poles may be anywhere: they and the equator have once, at least, exchanged places. The climatic changes now in progress, and the departure of the north star from its old post in the sky, indicate that, if the earth stands long enough, they will do so again. The Cuban and the Australian will become fir-clad Icelanders. Spitzbergen will cultivate the orange, and its inhabitants will swelter under one hundred and twenty degrees Fahrenheit.

Some author has remarked that, from the earliest times, there has been in this world a loud and ever-repeated cry of "Fire!" It was begun by the Egyptians, continued by the Greeks; and in our own day it has waxed so loud and clear that no man of science can say it is a false alarm. The existence of fire within the earth may have been in part conjecture with the Egyptians; with us it is no longer conjecture, but certainty; the pliable character of the earth's surface proves it. Three hundred active volcanoes, and numerous extinct ones; the remarkable eruptions of Vesuvius from 63 to 79 A.D., which "devastated the fair and fertile fields adorning its sides, scattering the numerous populations which had been engaged in all the various occupations of life;" and still more recent eruptions,—are evidences that this world has been, and still is, on fire throughout its inner courts and compartments. These and other facts prove the existence of internal fires with as much certainty as we should know, upon entering a house, where, from every crack and seam, fitful flames and black smoke were issuing, that some hall or room within was wrapped in destructive flames.

Herculaneum, Pompeii, and Stabiæ, are solemn and sombre witnesses of facts. Look at those cities for a moment. Herculaneum was buried underneath one hundred feet of mud and ashes, sand and lava. There it slumbered unknown nearly seventeen hundred years. One hundred and fifty years ago its grave was entered and its history read. The streets and shops were found just as the flying inhabitants left them. The ruts made by carriages on the streets bore the impress of wheels, as perfectly as they do in our own day. The names of the owners were found over the doors of their houses. Fabrics in the shop windows, vessels of fruit on the shelves, and medicine on the apothecary's counter, showed their texture and nature as accurately as if they had been left there the day before. There were found statues and vases bearing the impressions of the minutest lines, and loaves of bread with the impress of the baker's name. Soldiers were found standing on guard, with spear in hand; and in one of the halls of the city was found the skeleton of a woman with an infant skeleton in her arms. Her bones were encircled with the rings and ornamental chains of gold which she wore in life. What a thrilling history these discoveries suggest!

"After nearly seventeen centuries had rolled away," says a modern writer, "the city of Pompeii was disinterred from its silent tombs, all vivid with undimmed hues; its walls fresh as if painted yesterday; not a tint faded on the rich mosaic of its floors; in its forum, the half-finished columns, as left by the workman's hands; before the trees in its gardens, the sacrificial tripod; in its halls, the chest of treasure; in its baths, the strigil; in its theatres, the counter of admission; in its saloons, the furniture and lamps; in its triclinia, the fragments of the last feast; in its cubicula, the perfumes and the rouge of faded beauty; and everywhere, the skeletons of those who once moved the springs of that minute yet gorgeous machine of luxury and life. The remarkable preservation, for nearly two thousand years, of these cities, with their houses, furniture, and even the most perishable substances, beneath beds of volcanic rocks, may be compared to those geological changes by which the forests of an earlier world, and the remains of the colossal dragon-forms which inhabited the ancient land and waters, have been perpetuated."

What is there to prevent a repetition of these scenes on a grander and far more extensive scale, in which will be involved, not the fate of single cities, but of the world itself—nay, of the planetary system of which we form a part? Are not the elements at command? Is there any scientific improbability?

On the 5th of June, 1835, there was an eruption from the crater of Mauna Loa, which sent a mighty cataract of fire,—in some places two hundred feet deep and from one to five miles broad,—with resistless energy, a distance of forty miles to the sea. Here leaping a precipice of fifty feet, it plunged for twenty days and nights its liquid mass of fused rocks and minerals, with the depth and breadth of Niagara, in one emblazoned sheet, one raging torrent of gory red, into the ocean beneath. The atmosphere was filled in all directions with ashes, spray, and gases. The waters were heated for twenty miles along the coast. Night was converted into day for a distance of fifty miles at sea; and the light from it rose and spread itself like morning upon the distant mountain-tops.

Pass from 1835 to 1868. We take the following account from a published letter of a missionary, respecting an eruption of this mountain, which occurred in the latter year. "March 27, early in the morning, we discovered," he says, "an immense column of smoke and gas, which in a few minutes attained the height of several miles, forming huge pillars, grand beyond description. A few minutes after one o'clock, on Saturday, the foundations of the everlasting hills seemed to give way. The whole island seemed like a great ship loosened from her moorings, reeling to and fro, rising and falling and shaking terrifically, as if she were going to pieces. The oldest inhabitants unite their testimony that it was the most fearful and terrific earthquake ever known on these islands."

Why delay with isolated instances. The same facts are published, in one form or another, throughout the world, from Alps round to Alps again, and from the gleaming volcanoes of Iceland to the burning mountains of the Southern Polar Seas. Whole cities, with their elegant mansions and splendid churches, have been levelled to the ground in the space of a few minutes. The rising of the land in Scandinavia, and the depression in Greenland, are existing and long-continued warnings that we are on a crust, underneath which are chained and "*reserved*" the forces which, all science acknowledges, are sufficient to fulfil the conditions imposed by the prophecies respecting the end of the world. The conclusions of men of science, after the most careful investigations and explorations, are, that the interior of this earth is an ocean of fire, which begins at a depth variously estimated at from fifty to two hundred miles. Allowing that the diameter of the earth is eight thousand miles, should we pass through its centre, we should find on our journey at most only four hundred miles of earthy crust to seven thousand six hundred miles of liquid fire. What a precarious bridge is this upon which we are standing! What a hazardous journey is this we are making! We live in a house that has been fired, the flames of which are well under way.

"When we consider," says Lyell, "the combustible nature of the elements of the earth, the facility with which their compounds may be decomposed, and the quantity of heat which they evolve during the process; when we recollect the expansive power of steam, and that water itself is composed of two gases, which by their union produce intense heat; when we call to mind the number of explosive and deteriorating compounds which have been already discovered,—we may be allowed to share the astonishment of Pliny, that a single day should pass without a general conflagration."

Let but the order be issued to liberate those internal fires, to combine or separate certain chemical agents surrounding us, and the reserved forces would leap forth and swallow in their angry and fire-red jaws all traces of organic life and remains. The mighty pillars, and the vast mountain ranges of earth, from peak to base, would plunge into this ingulfing ocean of fire. The atmosphere, from a chemical necessity, would pass away with a great noise. The waters of the seas would be hurled from their beds. They would flash over the sky in trembling vapors and developed gases. They would flee away from the presence of Him that sitteth upon the throne. There would be "no more sea."

With these facts before us, with our feet upon the sciences, and, what is more than all else, with the sure word of prophecy in our hands, let the evangelical Christian world be charged no longer with lack of intelligence, when it asserts that the day of a general conflagration is on the wing, and that its morning and evening are known to God. The sciences do not present a single page which teaches that such a conclusion is in any way impossible or improbable. Analogically they prove that when the present system has culminated, a season of desolation (longer or shorter) will be followed by advancement and improvement.

The Psychologico-Scriptural Argument.—Many Christians *submit* to certain descriptions of their future abode. They neither believe nor are they satisfied with them. A few grand and expressive phrases take the place of substance and revelation. Madame De Gasparin has well spoken,—

"Splendor! Immensity! Eternity! Grand words! Great things! A little definite happiness would be more to the purpose." We now speak as a believer rather than a theorist. Revelation is the foundation on which we build.

As we enter this field of discussion, we are met by those who remind us that when so little is revealed, we must not seek to pry open closed gates. Such a course is thought to be profanation, The author of the "Physical Theory of Another Life" has well replied, "In truth, if the human family is to live anew, the future stage of its existence offers itself to our curiosity as a proper branch of the physiology of the species; and it only remains to be asked whether we are in possession of any sufficient materials for prosecuting the subject." For our own part, the more we study the Scriptures, the more they flood the other world with sunbeams. We are in possession of a clear, consistent, and beautiful revelation. Inspired "seers" not only clearly disclose the fact that the supernatural heavens and earth are to exist in the future, but that they do, in part at least, already exist.

A Syrian king sent troops to arrest the prophet Elisha. They surrounded the village where the prophet abode. He had but one servant for defence. "Alas, my master," inquired the servant, "what can we do?" The prophet saw that instant what his servant could not see. Once before he had seen what fifty witnesses, watching over the river, could not see—the translation (rather the transfiguration) of Elijah. "Fear not," replied the prophet, "for they that be with us are more than they that be with them." To the natural eye the dawn-light of that morning disclosed nothing except an immense Syrian army. "And Elisha prayed and said, "Lord, I pray thee, open his eyes, that he may see." A new sense or faculty was conferred. The young man saw a new order of intelligences—also "horses and chariots of fire." They were there before, but were previously invisible.

Ascend the Mount of Transfiguration. Certain forms then appeared which bodied forth the fulness of life. They were not transient visitors to earth.

Those glorified inhabitants of the other world assumed nothing extraordinary on that occasion. The change was in the observers. The natural physical senses of the disciples were locked up. Others were temporarily conferred or awakened. They saw — "*eidon*" (a word which implies the veritable sight of a veritable object) — what the natural eye could not see. Take another illustration. The same phenomenon occurred in the case of Stephen. While he was falling to the earth under the cruel blows of his murderers, this supernatural sense was conferred. The eternal gates *seemed* to open. It was really the opening of his eyes upon the immortal life. The same thing was true of Paul on the road to Damascus. He saw objects which fall not within the range of natural sensation. Christ did not then descend from some place beyond the stars; he is ever present and omnipresent, but he seemed to break in upon the inner sight of the persecutor. He came from a sphere above the natural, but within the range of immortality, and within the visual range of eyesight, but beyond its power. These disclosures can be accounted for by the suspension of the natural perception, or by the exercise of one which can look upon countenances whose radiance is above the dazzling brightness of the lightning stroke, and upon raiments which glisten above the whiteness of the snow under sunbeams. The angels which appeared amid the scenes of our Saviour's resurrection, and those which visited the patriarchs on various occasions, assumed no new attribute themselves. Their faces were all the while present and radiant. The change was entirely with the beholder.

Perhaps the most remarkable instance of the gift of supernatural discernment recorded in the Scriptures occurred at the resurrection of our Saviour. His crucifixion was attended with violent earthquakes. The limestone caverns, in which graves had been excavated, were wrenched asunder. The graves were opened. On the third day following, many saints appeared. Tradition informs us that the twelve patriarchs were among the number, "and came out of the graves after his resurrection, and went into the holy city, and appeared unto many." (Matt. xxvii. 53.) We think no violence is done to the laws of Scripture interpretation, when we say that the "many" referred to looked in upon the immortal world. The dust and material corruption of those patriarchs did not return to the tombs, indeed they did not quit the tombs even temporarily. The change, as in case of Elisha, of Paul, and the Revelator in Patmos, was unconsciously in the beholders. They beheld the dead as risen and alive.

It is the practice of the inspired writers to represent an appearance as the thing itself. These saints appeared to have just come from their graves. In reality, they had frequently walked the streets of Jerusalem, entered the temple, and visited the homes of the people. The transaction itself was nothing new. The people were now permitted, for the first time, to become "seers" in the prophetic sense. To the thousands who were in Jerusalem, these disclosures were attestations that Christ had risen, that he had pierced the domain of death, and awakened to immortal life the blessed saints who were precious in his sight.

But why delay to recount individual instances? The Scriptures are pervaded with evidence that we dwell among invisible but eternal verities — personalities and substances.

The disclosures of the Scriptures are supported by science. "The conjecture concerning an invisible, sentient, and rational economy, coexistent with the visible universe, and occupying corporeally the same field, comports well enough, as we shall presently see, with the intimations of Scripture regarding the spiritual world; and it consists also with every analogy of the physical system, as understood by modern science; for it has been ascertained that ponderable elements pervade one the other; that the imponderable pervade all; that different kinds of emanations or vibrations are always passing and repassing, in the most intricate manner, through the same spaces, without in the least degree disturbing each other; and finally, that the most powerful agencies are perpetually in operation around us, of which we have not the faintest perception, and which we detect only by deductions from circuitous experiments." *

The universe is one system, but there are different involved systems — "bodies celestial" and "bodies terrestrial." Some are ponderable; others are not. The surgeon may amputate the physical limb; the invisible limb remains untouched. It is felt to remain in all its perfection.† There is a substance which chains the needle to the pole, but it is invisible. Invisible forces will always produce either visible or invisible substances. We inhabit miniature taberna-

* J. Taylor. † Dr. Holcombe.

cles, which are built under the eaves and shadow of everlasting palaces. Blind and deaf men may be in a world which is filled with beauty and music, without seeing the one or hearing the other. All mortals are blind and deaf; all are asleep. A word will remove our blindness, and rouse us to consciousness.

Let God speak, and the *prepared* mansions would be seen as in the atmosphere about us. The planets make their revolutions through a substantial abode which envelops them. When the world and stars are rolled up like a scroll, and pass away, the new earth and heavens remain in their place undisturbed. It is only a line which separates us from the objective scenery of another world. When our planetary and suburban existence ends, our immortal and metropolitan begins. It is but a step from things which are "seen and temporal" to things which are "not seen and eternal." Death will be to us that step — a step into light. "Whosoever liveth and believeth in me shall never die. Believest thou this?"

Of the character of our future abode, and its occupations, we know only "in part." Its material character will differ from that of the present. It will lack, however, none of its *essential* excellences. The new earth will not crumble, or be on fire. It will contain neither the remains nor images of death. It will be swept and garnished. It will be substantial and beautiful.

Look upon our present earth, with its grace and grandeur. See the sky, adorned with the lamps of night; see the blue morning creeping over the hills; see the great dome lit up in midday. Is there to be nothing that resembles this loveliness in the new earth? Then let the old one remain.

Go into a deep primeval forest, where the giant arms of lofty trees hold their leafy tenting over us, where one can drink in melody from the sublime solitudes of the infinite. Go to the summit of a lofty mountain range, where the enchanting smiles and beauty of lesser hills, and lakes, and streams blend into a perfect picture, which bears the stamp of the presence and image of the great Creator. Is there to be nothing like this in the future abode? Are we to stand forever upon a dead level? Is there to be but one building, and that an immense temple? The thought is painful to us. Ah, but our natures are to be changed! That we are to be improved is doubtless true; but that human nature is to be changed into any other kind of nature, we deny. It is to be rounded out and completed, redeemed and purified; that is all.

"I do not believe in a gross heaven," says Dr. Chalmers, "but I do believe in a reasonable one." The fixed and immovable choirs, dressed in plain white, are not the most pleasing to us.* The glory of that abode will not continually dazzle with its ineffable brightness, but will be supremely enjoyable. The future heaven is not an abstract grandeur, but a pleasant place. It is not filled with shadows and ghosts, but is the abode of the most tangible substances, and the most visible and friendly personalities that exist. The God who rules it is not an overwhelming and sublime abstraction, but a real and dear friend in the person of Christ our Saviour.

* Gates Ajar.

John saw therein a beautiful stream; it flowed down from some hill-side. He saw trees of wonderful foliage, from which the people plucked their palm branches. He saw wonderful fruit. We need not particularize. The impression which revelation leaves is that the new heavens and earth are purely *objective*. The forms and bodies in it glow and pulsate with the reality of life. A brilliant, happy life, in the smiling light of a Redeemer's countenance, takes the place of cold formalities. Songs gladden the atmosphere. The Lord God Almighty, which is the Lamb, lights up its everlasting archways; every corridor of the temple, every vale and hill-side of the landscape, is mantled with his smiling presence.

Revelation also assures us that our associations in the immortal world are to be eminently social.

The sentiment expressed by our Saviour in his "high priestly" prayer, involving the desire to please himself and friends by showing them the glory he had with the Father before the world was, discloses an element in our human character which will never be separated from it. "I go," said Christ, "to prepare a *place* for you." "In my Father's house are many mansions" — homes. The new earth is a place for homes. It would be any place but heaven without them. The breaking up of vast congregations will be the signal for returning to joyous homes. "Be with me where I am" presents a picture of intimate and happy associations. "Neither marry nor given in marriage, but as the angels in heaven" — how is that? Yes, the carnal disappears, but the heart is none the less knit to the heart it loves.

The family circle, the restoration of missing links, the being together, the being where *He* is, the converse of friends, the old smile that ever played upon the face, the familiar voice, — these go to make up the heaven of revelation. It exists now. It will exist in perfection when the earth is removed out of its place, when the resurrection body is received, and the final judgment is passed.

But who is he that is able to doff the working garments of the old world after it has been baptized in an ocean of fire? Who can deck the universe in all the splendor of everlasting robes? Who can furnish those rich and fascinating fields which shall fill the mind with ecstasy, as it flies onward and onward world without end? Who is able to provide the city which hath foundations, not of fire, but those which are eternal — that country and city of which the prophets spoke, and for which their hearts were ever sighing? Who can furnish those immortal and spiritualized bodies promised to the servants of God, in which they shall be able to behold scenes far more enchanting, and objects far more glorious, than can possibly come within the range of mortal vision, and possessed of a power which will enable them in a moment to soar away far beyond the ken of the telescope? "The depth saith, It is not in me; and the sea saith, It is not with me." "Destruction and death" say of it, as of wisdom, "We have heard the fame thereof with our ears." Has any being the power? Yes. Thou art able, thou Word and Christ of the world and of God. In thee and in thy word we trust. To the hem of thy garment we fondly cling. In thee is eternal life. United to thee, we fear nothing and expect all things.

Without thee was not anything made that was made. Thou, who hast wrought the mighty changes of the past, canst work this final consummation also.

Then shall be brought to pass the saying written, "And I heard a great voice out of heaven, saying, Behold, the tabernacle of God is with men, and he will dwell with them, and they shall be his people, and God himself shall be with them, and be their God. And God shall wipe away all tears from their eyes; and there shall be no more death, neither sorrow nor crying; neither shall there be any more pain: for the former things are passed away. And he that sat upon the throne said, Behold, I make all things new. And he said unto me, Write: for these words are true and faithful. And he said unto me, It is done. I am Alpha and Omega, the beginning and the end. I will give unto him that is athirst of the fountain of the water of life freely. He that overcometh shall inherit all things; and I will be his God, and he shall be my son. But the fearful, and unbelieving, and the abominable, and murderers, and whoremongers, and sorcerers, and idolaters, and all liars, shall have their part in the lake which burneth with fire and brimstone; which is the second death." The good remain, the wicked are banished.

All things are beseeching the race of mortals to kneel at the cross and live forever?

"Seeing that all these things shall be dissolved, what manner of persons ought ye to be in all holy conversation and godliness? Wherefore, beloved, seeing that ye look for such things, be diligent that ye may be found of him in peace, without spot, and blameless."

"But Thomas, one of the twelve, called Didymus, was not with them when Jesus came. The other disciples, therefore, said unto him, We have seen the Lord. But he said unto them, Except I shall see in his hands the print of the nails, and put my finger into the print of the nails, and thrust my hand into his side, I will not believe. And after eight days again his disciples were within, and Thomas with them: then came Jesus, the doors being shut, and stood in the midst, and said, Peace be unto you.

"Then saith he to Thomas, Reach hither thy finger, and behold my hands; and reach hither thy hand, and thrust it into my side; and be not faithless, but believing. And Thomas answered and said unto him, My Lord and my God. Jesus saith unto him, Thomas, because thou hast seen me, thou hast believed: blessed are they that have not seen, and yet have believed." *John* xx. 24–30.

"I am the resurrection and the life. Whosoever liveth and believeth in me shall never die. Believest thou this?" *John* xi. 25, 26.

"The ground occupied by the sceptic is the vestibule of the temple. Knowledge is the knowing we cannot know."

EMERSON.

"The clear, cold question chills to frozen doubt;
Tired of beliefs, we dread to live without;
O, then, if Reason waver at thy side,
Let humble Memory be thy gentle guide;
Go to thy birthplace, and, if faith was there,
Repeat thy father's creed, thy mother's prayer."

O. W. HOLMES.

THE SCEPTIC AMONG THE DISCIPLES.

WITHIN a few days after our Saviour had risen from the dead, there might have been seen a company of eleven men, in earnest conversation, met within private rooms in the city of Jerusalem. Ten of the number were making an effort to convince the eleventh of the resurrection of their Master and Teacher, who, a few days before, had been publicly executed. They based their argument upon the fact, that during the absence of this disciple they had seen and conversed with their Master, having received from him also many and strong evidences of his identity. This disciple, whom all recognize as Thomas, listened at first patiently to the statement of the case; but as his brethren proceeded, so many and fresh difficulties suggested themselves, that he became impatient and thoroughly sceptical. That they had seen something, he did no doubt; but in his judgment that something was *not* Christ, but was, perchance, a ghost. He did not charge them with falsehood, but with illusion; not with an effort to deceive him, but with self-deception. We can easily imagine the scene during this discussion. On the one side there were the earnest tones and gestures of men who know what they have seen, and think it strange that others will not believe them; on the other side a man, tall in stature, the reflective faculties predominating, of calm and searching eye, of high and pale forehead, who stood unmoved by what, to him, seemed improbable testimony, or, rather, testimony as to things improbable. His opponents reaffirmed, again and again, "We have seen him! We have seen him!" He again and again objected to the evidence as unsatisfactory. They thought him unduly sceptical; he thought them unduly credulous. Like many others, these men, the same at heart, differed widely in judgment. At length, after many words, only an abstract of which is here given, Thomas closed the controversy by assuring them that he could not believe in his Master's resurrection until he had seen the "print of the nails." The language employed to express his position, and the subsequent events of his life, disclose the fact that there was an earnest sceptic among the disciples, and suggest to us the method of overcoming the scepticism which is not unfrequently found among sincere Christian people. The term sceptic, however, is not here employed in its repulsive, but in its original sense. One with a covered or a shaded eye is the real sceptic. He looks at a subject intently, and scans it closely before he is prepared to believe; he doubts, not because he chooses to, but because he cannot help it; to him the testimony ordinarily given is not satisfactory, and the evidence produced is not attested by the senses or approved by the judgment. There is much truth in the following statement of Emerson: "This, then, is the right ground of the sceptic, this of consideration, of self-containing; not at all of unbelief; not at all of universal denying, nor of universal doubting, — doubting even that he doubts; least of all, of scoffing and profligate jeering at all that is stable and good. These are no more his moods than are those of religion and philosophy. He is the considerer, the prudent, taking in sail, counting stock, husbanding his means, believing that a man has too many enemies than that he can afford to be his own; that we cannot give ourselves too many advantages in this unequal conflict, with powers so vast and unweariable ranged on one side, and this little conceited, vulnerable popinjay that a man is, bobbing up and down into every danger, on the other. It is a position taken up for better defence, as of more safety, and one that can be maintained; and it is one of more opportunity and range; as, when we build a house, the rule is, to set it not too high nor too low, under the wind, but out of the dirt." Such a man is the one to whom the term *sceptic* originally applied; and such, in this respect, precisely was the character of Thomas. He was constitutionally thoughtful and meditative. He required strong evidence in order to establish belief. He was a natural doubter. He was ever inclined to look upon the dark and uncertain side of every question, but had in his bosom a noble and an heroic heart.

Of the early life and character of this disciple inspiration is silent. The traditionary evidence, however, goes to show that he was born in Antioch, nearly contemporaneous with our Saviour's birth. It would appear that he met Jesus somewhere in Palestine, during his early Judean ministry, and subsequently, upon the Master's invitation, became his disciple. The New Testament notices respecting him, as respecting others, are not voluminous, but brief and definite. They nevertheless involved all that is necessary for us to form an accurate estimate of his character and mental peculiarities. God works in revelation as in nature. Comparative philology, from a single obsolete word, will disclose to us the structure of a dead language. Comparative anatomy, from a single fossil bone, will restore an extinct species. Thus a single word, and attendant expressions, with careful study, may tell us all that we need know of the man with whom we do our business, or whom we meet in the streets.

The first notice we have of the disciple Thomas was his speech when our Lord determined to face the dangers which awaited him in Judea, on his journey to Bethany. It was only a few months before the crucifixion, and shortly after our Saviour's escape, by going beyond Jordan, from the Jews who were about to stone him. While teaching in that region, the sisters of Lazarus sent to Jesus that their brother was sick. After remaining two days, he said to his disciples, "Let us go into Judea again." This proposition met with immediate and positive opposition. "Master," replied the disciples, "the Jews of late sought to stone thee, and goest thou thither again?" It was at this crisis, when the other disciples were hesitating and throwing every obstacle in the path of Christ, that Thomas comes first into notice; and, "Let us also go, that we may die with him," was his earnest but desponding plea. Two traits of character are here apparent: first, the most entire devotion to his Master; and, second, his constitutional tendency to view things on the dark side. This expression indicates that he saw nothing but night and death before him. He entertained not the slightest hope of escape. He looked on the journey to Bethany as leading to total and irretrievable ruin; but he was none the less resolved to go, and share the peril of it with his Master.

The second notice we have of Thomas was his speech during the Last Supper. Our Saviour had been endeavoring to comfort the troubled hearts of the disciples with the hope of heaven. He was just saying to them, "Whither I go ye know, and the way ye know," when he was suddenly interrupted by Thomas, who said, "Lord, we know not whither thou goest; and how can we know the way?" This question brings before us another characteristic of the disciple — that of prosaic but honest doubt. Here were the tearful eye and trembling heart of one who goes to the altar for prayer, not knowing that it will avail anything, not knowing how it can avail anything; evincing often a hesitating incredulity as to moving a single step in the unseen way, but all the while expressing an eager inquiry, that breaks in upon what is passing, to know how that step is to be taken, if it can be taken at all. I will go; but *how*, and where, and when? are the questions.

The third and last important notice we have of

Thomas is the one already referred to. On this occasion the apostle gave expression, not to his characteristic devotion, as in the first instance, nor to his constitutional despondency, as in the second, but to the vehemence of his natural scepticism. While the other disciples were trying to argue him into a belief of Christ's resurrection, the vivid image that his last view of Christ upon the cross had made upon his mind, the nails in his hands and the gash in his side, refuted all their arguments, and neutralized every assertion. The intensity of doubt seized upon him. With all the earnestness of his soul he exclaimed, "Except I see the print of the nails, and put my finger into the print of the nails, and thrust my hand into his side, I will not believe." This is the earnest expression of an inability to believe. It is not the language of obduracy, but is rather that classical use of the simple future, which would be better translated, "I cannot believe;" meaning, I have not the moral ability to believe such an event upon your testimony. "I wish I could, but I cannot," is the embodied sentiment. It also partakes of the character of language used in animated discussion — a sudden retort. This is not the incredulity of one who asks for reasons only to combat and reject them, but that kind of intemperate exclamation which arises when one is attacked on all sides at once. It was ten against one, and led to the use of stronger language than was really meant — a demand for evidence, as the sequel shows, stronger than was really required. It was, on his lips, characteristic language. It gives us a true insight into the make of his mind and drift of his thoughts.

The doubts of Thomas and those of which we speak arise not from an indisposition of the heart, but of the head. The affections are aglow; the thoughts are befogged.

There are two classes of devout minds in the world: first, those who *feel out* their religion, liable sometimes, especially in their earlier experience, to excesses and deceptions; and, second, those who *think out* their religion, who are liable to live in the realm of doubt and cloud. Those of the first class believe easily; they are admitted at once into the light; they see no night; there are no barriers to their initiation and progression; there is heaven within heaven, sky above sky, star beyond star; the whole upper dome is ever seen glistening and trembling with truth and beauty. The second class are often enveloped in clouds black as ink. The sky nowhere gleams with the smile of a golden sunset, or the triumph of a rosy morning. "The gates" are neither "wide open," nor "ajar." Those of the first class never examine evidence, take no interest in carefully balancing testimony. They are neither lawyers nor philosophers: they do not necessarily receive what they *hear*, but what they *feel* to be true. Religious truth enters the hearts of such persons, not through the head, but *direct*, as by intuition. It cannot be said that they believe thus and so because others do, nor that others think for them. They care less about thinking, and more about conviction. They know truth by feeling it. They are so in sympathy with Christ, and so mentally constituted, that they need no external, but are satisfied with internal evidence. The resurrection of Christ to them is a fact. Arguments against will not shake, arguments for will not strengthen, their confidence. Their own resurrection is as real as if the clay were already falling off, and the new material forming upon the body. Such a faith affords a confidence which all the arguments and objections in the world cannot shake. One who can thus believe is "blessed" as no other on earth.

Such a state of mind is the repose of John upon the bosom of Christ, the confidence of a child in the arms of its mother; while the opposite characteristic is the struggle of Thomas before the disciples.

"Blessed," said our Saviour, — and this was precisely the principle he meant; not the imputation of blame to Thomas, but the simple statement of a fact, — "Blessed are they who have not seen, and yet have believed;" that is, blessed are those who feel their religion, and know it because they feel it. It was so in the days of Christ; it is none the less so now. It will be a sad day for our Christianity, and more sad for many in the church, if the head, in this respect, were required or allowed to take the place of the heart, or if sight undertake to do the work of faith. The head cannot safely say to the heart, more than the heart can to the head, "I have no need of thee." But these who feel out their religion cannot be said, on that account, to be better men, or more devout: they are more cheerful Christians; that is all. On the other hand, those who think out their religion cannot be said, on that account, to be less faithful or evangelical. As a rule, they can be depended upon in times of peril. They instantly fly to the rescue of the church whenever it is assailed. They are the sounder theologians. They are the deeply earnest souls of the world, who love the truth none the less because it is not seen, but who navigate the ship through tempest, storm, and night, to the haven, believing there is some place where anchor can be cast and sails furled. They love solitude. They shun the world to find in their own mysterious thoughts their companions and their hopes.

It is this characteristic which best explains the absence of Thomas during the first visit of his Master. We do not say but it would have been better for him to have been with the disciples; we cannot tell; we only know that Christ did not condemn him. Thomas was so like that earnest, thinking John Foster that we pause for a moment to note the comparison. Foster was often alone, often absent from society, but never idle, never thoughtless. He used to walk the aisles of his church at Chichester, often by moonlight and by starlight, until, at length, he wore his path in the solid pavements. He wrestled by the hour in prayer, struggling with eternity and immortality, and fashioning those mighty thoughts, "which," says Robert Hall, "are like a great lumber-wagon loaded with gold." They were given to the world, and ever since have fired the hearts of young men to meet duty and fear God. He used to kneel in charnel-houses, and pray the dead to break the silence, and speak to him of the Invisible. He used to cry aloud to the midnight hills for some wandering spirit to render up its secrets, and tell him what to do. "We know not whither thou goest, and how can we know the way?" was the burden of his prayer.

Such men, we repeat, cannot be so truly happy as others. Foster, Cowper, Thomas, were not happy men; they could not be; but they were thinkers and servants of God.

Consider the conduct and language of Thomas, as he stood before the disciples on the occasion in question. He was then and there the embodiment of a pure rationalism. They stated to him a fact which, more than anything else in the world, he wished were true. No one of his ten brethren desired any more intensely that the fact might be true; but to him it was dark — all dark. One hundred and fifty generations had passed away. He could think of no one who had returned from the invisible world to walk among men. Whole armies had daily set sail upon that ocean which has no shore, but no friendly sail had returned until now. The statement of his brethren staggered him. The bloody gash in the side of his Master haunted him. He listened; he heard what was said; he struggled; his heart throbbed to receive it. O that it were true! But his head was among the clouds; the empty tomb and living Christ were hid from view. Whatever may have been his personal choice, he had not the moral power to believe upon the evidence given. A simple assertion was not sufficient, though repeated a thousand times. The prophecies and the statements of Christ had been overlooked or forgotten by him and his companions amid the terrible scenes of the crucifixion, and "we have seen him" was the only argument employed. For Thomas to have believed upon that testimony solely would have been to *make* believe. That he could not do. His mind was of an order too high and too pure to deceive itself. In consequence, the splendid truth of Christ's resurrection fell at his feet unembraced and unbelieved. The company of the disciples separated, and Thomas returned to his abode sad and disconsolate.

All remember the disciple whose heart was bruised the most sorely at the trial of Christ, and the message that came within a few days, "Go, tell the disciples *and* Peter that he is arisen and goeth before them to Galilee"! So is it always. Christ never forgets his distressed but honest followers.

It was a delightful Sabbath morning in the month of March, the first after the one which had witnessed the resurrection of the Son of God, that the Jewish people might have been seen slowly approaching the temple, or turning their faces towards Jerusalem, for worship. The disciples had again met, and Thomas with them. Ten of his companions, and certain women, gave in their testimony anew, but he yielded not. He dreaded delusion. A few moments later, without a window opened or a bolt drawn, silent as a spirit, but real as life, the Master was again before them. We can almost hear the workings of the thoughts of that meditative disciple, as a score of conflicting emotions thrill his soul. His lips are silent, his eyes tearful, and his heart is throbbing to be pressed to the Master.

"Thomas!" How the well-known voice thrills him! "Thomas, reach hither thy finger, and behold my hands; reach hither thy hand, and thrust it into my side; and be not faithless, but believing." "My

Lord *and* my God!" How much is involved in that reply! What a testimony to the world! It is the cautious verdict of an enlightened, suspicious, most honest, and most earnest sceptic. He was eye-witness to the resurrection of Christ. Can the world ask more? We said that this truth of the resurrection fell at the sceptical disciple's feet; but it fell to be lifted again by One who is able to dissipate all doubts from every faithful heart, and so to strengthen this doubting disciple, that he may be able, by his peculiarity of mind, to make an advance far beyond and far above any of his fellow-disciples. He was enabled to comprehend, as the necessary outgrowth of the resurrection, the identity of God and Christ. His mind alone seized upon the fact that, if Christ could rise from the dead, he could do anything else, and was divine. This was a new step in the theological world. Thomas stands before us as the soundest and most advanced theologian of the twelve — "the rationalist among the disciples."* He was in spiritual darkness until a rational and intellectual light dawned upon him. He thought out his religious belief. In his heart his convictions found their moorings. Christ afterwards confirmed them as the reward of love and faithfulness.

We may here pause for a moment to consider certain inquiries, which, doubtless, at one time or another, have entered the mind of every Christian. Why cannot some persons believe as easily as others? Why cannot this man enjoy his religion as that man does his? Why are not the evidences of Christianity

* Oldshausen.

equally clear to all minds? Is it because the one is better than the other, or not?

It has been well remarked,* that some of the highest and purest Christian lives on earth have been unproductive of Christian enjoyment and assurance. It becomes us, therefore, to pity the blind, not to be angry with them. We speak in behalf of those who doubt their religion because they lack religious enjoyment. There are Christians who make no professions, simply because they have none to make. They express no assurances, because they have none. They do not preach to the world joy and hope, because they have no joy or hope. They would be hypocrites if they made such professions. Their inner Christian life they conceal, because it is as the valley and shadow of death. They are sometimes reproached by well-meaning but inconsiderate Christian people, but bear the reproach with the composure of Christ. They are so pitiful when they mention God's dealings with them that we weep. Their despair is so frightful and hideous that we shrink from them. But are these the worst people in society? Nay, they are sometimes the best, and serve God under circumstances in which others would rebel against him. In the end they often believe religious truths far more firmly and consistently than those who had previously condemned them. The mistake of Job's friends is the mistake of the world. They thought his sufferings indicated the depravity of his heart. "Who ever perished being innocent?" pointed the arguments they employed, and the

* Phelps.

charges they hurled against him. The despondency of William Cowper led those who knew him to speak of him as "Poor Cowper!" The gloom of John Foster startles us. Why? Because these men were the worst characters in the world? Nay, far otherwise. Job, the perfect man, met with complicated and repeated reverses, not because he had done anything to merit such treatment, but that he might demonstrate to the world and the universe that a mortal is able to conquer the devil on his own grounds and with his own weapons. Cowper was left to weep in darkness for eleven years, in which, he tells us, not a solitary moment of hope of his own salvation ever cheered his soul; not that he deserved such treatment more than other men, but that in all coming time the fragrance of his hymns might cheer the hearts of others, and that his plaintive wailings — "God moves in a mysterious way," and "There is a fountain filled with blood" — might be heard in a thousand sanctuaries of Zion on every returning Sabbath, inspiring suffering hearts with the very hope and confidence which were denied him.

Christ made his first visit during the absence of the sceptical disciple, leaving him to contend with his own doubts and with his fellow-disciples, not by chance or accident, not because he was less worthy of the visit, but that the world might have from him the most overwhelming testimony to the identity of the Christ risen with the Christ dead. And thus the downcast, afflicted, sorrowing, despairing Christians throughout the world to-day may be depressed, not because they have sinned above others who are thrilled with joy, not because they are sinners at all, but in order to glorify God in the shock and struggle of a warfare in which "man contends with dreadful though unseen belligerents," and unconsciously fulfils a prophecy in which he demonstrates the fact that the seed of the woman of Eden still has power to bruise the bruised head of Satan. Or it may be they are thus left to be lights and beacons to others who are less able, alone and unguided, to navigate the rough and stormy sea of life and of Christian experience. If any of our readers are thus depressed, if God has seemed to withdraw his face and favor, "be not faithless, but believing." Beat up and down through the regions of night a while longer; light shall come — if not at eventide, certainly in the morning.

The Method by which the Scepticism or Doubts of Christians may be overcome. — There is a celebrated statue of Thomas, by Thorwaldsen, in the church at Copenhagen. He stands as a thoughtful, meditative sceptic. He holds a rule in his hand for the due measurement of evidence and argument. In every feature, the glance of the eye, the attitude of the body, the cast of the head, is seen that restless search for truth which clearly marks the "*inquirer.*" Who has not felt that there is a world of force and grandeur wrapped up in that single word? or what witness has not been touched by the sublimity that rests upon and above the altar in the Christian church erected for the *inquiring spirit?* The world is filled with barred doors and bolted windows. Who should not be an inquirer? We cannot doubt that the representation at Copenhagen is correct. Thomas was an earnest man in every thought and expression. He found himself in a world of mystery; eternity rushing on to view, and the cry of his troubled soul was heard for "the way" and "the truth."

There are two kinds of scepticism in the world — that earnest, inquiring scepticism which is faithful, and that which cares little or nothing for the truth, and which rejects it when presented. The one says, "Lord, we know not the way," and awaits the answer. It fastens the troubled eye upon the Teacher. The soul is aroused as for life and eternity. The other asks the question, folds the arms, and falls asleep. The one asks, "What is truth?" and waits until early dawn, if need be, for the answer. The other asks, like Pilate, and turns away before the reply is given. The one is earnest, the other frivolous. The one seeks only for checks and balances against exaggeration, the other for obstacles and objections as excuses. The one is innocent, the other guilty. The one course is dangerous, because it becomes chronic. Says Mackintosh, "Those who are accustomed to dispute first principles are never likely to acquire love for the truth." That is fatal to the life and activity of the soul. The other is harmless, because a night will have a morning, and the darker and longer the night, the brighter and more cheerful the morning. To the one the seal is fixed upon the book; the other shall be worthy to loose it, because it is willing to grapple with difficulties if they come, and still be earnest and devout. If the doubting man is only an earnest and faithful man, there is no trouble or danger. Every class of mind, even the sceptical, if devout, has its peculiar advantage to itself and to the world. God receives all, and needs all. Let a man be serious, let him grapple in real earnest with the great problems of life and death, though borne down before the awful shroud that hides an endless future, let him look intently before and above him for the way and the truth, though often compelled to put his fingers on his lips and weep in silence; let him be devout, and pray, and weep, and struggle; soon the painful silence to his questions of the Infinite shall be broken. God, in due time, will cleave the solid heavens, if need be, throw open the broad gates of the temple, bid him enter, reach forth his finger, and touch the living Christ of the universe, and live forever. This experience occurs daily. Such, precisely, were the character and the reward of the apostle Thomas. It is only the cold doubt of the Sadducee which demands a sign, being unworthy of it, upon whose soul the answer shall fall back like ice, "There shall no sign be given," except one full of perplexity, like that of Jonas. If men will continue faithless in life or heart; if they doubt and scoff, or, with David Hume, assume a boyish frivolousness, ask for cards, and bequeath Port and Sherry, when dying; if they will be satisfied only with gross weight in everything, and the pound of flesh; if they care only "to go, and mix, and leave, and get, and have;" if they decide to decide nothing; if they will have nothing to do with faith, because it enjoins duty; if they will live in doubt of religion, and act as though it were not true; if they remain contented, without knowing whether the ship in which they sail is sound or rotten, whether the chart and compass they hold in their hands are reliable or worthless, whether the hoarse murmur they hear is the howling of the wind or the surf of the breakers on the fatal rocks; if they choose spiritual paralysis, rather than spiritual life,—then they can never, *never* hear the voice of the Infinite. How different the conduct of the apostle whose character we have been considering! Whatever he believed to be his duty, that he fearlessly performed. Though often under the cloud, he never, intentionally, deserted his post. Had Christ commanded him to be present on his first visit to the disciples, he would have obeyed, had it cost him his life. It was this devotion and faithfulness to Christ and duty which at length triumphed over his scepticism, and made him the most convincing witness of a risen Redeemer.

Consider the closing scene of this apostle's life. While on a missionary tour at Maliper, not far from the present city of Madras, he suffered martyrdom. His reasoning had been so cogent, and his statements so clear, as to the life, death, and resurrection of Christ, that he had gained many converts, and confounded the subtle Brahmins, who were not able to answer him. At length they ordered him to remain silent, or leave their city. But the preaching of Christ was dearer to him than life. He refused to comply with the demand, and, in consequence, was shortly after murdered, as he was kneeling at his devotions. His whole missionary work,—which extended from Jerusalem to Indostan and the coasts of Ceylon,—his life and death, attest the same devotion and faithfulness. And yet this disciple, who was ready to risk his life in order to accompany Christ to Judea, at a time when the journey was beset by every peril, and who, by his position and language, inspired the same heroism in his fellow-disciples, and who, at last, died for his devotion, — this man has been held up to the world as an example of unfaithfulness. The charge is false and groundless. How frequently Christians misjudge one another! Thomas is the last man upon whom we can base the accusation. Many who are regarded as last may be honored as first. With all his doubts, in the strictest theological sense Thomas was a man of faith. "PISTIS," which is the word Paul uses for *faith*, in some of the voices of the verb means to *obey*. Obedience, then, is victorious faith — the faith in which God takes delight. When the soul stands before his judgment, the question will not be one of doubts and fears, but of *faith*-ful-ness.

Is any Christian in doubt, or sometimes troubled, as to the divinity of Christ, his resurrection and ascension — troubled sometimes with doubts as to the truth of revelation, the reality of heaven, the existence of hell, the resurrection of the body, and the immortality of the soul? Is the "supernatural book" at times a sealed book? do "supernatural beings" sometimes appear to be only imaginary beings? does the "supernatural life" occasionally present itself as a visionary life? and does the "supernatural destiny" ofttimes conceal itself under a myth? There is something worse than these temporary doubts. It is not a faithless head, but a faithless life and a faithless heart that are most to be feared. How are men living? is the question, — as if their doubts were true, or false — which? Are they struggling to know the truth and do right? If so,

> "Give to the winds thy fears;
> Hope, and be undismayed."

A faithful man's doubts are transitory, not permanent; disciplinary, not penal; temporal, not eternal.

If the facts of life, death, and a conscious immortality, press heavily upon us; if we are overwhelmed as child or friend slips our hand, and drops into the great unseen and unknown, we must not despair. We should not be frivolous, but must struggle and pray, and keep knocking at the door of the temple, and shouting to the keeper. Our cry should be heard echoing along the walls of the city, "Lift up your heads, O ye gates! and be ye lifted up, ye everlasting doors!" The "Lo, I come," will at length be heard from the City of God.

> "God liveth ever!
> Wherefore, soul, despair thou never!
> What though thou tread, with bleeding feet,
> A thorny path of grief and gloom?
> Thy God will choose the way most meet
> To lead thee heavenward — lead thee home.
> For this life's long night of sadness
> He will give thee peace and gladness;
> Soul, forget not, in thy pains,
> God o'er all forever reigns."